THE YEARS OF HIGH THEORY

INVENTION AND TRADITION IN
ECONOMIC THOUGHT
1926–1939

THE YEARS OF HIGH THEORY

INVENTION AND TRADITION IN ECONOMIC THOUGHT
1926–1939

BY

G. L. S. SHACKLE

Brunner Professor of Economic Science in the
University of Liverpool

CAMBRIDGE
AT THE UNIVERSITY PRESS
1967

Published by the Syndics of the Cambridge University Press
Bentley House, 200 Euston Road, London, N.W. 1
American Branch: 32 East 57th Street, New York, N.Y. 10022

Library of Congress Catalogue Card Number: 67–12320

Printed in Great Britain
at the University Printing House, Cambridge
(Brooke Crutchley, University Printer)

To
S. B. SAUL
A. J. YOUNGSON

ACKNOWLEDGEMENT

I wish to record my gratitude to Mrs E. C. Harris for typing my manuscript, putting in order the items of the index, and correcting the proofs, with such great patience, skill and care.

G. L. S. SHACKLE

CONTENTS

CHAPTER I

THE ORIGIN OF THEORIES: A CASE-STUDY PROCEDURE

If the activities of men were arranged in sequence according to the degree in which he shares them with other parts of the animal creation, theory-making would surely rank amongst the most exclusively human. Younger than art and religion, and younger even than complex and exact technology, it is a latecomer to the human scene. Fire and the cutting edge, the boat, the wheel, the sail, animal husbandry, agriculture, the computation of the seasons, architecture, writing and the alphabet: all are technology. Each involves principles, but these are each self-satisfying, self-subsistent, self-contained, a rule of thumb picked up like a tool and laid down again as soon as it has served its purpose. They are not, in their own right, strands in the great web of scientific speculation; their claim upon men's minds is practical, not the claim, by which all theory ultimately stands or falls, of imaginative splendour lifting thought above itself.

Cosmology and astronomy have produced theories of arresting majesty, so stupendous in their scale of time and space as to be beyond any genuine apprehension, and to have for us only a formal meaning. Physics is said to have grounded the entire material cosmos in no more than three ultimately elementary particles. Despite appearances there is, at any rate on earth, only one form of life, its basic chemistry being the same for all living creatures. In the description of the world, a universal, all-pervasive uniformity, simplicity, and unity is assuredly the aim of science, and various sciences at various times appear to take long strides towards its attainment. Against these aims and achievements, in the midst of an architecture of ideas so overwhelming in conception, the sciences, if such they are, of human nature, conduct, policy, and institutions must seem at first glance to be dwarfed in scope and altogether outclassed in professional technique and assurance. Yet it is a truth so obvious as to be banal that science exists only in the minds of men. It cannot then, after all, be so negligible a task to study mankind itself, 'man the measure of all things'. Economics is a part of the study of mankind, and we do not apologize for it. Economic theorizing is one (even if artificially demarcated) department of thought, and the manner and style of this thinking, the impulses which from time to time accelerate its evolution, the circumstances which shape it, the means, materials and mechanism it employs, the technics peculiar to it (if any such is peculiar), the frictions, traps, misfortunes, and frustrations which afflict it, are, we believe, a worthy and useful object of investigation. In the spirit of the times, in the track of natural science, in the exclusively respectable and acceptable tradition, and in face of the invincible evidence that there is no other method which succeeds, such investigation must be empirical. Where, then, can we find a suitably definite and limited field?

There is something to be said for the notion that theory prospers and marches forward in any subject if that subject happens to attract a particularly able group of many young contemporaries, who, if not in touch with each other, are at least conscious of being part of a company advancing together. The most famous example is doubtless that of the founders of the Royal Society. In economics there have been at least three episodes of the kind. In the mid-eighteenth century our subject was founded as a distinct systematic discipline by Cantillon, the Physiocrats and Adam Smith. In the last third of the nineteenth, it suddenly took on a new unity and elegance in the hands of a very remarkable group of men of many countries, all born in the years 1840–51, who founded the notion of general equilibrium on the three pillars of a subjective theory of value, the application of the differential calculus to moral science, and the conception of the universal inter-penetrating influence of every economic quantity on every other. Their work and outlook were dominant for more than half a century, and, of course, it lies still at the heart of economics. But in the 1920s and 1930s it was suddenly found to be not enough. Attention was called by contemporary fact to the vagaries of money and the general price level, and then to the bewildering phenomenon of general heavy unemployment. These problems attracted a number of highly gifted minds from diverse scholarly beginnings, not only economics itself but mathematics, classics, and physics, and the result was a great ferment of new work at the heart of economic theory. This episode is now distant enough to be seen in some perspective, yet most of its chief participants are still alive. This moment, then, of the mid-1960s is perhaps the right one to make use of that episode to cut a few sods in aid of an eventual theory of the origin of theories.

CHAPTER 2

ECONOMIC HARD TIMES AND THE RICHES OF IDEAS

The forty years from 1870 saw the creation of a Great Theory or Grand System of Economics, in one sense complete and self-sufficient, able, on its own terms, to answer all questions which those terms allowed. The briefest statement of those terms may be that they took as the sole purpose of economic theory the demonstration of the logical implications of given tastes or needs combined with perfect knowledge and confronted with a scarcity and versatility of resources. Scarcity and versatility of resources, combined with perfect and universal knowledge of the satisfactions to be derived from each use of these resources throughout the entire range of possibilities revealed by a given state of technology, ensured that these resources would always be fully employed. Perfect knowledge also carried with it perfection of markets, so that every good was produced by a great number of evenly sized firms amongst which buyers were completely indifferent. Perfect knowledge further abolished the need for any means of storing general purchasing power (as distinct from wealth embodied in concrete forms capable of yielding direct consumer-satisfactions or of aiding physically in production), and so there was no real money (whose function, as a store of value, is to make possible postponement of detailed decision for those whose knowledge is *imperfect*). The theory eschewed consideration of growth in any form. It analysed the process of production into time-sequential stages, but not in such a way as to show precisely how the quantity required of each 'intermediate product' emerging at each such stage would be altered by an alteration in the 'bill of goods' wanted for final use. The Austrian theory of capital (in any case somewhat of an appendix to the main theory) in fact neglected the inter-dependence of industries and the feed-back or reflexive aspects of roundabout production, and concerned itself only with the consequences of its time-consuming aspect. This Great Theory was thus the theory of general, perfectly competitive, full-employment stationary (or better, timeless) equilibrium. It was complete in essentials by the time that Wicksteed, Wicksell, and John Bates Clark had solved the 'adding-up problem' of the matching of factor-shares in total with the total result of their collaborative effort, and this had happened before the end of the century. In its arresting beauty and completeness this theory seemed to need no corroborative evidence from observation. It seemed to derive from these aesthetic qualities its own stamp of authentication and an independent ascendancy over men's minds. The intellectual Establishment were basically content, and therefore passive. Only a few questions, that lay outside the terms on which the Great Theory allowed itself to be consulted, remained as scraps to satisfy the prowlers round the edge of the camp. The overwhelming concentration of intellectual power within the camp was such as to daunt any possible attacker, and the Great Theory, thus guarded, remained inviolate for two decades. But the second of those decades brought to an end the Pax Britannica and the tranquil generation-and-a-half which had favoured and fostered a belief in a self-regulating, inherently and naturally self-optimizing, stable and coherent economic system. When men had got back their breath after the war and turned to apply their conceptual tools to repair the ruins of European organization, their failure (which a few years of endeavour forced them to acknowledge) to bring back the old order of things made them begin to ask for new tools. A new generation of students, which went seriously to college only in 1919 or after, had graduated and begun to think, impelled by new questions and freed in some degree from old pre-conceptions. Thus there began in the mid-1920s an immense creative spasm, lasting for fourteen years until the Second World War, and yielding six or seven major innovations of theory, which together have completely altered the orientation and character of economics. This extraordinary temporal concentration of innovative intellectual effort in one limited sphere seems to present a special empiric field for the study of theoretical creation itself, in a general sense and context. It is this opportunity which, in this book, I seek to explore and exploit in some tentative and preliminary fashion.

At the opening of the 1930s economic theory still rested on the assumption of a basically orderly and tranquil world. At their end it had come to terms with the restless anarchy and disorder of the world of fact. Partly this transformation was effected by the brutal force of events: by a slump without parallel and the unnerving spectacle of the rise of Nazism in a world cheated of the hope of peace. But partly it was the work of a mere handful of great theoreticians. One thing above all divided the new theory from the old: the discarding of the assumption (which had often been quite tacit) of universal perfect knowledge. What sense did it make to assume perfect knowledge in a world where every morning's newspaper was opened in fear and scanned with foreboding? But the ferment had been working in the world of theory from the beginning of the 1920s. Frank Knight's *Risk Uncertainty and Profit* of 1921 puts entrepreneurship in the forefront of a treatise on value theory which largely sets forth the old orthodoxy. But perhaps its title was a portent. It was in Sweden that *expectation* was first taken seriously as a prime mover in the economic process. (Marshall, as always, was with the angels, but he did not blow this particular trumpet very loud.) Erik Lindahl and, more incisively and with one brilliant and epoch-marking stroke, Gunnar Myrdal, developed the first 'economics of expectation'. Myrdal's essay, published in Swedish in 1931, in German in 1933, and in English only in 1939, would have served very well as the launching-pad for a theory of general output and employment, had the *General Theory* never been written. 1937 was the year of intensive Keynesian critical debate. In February Keynes himself declared in the *Quarterly Journal of Economics* that the *General Theory* was concerned with the consequences of our modes of coping with, or of concealing from our conscious selves, our ignorance of the future. Hugh Townshend, his intellectually most radical interpreter, simultaneously expressed the matter (in the *Economic Journal* for March) in terms, if anything, even more uncompromising. Uncertainty was the new strand placed gleamingly in the skein of economic ideas in the 1930s.

It is uncertainty which gives to money every character and capability which distinguish it from a mere numéraire. Money is the refuge from specialized commitment, the postponer of the need to take far-reaching decisions. Money is liquidity. Money is not mechanical nor hydraulic, but psychological. The beginning of new things in monetary theory came with Sir Dennis

Robertson's *Banking Policy and the Price Level* in 1926, and this is one of our two reasons for starting our period with that year.

Until the 1930s, economics was the science of coping with basic scarcity. After the 1930s, it was the account of how men cope with scarcity and uncertainty. This was far the greatest of the achievements of the 1930s in economic theory. There was just time for the first emergence of another idea of comparable importance, namely, that the natural condition of efficient economies is not a static optimum, the best use of *given* resources, but growth, the continually improving use of steadily increasing resources. The insistence on the need for a theory of growth, as general in application and as abstract in character as that of general equilibrium, was the contribution of Sir Roy Harrod.

Harrod seized upon and essentially answered the root question from which all theory of growth must spring: what are the implications of the double, two-way relation between investment and general output, namely, the theorem that the pace of investment (the net flow of expenditure on augmenting and improving equipment) governs the pace, or size of flow, of general output, and the acceleration of general output governs the pace of investment? Or: what consequences flow from the co-existence of the multiplier and the accelerator? For 'regular' or unfluctuating growth, Harrod showed, the ratio of capital (equipment) to a month's production, times the percentage by which output (monthly production) grows in a month, has to be equal to the proportion of income voluntarily saved. He did not express his theorem in *ex ante* terms, but the translation into that language is easily made. Harrod's theorem is one of the great simplicities. On its own level of high abstraction, it is wonderfully fruitful of insight into sources and consequences of instability, of stagnation, and of inflation, and it provides in this way the basis of Sir John Hicks's refined 'explosion–collapse' model of the business cycle. It is, of course, a macro-economic theory, not concerning itself with the Leontief problem, the balance of different *sorts* of production, the internal coherence, that is, of the multifarious and involuted productive process as a whole. The study of multi-sectoral growth had to be left until after the war, but multi-sectoral production itself had suggested to Wassily Leontief at the outset of the 1930s a most beautiful, simple, and powerful use of matrix algebra, which was thus brought into economics at the same moment as it was brought (by Max Born) into quantum physics, a whole human life-span after Arthur Cayley and others had invented it. One thing we shall ask ourselves in later chapters is why, in economics, the seeds of theory seem in so many instances to have taken decades, generations and centuries to germinate.

Myrdal, Keynes and Harrod each in his way changed the content and purposes of economic theory. Leontief exposed a problem and invented a tool for solving it. The problem was not a theoretical enigma, where we feel a need for insight in a situation such that even the right questions to ask are not obvious, but a highly practical desire for a means of calculation in a matter which was not mysterious but only intricate. Firms and industries supply things to each other as well as to consumers or the buyers of long-lasting equipment. For a given 'bill of goods'—list of (say) annual quantities to be supplied to those 'final' buyers—the sizes of the flows of intermediate products required by each firm or industry from others is, in a given state of technology and in given market conditions, determinate. Thus the required output of each and every firm's, or industry's product will be composed of the part it sells to consumers, etc., and the part it sells to other firms. Any change whatsoever in the list of annual quantities taken by 'final' buyers will in general require a change in the output of every firm or industry. Even if its direct sale to consumers is unaffected, the demands from other firms for intermediate products from this firm or industry will change. But the degree of this change is wrapped in an immensely complex shift of the whole quantitative pattern of inter-industrial flows. How can it be calculated? The fact of the intricate inter-dependence of industries has, of course, been clearly recognized from the beginnings of economics. The Physiocrats were centrally concerned with it, at any rate at an aggregative level, and Walter Bagehot, for example, a century after them has a celebrated passage on its effects in transmitting and propagating prosperity and depression. Leontief, by expressing the genetic tree of inter-industry production as a matrix, equipped it at once with the whole armoury of manipulations which constitute matrix algebra (only one of them is essentially required) and in principle thus solved it at a blow. His input–output analysis fuses theoretical clarity, mathematical manipulation and statistical fact into a tool of great beauty and practical power, one of the most impressive that economists have ever offered to the statesman, and already in world-wide use. It is the paradigm of genuine and worth-while 'econometrics'. But it offers us one more example of the central mystery of the time which the evolution of theories takes. All three elements in Leontief's scheme were ready to its inventor's hand. And they had been ready to anybody's hand for a lifetime. Anybody could have combined them. The matrix notation, by hind sight, is a self-suggesting 'natural' for the purpose. Many an economist with mathematical propensities must have been aware of matrix algebra, at least under the guise of determinants which are functions of the elements of a matrix. What might not have resulted from a mutual influence, should it have occurred, of two Cambridge men, Arthur Cayley and Alfred Marshall, belonging to nearly the same generation?

One more of the six chief developments of theory in our period was a matter of a tool. The real achievement of Hicks and Allen in their articles on consumer's behaviour, in *Economica* for 1934, was to make known the indifference-map to the Anglo-Saxon world. Of course the indifference-curve had been invented in that world. It was originated by Edgeworth in *Mathematical Psychics* in 1881. But there it was a means of insight only into bilateral monopoly. It was Pareto who seized upon it as a means of escape for theory from the non-observable and non-measurable, yet assumedly quantifiable notion of utility. Pareto, however, never achieved the complete Hicksian diagram where indifference-curves, the picture of the individual's tastes, are confronted with the budget-line, the picture of his circumstances. The tangencies in Pareto's diagrams are between indifference-curves and the technological 'paths' whose nature and constraints are not made fully clear. Nonetheless Pareto sought to place the notion of indifference-curve at the heart of his expression of a general theory of economic action (in more usual language, which Pareto seems to wish to eschew, a theory of 'value'), where the choice of action arises from the mutual confrontation of tastes and the obstacles to their fulfilment. Still the full apparatus, of indifference-curves and budget-line, is already present in Barone, who showed by its means the superiority of direct over indirect taxation in his article 'Studi di economia finanziaria', *Giornale degli Economisti* (1912).* Thus it was not the tool itself but its possibilities which were revealed or hinted at by Sir John Hicks and Professor Sir Roy Allen. They showed what could be done, in a form of argument which anyone, mathematician or not, could follow, with this tool which carries problems half-way to solution by the mere visual stating of them, and which performed this service for problems involving *three* variables, a vital and as it were a qualitative advance as compared with two-dimensional methods. Why, once more, did it take more than fifty years for the means of a notable advance to be fully exploited? And is it, in this case, a mere fifty years? The indifference-map is, of course, in form a *contour map* and contour-maps have been used in geography since at least 1700. Once Hicks and Allen had demonstrated it, the contour map sprang into vast popularity as a means of expressing production functions, factor-supply conditions, and many other things, all of which could have been thought of in contour-map terms at any moment for a hundred years past. What vivid, versatile, and suggestive tool is lying unrecognized beneath economists' eyes at this moment?

There is a sense in which our period saw not only the eclipse of value theory by new branches of economics, but its veritable destruction. For value theory as an account of the mode of allocation of versatile scarce resources in the *perfect knowledge* economy, is the theory of a *perfectly competitive* economy. The abandonment of the perfectly competitive assumption is part of the abandonment of the perfect knowledge assumption, and its consequences were enormously more far reaching than its authors seem to have dreamed at the outset. Paradoxically, their writing looks constantly back, seeking merely to adapt and complete the old structures, not to discard them. Yet 'imperfect competition' renders the supply curve unworkable and undermines the stable, self-adjusting mechanism of 'supply and demand'. 'The threatened wreckage', said Sir John Hicks, 'is that of the greater part of economic theory.'†

---

* Quoted by Mauro Fasiani in 'Di un particulare aspetto delle imposte sul consumo', *La Riforma Sociale*, vol. XLI (1930), reproduced in English in *International Economic Papers*, no. 6 (Peacock, Stolper, Turvey, Elizabeth Henderson, eds.).

† *Value and Capital*, chapter VI, p. 84 (1st edn).

In 1926 Mr Piero Sraffa took by the horns a dilemma made explicit by Marshall in the *Principles* (footnote to 8th edn. p. 459), namely, that economies of large scale, internal to the firm, are difficult to reconcile with 'competition'. Mr Sraffa's solution (like Marshall's, though Marshall did not argue strictly enough to be embarrassed by the situation) was to abandon perfect competition. In seven years this policy, followed out with a fertile and eclectic ingenuity by Sir Roy Harrod and later with more ruthlessness by Mrs Robinson, had shown that value theory, in the sense of a simple, symmetrical body of universal principles, could not survive. Mrs Robinson therefore carried the policy a stage further, and abandoned value theory itself in favour of her new invention, the theory of the firm. This she did without quite acknowledging it, and both she and Professor Chamberlin papered-over the gaping rents they had hewn in the old fabric by assuming that firms, which were monopolists because their products were *distinct*, nevertheless were *identical* in respect of the demand-conditions and the cost-conditions facing them, so that they could still be grouped into an industry. The 'industry', the (technologically defined) 'commodity', the supply curve; these, and 'particular equilibrium' other than that of the mere firm, were the chief casualties, and the work of destruction caused misgivings in those who performed it and many an effort to prop up the ruins. The whole episode is full of puzzles. Why did the dilemma lie untouched from Cournot to Marshall, and from Marshall to Sraffa? Why, at that moment in the 1920s, did a half-dozen or more people suddenly start to work on it, so that while Sir Roy Harrod was putting the marginal revenue curve in print, people at Cambridge were suggesting it to their supervisors and Professor Yntema in 1928, like Marshall in 1890, had written it down with casual mathematical ease as a by-product of a different study? Why, in so many instances in economics, does the winter last so long between seed time and the bursting forth of the crop?

These, then, are the innovations in economic theory which are to serve as our empiric field for the study of the genesis and mutation of thought-schemes in the 'moral sciences', the sciences of human nature, human deliberative conduct and human history. It seems possible that economic action is sufficiently typical of human decisive action in general to throw light beyond its own borders, into the fields of political, intellectual and even imaginative and artistic action. It is much more doubtful whether the insights we may gain will be relevant to those sciences where 'decision' is absent and 'learning' by the objects of study impossible. Evolution, however, if in truth it results from Nature's random trial-and-error coupled with that 'learning' which consists in the proliferation of mutants in congenial environments, may be a sort of borderline science, leaning perhaps towards the physical, but hinting at the eventually psychic problems. Our method of exploiting the field will require the most exact insight and complete understanding of these particular new or evolved economic theories, from an almost clinical viewpoint. A programme of intellectual surgery may be deemed to be in hand, and a study of comparative conceptual anatomy to be one of its main purposes.

Our period opens with the Sraffian Manifesto of 1926, demanding the revision of value theory. We shall try to trace the struggle to dispense with perfect competition and the gradual recognition that value theory, in the old sweeping, unified, and universal sense, stands or falls with the perfectly competitive assumption. Next, it is convenient to take the other value-theory development of our period, the brilliant demonstration of the indifference-map by Sir John Hicks and Professor Sir Roy Allen (as they have become). The other great traditional branch of economics is monetary theory, and our period sees it transformed by Myrdal, Keynes and their company into an expectational theory of general output and employment. Partly from this, partly from the independent work of Frisch and Kalecki, there sprang new and powerful theories of the business cycle. Sir Roy Harrod's was the first, and we might stretch our limits to include that of Professor Kaldor. The proper close of our period in 1939 is marked by Sir Roy Harrod's first proposal of the conditions of regular growth of general output. Lastly we must turn back to 1931 for Leontief's introduction of input–output analysis. This marvellous decade, into which, perhaps, more invention was crammed than into the whole generation from 1870 to 1900, should offer rich suggestions of the nature of that process of artistic creation which results in theories instead of fictions. We cannot formulate our questions in advance. Questions and answering hypotheses must arise together from the material.

CHAPTER 3

SRAFFA AND THE STATE OF VALUE THEORY, 1926

In the tranquil view which the modern theory of value presents us there is one dark spot which disturbs the harmony of the whole. This is represented by the supply curve, based upon the laws of increasing and diminishing returns... [In the law of increasing returns] consideration of that greater internal division of labour, which is rendered possible by an increase in the dimensions of an individual firm, was entirely abandoned, as it was seen to be incompatible with competitive conditions.*

Perfect competition is that state of affairs where the individual firm can sell 'as much as it likes' at a price which the market determines independently of this firm's output. If at each larger output the firm's cost of production per unit of product is lower, what is there to prevent the firm's indefinite expansion? But if the firm expands indefinitely, and thus swallows the whole market, where is perfect competition? This is what we shall call Sraffa's dilemma, and perhaps we ought rather to call it Marshall's dilemma, for in the *Principles of Economics*, 8th edn, footnote to p. 459, Marshall himself speaks of a dilemma:

Some, among whom Cournot himself is to be counted, have before them what is in effect the supply schedule of an individual firm; representing that an increase in its output gives it command over so great internal economies as much to diminish its expenses of production; and they follow their mathematics boldly, but apparently without noticing that their premises lead inevitably to the conclusion that, whatever firm first gets a good start will obtain a monopoly of the whole business of its trade in its district. While others avoiding this horn of the dilemma, maintain that there is no equilibrium at all for commodities which obey the law of increasing return.

At the end of this footnote, Marshall refers us to his mathematical note xiv, and in that note we find, in calculus notation,

* Piero Sraffa, 'The Laws of Returns under Competitive Conditions', *Economic Journal*, vol. xxxvi, pp. 536, 537.

the idea nowadays known as *marginal revenue* most explicitly set forth:

Now if p be the price per unit, which he receives for an amount β of villa accommodation, and therefore $p\beta$ the price which he receives for the whole amount β; and if we put for shortness $\Delta\beta$ in place of $(d\beta/dx_1)\,dx_1$, the increase of villa accommodation due to the additional element of labour dx_1; then the net product we are seeking is not $p\Delta\beta$, but $p\Delta\beta+\beta\Delta p$; where Δp is a negative quantity, and is the fall in demand price caused by the increase in the amount of villa accommodation offered by the builder.

Marshall in his footnote seems a little unjust to Cournot, who expresses in his own fashion the very same dilemma noticed by Marshall and by Sraffa:

It is, moreover, plain under the hypothesis of unlimited competition, and where, at the same time, the function $\phi_k'(D_k)$ [viz. the marginal cost function of firm k for an output D_k] should be a decreasing one, that nothing would limit the production of the article. Thus, wherever there is a return on property, or a rent payable for a plant of which the operation involves expenses of such a kind that the function $\phi_k'(D_k)$ is a decreasing one, it proves that the effect of monopoly is not wholly extinct, or that competition is not so great but that the variation of the amount produced by each individual producer affects the total production of the article, and its price, to a perceptible extent.*

Cournot here clearly envisages a downward-sloping demand curve for the firm's products, and may be said to have essentially solved as well as posed the dilemma. One page before his announcement of the dilemma Marshall seems to offer the essence of its modern solution. In the first footnote to p. 458 he says:

This may be expressed by saying that when we are considering an individual producer, we must couple his supply curve—not with the general demand curve for his commodity in a wide market, but— with the particular demand curve of his own special market. And this particular demand curve will generally be very steep; perhaps as steep as his supply curve is likely to be, even when an increased output will give him an important increase of internal economies.

* Augustin Cournot, *Researches in the Mathematical Principles of the Theory of Wealth* (1838), translated from the French by Nathaniel T. Bacon (New York: The Macmillan Company, 1927).

Everything needful seems at hand to enunciate the modern theorem. And yet some final coalescence of thought escapes him. Marshall isolated marginal revenue only in algebra and not in words, and in Appendix H, on p. 805, he seems also to lose grip on marginal cost:

The term 'margin of production' has no significance for long periods in relation to commodities the cost of production of which diminishes with a gradual increase in the output: and a tendency to increasing return does not exist generally for short periods.

It may be thought that we are here watching a process rather than testing the possibility of an equilibrium. But, if so, we are later shown two stages of this process; the first, where the demand curve has shifted so as to offer great economies of scale, only a part of which have so far been exploited; and the second, where output has been increased to the full extent allowed by the shift of the demand curve:

Let us turn to the case in which the long-period supply price for the increased output fell so far that the demand price remained above it.... Capital and labour would stream rapidly into the trade; and the production might perhaps be increased tenfold before the fall in the demand price became as great as the fall in the long-period supply price, and a position of stable equilibrium had been found (Appendix H, p. 806).

The real source of Marshall's difficulty is glimpsed in this last sentence. He seeks in the case of increasing return an equilibrium like that of diminishing return, where in perfect competition price is equal to marginal cost. The key idea of the theory of imperfect competition is the one which resolves this difficulty. It is the idea of the separation, conceptually and quantitatively, of supply price from marginal cost.

In his famous chapter on monopoly, Cournot differentiates with respect to price instead of quantity, and so his main equation does not exhibit marginal revenue as such. The latter is, however, very easily derived. Writing $F(p)$ for the quantity demanded at price p, Cournot discusses the case where production costs are not zero:

It will no longer be the function $pF(p)$, or the annual *gross receipts*, which the producer should strive to carry to its maximum value, but the *net receipts*, or the function $pF(p) - \phi(D)$, in which $\phi(D)$ denotes the cost of making a number of litres equal to D. Since D is connected with p by the relation $D = F(p)$, the function $pF(p) - \phi(D)$ can be regarded as depending implicitly on the single variable p, although generally the cost of production is an explicit function, not of the price of the article produced, but of the quantity produced. Consequently the price to which the producer should bring his article will be determined by the equation

$$(2) \qquad D + \frac{dD}{dp}\left[p - \frac{d[\phi(D)]}{dD}\right] = 0.$$

If we write F throughout instead of D (to which in equilibrium it is equal), net revenue will be the greatest attainable where

$$\frac{d[pF(p) - \phi\{F(p)\}]}{dp} = 0,$$

that is, where

$$\frac{dp}{dp}F + p\frac{dF}{dp} - \frac{d\phi}{dF}\frac{dF}{dp} = 0.$$

Multiplying through by dp we have

$$dp\,F + p\,dF - \frac{d\phi}{dF}dF = 0,$$

where $dp\,F + p\,dF$ can be looked on as the increment of gross receipts due to a small increment dF in the quantity sold, and $(d\phi/dF)\,dF$ as the increment of total cost due to this same increment. In the form

$$dp\,F + p\,dF = \frac{d\phi}{dF}dF$$

this equation expresses the equivalent of our familiar test for the monopolist's most profitable output, viz. that marginal revenue must equal marginal cost. By a strange oversight, Cournot himself wrongly expresses in his notation the equivalent of marginal revenue. Marshall, his great admirer, might nonetheless have taken more note of this passage:

We shall observe that the co-efficient $d[\phi(D)]/dD$ though it may increase or decrease as D increases, must be supposed to be positive, for it would be absurd that the *absolute* [i.e. total] expense of production should decrease as production increases. We shall call attention also to the fact that necessarily $p > d[\phi(D)]/dD$, for dD being the increase of production, $d[\phi(D)]$ is the increase in the cost,

pdD is the increase in the gross receipts, and whatever may be the abundance of the source of production, the producer will always stop [increasing his output] when the increase in expense exceeds the increase in receipts.

This fallacious argument, where pdD, instead of $pdD + Ddp$, is wrongly called the 'increase in gross receipts', is followed by a correct one where Cournot reaches, in the 1830s, the result which was so painfully re-discovered in the 1930s, that at the equilibrium of a *monopolist*, whatever the degree of competition to which he is subjected, short of the disappearance of his monopoly under perfect competition, price is *greater* than marginal cost:

This is abundantly evident from equation (2), since D is always a positive quantity, and dD/dp is a negative quantity.*

In his chapter 'Of Monopoly', Cournot treats his monopolist as a price-adjuster, and so a trivial rearrangement of his algebra is needed in order to get in explicit form the statement that profit will be a maximum at that output where marginal cost equals marginal revenue. Since Cournot's monopolist or Proprietor recognizes that the annual quantity demanded is a function of price asked, the question whether he is looked on as a price-adjuster or a quantity-adjuster is of no significance. When in his chapter VII Cournot comes to discuss oligopoly, he expresses the condition of maximum profit for each proprietor by differentiating net revenue with respect to quantity, or in other words, by treating his proprietor as a quantity-adjuster. Writing D_1, D_2,...for the quantities offered respectively by Proprietors (1), (2), ...; D for the sum of all these quantities; $f(D)$ for the price per unit, assumed equal for all producers; and $\phi(D_1)$ for the total cost to Proprietor (1) of producing an annual quantity D_1, and so on; Cournot expresses as follows the condition for maximum profit for Proprietor (1)(Bacon's translation, p. 85):

$$f(D) + D_1 f'(D) - \phi_1'(D_1) = 0.$$

* Augustin Cournot, *Recherches sur les principes mathématiques de la théorie des richesses*, translated by Nathaniel T. Bacon, edited by Irving Fisher (New York: The Macmillan Company, 1927). This and the previous passages of Cournot are from chapter V: 'Of Monopoly'.

Here we have nothing else than the explicit statement that for maximum profit, marginal revenue, viz.

$$\frac{d[D_1 f(D)]}{dD_1} = f(D) + D_1 f'(D)$$

has to be brought to equality with marginal cost, viz. $\phi_1'(D_1)$. Fifty years before Marshall, and nearly a hundred before the Imperfect Competition theorists of 1928–33, Cournot had provided the simple key to the whole matter.

Let us return to Sraffa. He next inquires what bounds we place upon our freedom of assumption, and our consequent results, when we adopt Marshall's method of particular equilibrium, that is, 'the study of the equilibrium value of single commodities produced under competitive conditions'. Here we require the demand conditions, and especially the income of the demanders and the prices of substitute or complementary commodities, to be unaffected by changes in the output of our commodity: demand curve and supply curve must each be able to be drawn with shape and position unaffected by movements *along* the other curve. But this mutual independence of supply and demand conditions, required by the method of particular equilibrium, cannot be assumed if the production of our commodity employs a considerable part of a factor fixed in total existing quantity. For any marked increase in the output of our commodity will necessarily then increase the unit price of the factor, by markedly competing for the use of it with the other goods which it helps to produce. Thus the prices of these other goods will be raised, and this, if they are substitutes or complements (as is likely), will alter the conditions of demand for our commodity. On the other hand, if our commodity employs only a very small proportion of the factor, the absorption of a little more will leave the factor price unaffected, and *thus also the unit cost of our commodity*. It is thus difficult, within the frame of competitive conditions in particular equilibrium analysis, to account for a unit cost curve, or a marginal cost curve, which slopes up with increase of supposed output. Thus 'the imposing structure of diminishing returns [that is, unit and marginal cost as increasing functions of output] is available only for the study of that minute class of commodities in the production of which the whole of a factor of production is employed'. Let us notice again that what this argument concerns is a method of analysis, a set of assumptions, namely the 'particular equilibrium' analysis of an industry operating in competition. Nowadays it seems likely that an analyst would go more directly to the result which Mr Sraffa has at this stage reached, by arguing that *perfect* competition applies to the factor market as well as to the product market, and so the industry must be supposed able to buy each of its factors, as well as sell its product, at a market price independent of its own output, and its long period marginal cost curve must be horizontal, if not downward-sloping.

Now a downward-sloping unit cost curve also, Mr Sraffa argued, is excluded by the assumptions. For economies external to the scale of manufacture of a particular commodity are, of course, irrelevant to the analysis of that industry's own isolated equilibrium, while economies of scale *internal to each firm* in that industry are incompatible with the industry's competitive character. But 'Those economies which are external from the point of view of the individual firm, but internal as regards the industry in its aggregate, constitute precisely the class which is most seldom to be met with'. If then it is not legitimate, within the assumptions of particular equilibrium of a competitive industry, to treat the unit cost of the product as either an increasing or a decreasing function of its output, we are left with the result that unit cost is independent of output. Now if unit cost is one and the same regardless of output, it is one and the same regardless of demand, and 'the old and now obsolete theory which makes [competitive value] dependent on cost of production appears to hold its ground'.*

If we allow ourselves to speak in modern terms of perfect competition, and mean by this that prices of both product and factors to the individual firm are independent of its output, then the conclusion of Mr Sraffa's argument at this stage is the failure of perfectly competitive assumptions to show any equilibrium of the individual firm. For both the demand curve for its product, and the curve relating unit cost to output, would be horizontal straight lines. This indictment of the perfectly competitive assumptions is Mr Sraffa's first objective.

* Piero Sraffa, *Economic Journal*, vol. XXXVI, p. 541.

His destructive purpose thus completed, he turns to his constructive one:

It is necessary, therefore, to abandon the path of free competition and turn in the opposite direction, namely, towards monopoly (p. 542).

Up to this point he has been examining a particular theoretical model and showing the consequences of its assumptions. Now he turns to examine the real world. In a single paragraph the whole basis and necessity of the modern theory of imperfect competition is set out with an ease and economy that have never been improved on:

Everyday experience shows that a very large number of undertakings work under conditions of individual diminishing costs. Almost any producer of [manufactured consumers'] goods, if he could rely upon the market in which he sells his products being prepared to take any quantity of them at the current price, without any trouble on his part except that of producing them, would extend his business enormously...Business men...would consider absurd the assertion that the limit to their production is to be found in the internal conditions of production in their firm, which do not permit of a greater quantity without an increase in [unit] cost. The chief obstacle against which they have to contend when they want gradually* to increase their production does not lie in the cost of production—which indeed generally favours them in that direction —but in the difficulty of selling the larger quantity of goods without reducing the price, or without having to face increased marketing expenses. This necessity of reducing prices in order to sell a larger quantity of one's own product is only an aspect of the usual descending demand curve, with the difference that instead of concerning the whole of a commodity, whatever its origin, it relates only to the goods produced by a particular firm (p. 543).

Again,

[What] renders a stable equilibrium possible even when the supply curve for the products of each individual firm is descending [is] the absence of indifference on the part of buyers of goods as between the different producers (p. 544).

Mr Sraffa proceeds to list all those natural and artificial circumstances which account for 'a willingness on the part of a group of buyers who constitute a firm's clientele to pay, if necessary, something extra in order to obtain the goods from a

* Let us note this word.

particular firm rather than from any other'. This willingness is manifested and measured in the elasticity, over the relevant segment, of the demand curve facing the firm, an elasticity less than the infinite elasticity of demand for the output of the firm under perfect competition. Mr Sraffa now quotes Marshall's footnote which we gave on p. 14 above, and indeed that footnote must make us wonder how it can have taken forty years, from the first publication of the *Principles*, for the great body of doctrine known as imperfect or monopolistic competition to start to be built up on the basis of hints so plainly present in Marshall. The fame of having assembled, out of the old confusing heap of notions concerning diminishing and increasing returns, and the scattered hints in Marshall, a clear mosaic picture of a new problem and the essence of its solution, belongs to Mr Sraffa. One essential piece only is missing. Mr Sraffa continues in his article to speak of the supply curve as though this expression could stand for cost conditions only, even when the firm's market is less than perfectly elastic. Marshall in his verbal text (as distinct from his mathematical note XIV) was puzzled to know *with what* the downward-sloping demand curve for the firm's products could intersect to determine the industry's equilibrium. He seems to have felt (see the passage quoted on p. 15 above, from *Principles*, Appendix H) that it could not simply intersect either the unit cost curve or the marginal cost curve. That at least is one interpretation of his remark that 'the term ''margin of production'' has no significance...[when] the cost of production diminishes with a gradual increase in the output'. The idea which Marshall groped for and even Sraffa did not supply was about to emerge in many quarters under various names. That we shall see in the next chapter. Meanwhile an important feature of the whole argument must be noticed. Marshall and Sraffa in our quoted passages repeatedly use the word 'gradually' and it is plain that 'Sraffa's (or Marshall's) dilemma' relates to the long period. For in the short enough period the firm can plainly experience marginal cost rising with output, as a consequence of the time required to install extra capacity. All the modern formulations of problems and their modern solutions are seen in the light of Marshall's great vision of the importance of time and the need to consider the *stages of evolution* of the ceaselessly changing economy.

CHAPTER 4

MARGINAL REVENUE

Marginal revenue results from differentiating price-times-output with respect to output, having regard to the dependence of price and output on each other. As such it was written down by Cournot and by Marshall. In their works it appears anonymously as a mere step of algebraic manipulation. Neither of them separated it from its context by giving it a distinctive name which would stay with it and make it a ready tool of verbal discussion. Cournot speaks (Bacon translation, p. 59) of 'the increase of the gross receipts', but then wrongly states this as price-times-increment of output. Marshall uses the formal notion to express 'the net product of an agent of production' (*Principles*, 8th edn, p. 849). To name a concept and thus fix it as an idea on its own is a considerable and essential part of the act of inventing it. It must, in our judgement, be doubtful on this ground whether either of these two writers can claim to have invented marginal revenue. Marshall's claim is better than Cournot's, for whereas Cournot actually forgot the second term of the expression, Marshall drew particular attention to the fact that there are two terms and that they are of opposite sign, and went on to discuss their relative numerical size (*Principles*, note XIV of Mathematical Appendix), concluding that in the ordinary competitive conditions of his day the second term may be neglected. Forty years, more or less, from the publication of the *Principles* this tool suddenly and simultaneously appeared in many hands, in the published or unpublished work of authors who had discovered it independently of each other. To find some explanation of such pieces of intellectual history by considering the nature of the problems and solutions involved is our main purpose in this book. What oral or printed sources of ideas may have been common to some of the early investigators of marginal revenue, what channels of communication may have linked them with each other, we cannot hope to establish. Such threads leading from mind to mind can be elusive beyond description. A word spoken by one pupil and repeated by the teacher to another, no one remembering or ever knowing the whole circumstances; a conversation at a college dinner table, casually overheard; a remark at a seminar, subconsciously noted; all this is largely gone beyond anyone's recall. The printed record alone is publicly beyond dispute, and its collation and analysis are all that will concern us.

Some notion of the degree of fame or of neglect that a given article has enjoyed can be gained by looking at the edges of the bound annual volume containing it, where the reader's fingers discolour them. By this test, few have read the article by Professor T. O. Yntema in the *Journal of Political Economy* for December 1928, called 'The Influence of Dumping on Monopoly Price', despite the reference to it in the Foreword of Mrs Joan Robinson's *Economics of Imperfect Competition*. Yet this is, it seems, the earliest printed occurrence of the phrase *marginal gross revenue*:

Let y_a be price in the domestic market; x_a be quantity taken in the domestic market;...y_c be average [i.e. unit] cost of production.... With operations restricted to the domestic market the monopoly will seek to maximize $(x_a y_a - x_a y_c)$, or total gross revenue less total cost. At this maximum point the marginal increment in gross revenue (hereafter called 'marginal gross revenue') will just be balanced by the marginal cost, or

$$\frac{d(x_a y_a)}{dx_a} = \frac{d(x_a y_c)}{dx_a}.$$

Let the quantity produced and sold, x_a, be plotted on the horizontal scale [of a diagram not here shown] and the marginal cost $[d(x_a y_c)]/dx_a$, and the marginal gross revenue, $[d(x_a y_a)]/dx_a$, be plotted on the vertical scale. Construct the marginal cost curve and the marginal gross revenue curve. The abscissa of [their] point of intersection represents the maximum profit volume of output; and the price, being a function of volume, is directly determinable from the originally assumed demand curve.

Professor Yntema's diagram shows the two marginal curves and no others. They are drawn as straight lines, both sloping down from left to right, the marginal revenue curve sloping the more steeply and duly intersecting the other from above. The demand curve, though not drawn, is referred to, and thus in the diagram and its descriptive passage we have all the elements of short-period equilibrium of the monopolistic firm.

England, and Oxford, next brought out marginal revenue in
print, for although Professor Edward Chamberlin filed his
thesis at Harvard in 1927, *The Theory of Monopolistic Competition* was not published until 1933. But at the same time the idea
had oral currency in Cambridge:

I first learned of it [says Mrs Joan Robinson] from Mr C. H. P.
Gifford, of Magdalene College, who was then reading for the
Economics Tripos. Shortly afterwards Mr P. A. Sloan, of Clare
College, showed me an unpublished essay in which it occurred.
Next it was published by Mr R. F. Harrod [Sir Roy Harrod] in the
Economic Journal of June 1930, in an article which must have been
written almost simultaneously with Mr Sloan's paper.

Marginal revenue was introduced by Sir Roy Harrod, independently of other writers, in his 'Notes on Supply' in the
Economic Journal of June 1930:

We shall now consider the case where the source [firm or plant] of
supply is not small in proportion to the whole industry. When that is
so, the source is confronted with a falling demand curve. When there
is one source, the demand with which it is confronted is that of the
whole market. Where the curve showing the demand for its output
is not horizontal, the output of a source is not determined by the
point of intersection of the demand curve and the marginal cost
curve. The demand curve of the market shows the price per unit
at which suppliers can find buyers for x units for all values of x.
From this curve may be deduced another, which I propose to call
the increment of aggregate demand curve, and which shows the
aggregate price that suppliers can obtain for x units of output less
the aggregate price that they can obtain for $(x-1)$ units for all
values of x...The output of a monopolistic source is determined by
the point at which the marginal cost curve cuts the increment of
aggregate demand curve.*

In this passage we see an author's struggle to disengage his
thought from habitual channels in order to achieve an innovation. In these few lines Harrod takes a step which was both
necessary and difficult, however obvious it may seem *ex post
facto*. He takes this step hesitantly, and, for his reader, somewhat
confusingly. This step consists in abandoning the notion of the
market demand curve for a commodity in favour of that of the
demand curve for the product of a particular firm. For a pure

* R. F. Harrod, 'Notes on Supply', *Economic Journal*, vol. XL, pp. 238, 239.

monopolist the two curves are, of course, one and the same, and it is by considering a pure monopoly that Harrod makes his transition. In the middle of this passage Harrod speaks in the plural of suppliers and defines his new curve as showing increments of *aggregate* demand. But marginal revenue is primarily relevant to the single firm or source of supply, not to the market or the industry, except in that case, viz. pure monopoly, where industry and firm are one. Marshall, in *Principles*, footnote to p. 458, had referred to a firm's particular market for its own product, and to the demand curve expressing that market, but he had not, perhaps, given this notion sufficient emphasis to make it a ready tool for later writers. But above all what relegated to obscurity the notion of a firm's particular demand curve for its product was the dominance of the notion of perfect competition, strictly defined, which obviated any need to consider such a curve.

When the type of objects produced by each firm in a collection of firms is physically and technically indistinguishable from the type produced by each other of these firms, and when no potential buyer of such goods has the least preference for one firm over another; when the number of these firms is so great, and their size so little dispersed, that no practicable change in the output of any one firm can noticeably affect the output of the collection as a whole, the type of objects can be unequivocally called a commodity and the collection of firms an industry, and this industry is producing and selling under perfect competition. In these circumstances the price per unit of the commodity is outside the control or influence of any one firm. This price is for each firm a datum, and it is one and the same datum for every firm. It is the sole datum, on the demand side, which the firm need take notice of in deciding the size of its output. A rise of price will induce every firm to increase its output, and a fall in price will induce each of them to reduce its output. Included in this last statement is the extreme type of case where a firm's output rises from, or falls to, zero; that is, the case where a firm enters or leaves the industry. These implications of perfect competition mean that, when the time allowed for adaptation is specified, the output of the industry as a whole is a single valued function of the price per unit of the commodity, provided incomes and other prices remain unchanged. In short, perfect competition gives logical existence to the *supply curve of a commodity*, allowing us, in given conditions of cost, to infer the output (i.e. the number of physical units produced per time unit) of this commodity from a knowledge of the *price alone*. Moreover, perfect competition assures us that price can, and will, find a level where daily or annual quantity demanded and daily or annual quantity supplied are equal: the market will be *stable*. All these clear-cut simplicities are lost when perfect competition is abandoned. It unifies each market where it applies; and since the market for any given, uniform factor of production may be co-extensive with the whole economy, the assumption of *general* perfect competition in all product and factor markets enables *general equilibrium* of the entire economy to be defined simply enough to make possible a study of the existence or non-existence, in a logical or mathematical sense, of *solutions* which would constitute such an equilibrium. To renounce the assumption of perfect competition was to risk the dissolution of value theory and even the whole fabric of economics as a deductive system. This was only realized gradually and even then only by the most clear-sighted and uncompromising minds.

Sir Roy Harrod and his co-pioneers during the next few years were like people inspecting the results of an earthquake. It was hard to realize at first that the old fabric of value theory had been destroyed. They picked their way amongst the old structures, calling them by their old names, but the masonry no longer fitted together on its old universal plan, the simplicity and unity had gone. Marshall had habitually spoken of competition and his pupils more rigorously of perfect competition. This phrase had seemed to them an approximate description of reality. In truth it was the wholly indispensable basis of that simple view by which the price and the output of a commodity, that is, some physically specified good produced by a group of firms called an industry, were determined in a manner of which the intersection of a single market demand curve and a single market supply curve was the diagrammatic illustration. It is the market supply curve which is killed outright by the abandonment of perfect competition; killed, paradoxically, not by anything which happens on the side of costs, but by what happens on the side of demand. Sir John Hicks, amongst all economists, has most openly stated what is involved in abandoning perfect competition as the working assumption of economists, and has consistently refused to abandon it:

> It has to be recognized that a general abandonment of the assumption of perfect competition, a universal adoption of the assumption of monopoly, must have very destructive consequences for economic theory. Under monopoly the stability conditions become indeterminate; and the basis on which economic laws can be constructed is therefore shorn away. Not only is falling average cost consistent with monopoly; falling marginal cost is consistent with monopoly too. There must indeed be something to stop the indefinite expansion of the firm; but it can just as well be stopped by the limitation of the market as by rising marginal costs...

> It is, I believe, only possible to save anything from this wreck—and it must be remembered that the threatened wreckage is that of the greater part of economic theory—if we can assume that the markets confronting most of the firms with which we shall be dealing do not differ very greatly from perfectly competitive markets...At least, this getaway seems worth trying.*

Sraffa's dilemma appeared at first as the simple question: What limits the size of the firm if its unit cost of physical production goes down with every increase of its output? Sraffa found the clue in Marshall: increased outputs can only be sold at unit prices which go down even faster, as output increases, than cost of physical production. Two paths were open to those who wished to follow up this hint. It could have been argued that the theory of monopoly had been provided by Cournot, and that if in Sraffa's words it was 'necessary... to abandon the path of free competition and turn...towards monopoly' it was only necessary to build upon Cournot's work, or at most to follow his example and apply mathematical analysis to a direct statement of monopoly conditions. By this latter policy Professor Yntema did in fact provide a brief, incisive, and almost complete theory of the firm parallel to Cournot's but using differentiation with respect to output instead of with respect to price. The other path, which it was necessary that someone should at some time trace out from one end or the other, consisted in finding, element by element, a counterpart to the model of the firm provided by

---

* John Richard Hicks, *Value and Capital* (Oxford, at the Clarendon Press, 1939), pp. 83–5.

the theory of perfect competition. This second approach, consisting in the piecemeal dismantling and replacement of the perfectly competitive model, was in a sense harder, for instead of 'placing free footsteps on untrodden ground',* the explorer had a field cluttered with existing theory. The explorer who opened this path was Harrod, while those who turned it into a highway were Mrs Joan Robinson and, in the role of her adviser, Mr (now Professor Lord) Kahn.

In order to carry the theory of the firm and of the industry from a perfectly competitive to a monopolistically competitive setting, it was necessary to answer the following questions:

(i) Whereas under perfect competition the firm's most profitable output is that which carries marginal cost up to equality with price, this rule will not serve for monopolistic competition, where the demand price for the firm's output diminishes as its output increases. For then an extra unit of output diminishes the price at which all existing units can be sold, and thus, to be profitable, it must command a price sufficient to cover not only the amount it adds to total cost but also the amount which it subtracts from the rest of total revenue. What, then, is to be the rule for determining monopolistic output? With what, if not with the demand curve for the firm's product, must marginal cost intersect?

(ii) At the firm's equilibrium in perfect competition, price is equal to marginal cost. What happens when the monopolistic assumption is applied to the Sraffian purpose of explaining the equilibrium of a firm which has decreasing unit costs? For where the firm's unit cost curve is downward-sloping, its marginal cost curve will lie below the unit cost curve and, if price were equal to marginal cost, unit cost would be greater than price and the firm would make a trading loss.

(iii) Question (i) having been answered by defining marginal revenue, and Question (ii) by showing that, since the demand curve for the monopolistic competitor's product is downward-sloping and therefore has its marginal curve lying below it, price at any output will be greater than marginal revenue and thus, at the point of intersection of the marginal revenue and marginal cost curves, greater than marginal cost, we are next led to ask what governs the relation between price and marginal revenue?

* Horace, *Epistles* I, xix, § 21.

(iv) Can a firm be in equilibrium at an output where its unit cost curve is falling and where, therefore, it is not producing at the lowest cost possible with its existing plant? Is such an equilibrium only a short-period one or can it be a long-period one? Can all the firms in an industry be simultaneously in such an equilibrium, so that it constitutes an equilibrium of the industry? What are the conditions for such an equilibrium of the industry?

(v) Under monopolistic competition, what becomes of the concept of the supply curve of the commodity?

(vi) There is finally a question which envelops and subsumes even that of the supply curve. For when every firm has its own particular market, expressed by a curve which manifests the preferences of customers for this firm's particular product, can we any longer regard the products of different firms as constituting a single commodity? What, in other words, has now happened to the concept of the *industry*?

Those whose minds, when they set out to construct a theory of monopolistic competition, were filled and dominated (for reasons we have explained) by the notions of perfect competition, found the path beset with traps and obstacles. Those who simply wrote down in algebra the conditions affecting a monopolist and sought their implications had no such trouble. Professor Yntema in his brilliant article obtained almost as by-products some results which a year or two later appeared to others vitally important principles and great milestones on the road. Amongst these by-products was his solution to our question (iii). In the course of relating the foreign to the domestic price of a firm's product, when this firm is a monopolist in the domestic but not in the foreign market, Professor Yntema pointed out that the respective quantities sold in the two markets must, for maximum profit, be such as to equalize marginal revenue in these markets. Using the notation we have quoted, he says

At equilibrium,
$$\frac{d(x_a y_a)}{dx_a} = \frac{d(x_b y_b)}{dx_b}.$$

Differentiating, factoring and substituting,
$$y_a \left(1 + \frac{1}{\eta_a} \right) = y_b \left(1 + \frac{1}{\eta_b} \right).$$

in which η, defined as $(y/x) \cdot (dx/dy)$, represents the elasticity of demand and has a negative value. Now if the foreign demand be the more elastic, i.e. if

$$|\eta_b| > |\eta_a| \quad \text{and if} \quad |\eta_a| > 1,$$

then

$$\left(1 + \frac{1}{\eta_b}\right) > \left(1 + \frac{1}{\eta_a}\right)$$

and

$$y_a > y_b$$

[that is, the domestic price is greater than the foreign price].

The formula

$$\frac{d(xy)}{dx} = y\left(1 + \frac{1}{\eta}\right)$$

expresses marginal revenue in terms of price, y, and elasticity of demand, η, for the firm's product. This formula is true of each and every output which the firm might produce. Suppose, then, that, by observing the firm during some period when its cost conditions do not change, we are able to write down for each of a number of prices respectively paid for its product on different occasions, the quantity bought from it per time unit at that price. Such a table would resemble superficially the *supply schedule* of a perfectly competitive industry, since although it would have been obtained by observation over a period, still our stipulation of unchanging cost conditions might, if we argued incautiously, lead us to think of it as revealing a pattern of response to changing price, valid so long as the cost conditions should continue unchanged. But our table would in fact be nothing of the kind. Output is at its most profitable size where one extra unit added to it would increase the firm's total costs by more than it would increase total revenue, while one unit subtracted from output would diminish total revenue by more than it would reduce total costs. Output is at its most profitable, that is to say, where *marginal revenue* equals marginal cost. It is marginal revenue which, on the demand side, determines output. And marginal revenue depends, as Professor Yntema's formula shows, not only on price but also on elasticity of demand for the firm's product. This intervention of elasticity in the relation between price and the firm's elected output destroys completely the possibility, in monopolistic competition, of a simple supply curve where each price would elicit from a firm, or an industry, one, and only one, output. Our answer to question (v), therefore, must be that the supply curve is destroyed. Sir John Hicks's dismay becomes easy to appreciate.

These almost casual creations and relegations of theory were not Professor Yntema's aim or concern. They were thrown off with the utmost economy of statement in the course of answering a special and narrow question, and he makes no reference at all, for example, to the supply curve. Such is one mode of intellectual invention, and an excellent one. Harrod's work was no less brilliant, but its laborious course was of a sort to give, in the end, a greater insight and a more extensive view.

In his 'Notes on Supply' Harrod defined, without knowledge of any similar formulation, the notion of the *increment of aggregate demand curve*, and stated the rule for a monopolistic maximum profit, viz. the choice of that output which equalizes marginal cost and the increment of aggregate demand. He further showed that this rule is a general one which includes, as a special case, the rule which requires a firm in perfect competition to equalize *price* and marginal cost:

The increment of aggregate demand curve shows the total price of x units less the total price of $(x-1)$ units for all values of x. When the sources are many and the demand for the products of a source is shown by a horizontal line, the demand curve and the increment of aggregate demand curve for the product of that source are coincident (R. F. Harrod, 'Notes on Supply', as previously cited).

In the perfectly competitive market the firm could sell at only one price, and at that price could sell as much or little, within its own productive capacity, as it liked. The output that it liked to sell was that which carried its marginal cost up to equality with this externally given price, for since an extra unit, no matter what the output to which it was added, could always be sold at this given price and since, therefore, it left unchanged the price of the units already being sold, it followed that price *was* marginal revenue. The firm in equilibrium in perfect competition was necessarily on a rising part of its marginal cost curve, and could therefore be on a rising part of its unit cost curve. But when both were rising, the unit cost curve would lie below the marginal cost curve, and at the latter's intersection with the (horizontal) price line, unit cost would then be below price, and the firm would make a profit on every unit sold. What, now, of monopolistic competition? If equilibrium of the firm had still consisted in equality of *price* and marginal cost, it might have seemed that the firm in equilibrium would be making a loss. For when monopolistic competition was serving its Sraffian purpose of explaining a falling unit cost curve, which would necessarily lie *above* its corresponding marginal curve, it would follow that any intersection of the price curve (that is, the demand curve for the firm's products) with the marginal cost curve would lie *below* the corresponding unit cost, and the firm would make a loss on each unit sold. The grip which the perfectly competitive set-up had, even on a mind so powerfully original as Harrod's, is shown by the tortuous struggle he became involved in to solve this non-existent difficulty.

The price per unit at which a firm in monopolistic competition is willing to supply a given quantity per unit time of its product depends, as we saw, on demand conditions as well as on cost conditions. Thus supply price is conceptually and numerically divorced from marginal cost, and is free to be equal to demand price even when the latter is greater than marginal cost. Indeed it is obvious that the price received by the monopolistic firm in equilibrium is bound just as essentially to be one which the buyers are willing, in all the circumstances of the case, to pay as it is to be one which the firm in these circumstances is willing to accept. It *can* lie on the demand curve, it *must* lie on the demand curve, and so this price will, of course, be represented by that ordinate of the demand curve whose abscissa is the firm's equilibrium output. To the 'direct analysts' like Yntema and indeed like Cournot, all this offered no difficulty. But Marshall, surprisingly, had baulked at it, and his followers teetered behind him, misguidedly appealing, in Harrod's case, to the quite separate idea of marketing costs which brings in enormous difficulties of its own.

In his famous article of 1926, Mr Sraffa had suggested by way of *reductio ad absurdum* that, even in the analysis of monopolistic competition, buyers' indifference might be formally preserved:

No doubt it is possible, from the formal point of view, to...regard every purchaser as being perfectly indifferent in his choice between the different producers, provided the latter, in order to approach him, are prepared to incur marketing expenses which vary greatly in different cases, and to reckon these increased marketing expenses in the cost of production of each...What is important is to ascertain how the various forces at work can be grouped in the most homogeneous manner, so that the influence of each of them on the equilibrium resulting from their opposition may be more readily estimated. From this point of view the method [indicated above] must be rejected, since it entirely conceals the effects which the circumstances from which the marketing expenses originate exercise in disturbing the unity of the market. It alters in a misleading way, moreover, the customary and well-defined significance of 'cost of production'.

Despite this warning, Harrod thought that a solution of Marshall's dilemma and all the attendant troubles might be found by constructions involving actual or notional marketing costs. We shall not trace out his (as we think) misdirected ingenuity. Marketing costs other than those consisting in a lowering of price are not the concern of this chapter. Moreover the objections which Sraffa pointed out hold true, and the purpose of the supply-and-demand analysis of value is only confused and frustrated by too early an introduction of the concept, quite alien to the nature of that analysis, of costs whose *raison d'être* is to distort and displace the very curves which are the frame of our conclusions. After following this false trail for several pages Harrod suddenly, and by a remarkable *volte-face*, totally abandons it and picks up what we must regard as the true scent. But in those early pages of his second article on supply, 'The Law of Decreasing Costs' (*Economic Journal*, vol. XLI, pp. 566–70), he reaches several important conclusions, even if by a not altogether satisfactory route:

[If a firm must take special measures to sell its output] a complete reconstruction of the notion of a supply schedule becomes necessary. In the usual analysis supply and demand schedules are regarded as independent of one another. On the new view every demand schedule has its own appropriate supply schedule. To determine equilibrium after a change in the former, the latter also must be changed. The customary graphical representation of supply is no longer possible.

In the paragraph following this passage, Harrod seems to forget his new invention, the increment of aggregate demand curve, and to be using an untenable picture of an equilibrium (of the firm) determined by the intersection of the firm's supply curve with a downward-sloping demand curve. Still pursuing marketing costs, he raises a little later what we have listed above as question (iii):

The second difficulty in supposing a competitive equilibrium to be compatible with the condition of short-period decreasing costs arises from the fact that if marginal costs are falling, the marginal prime cost will probably be less than the average prime cost, and if the price is equal to the marginal cost, total prime costs will not be covered.

In seeking to answer it, he plunges at first into an argument which loses all sight of the purpose of drawing demand and similar curves, namely, the simple representation of static and constant conditions whose confrontation determines an equilibrium. But deliverance is at hand. Suddenly marketing costs are thrown overboard:

To illustrate how a particular falling demand curve affects the relation of costs to price, we may suppose that the whole manipulation of the market at the disposal of the individual firm consists of price regulation, and that the selling expenses are null. In such a case the marginal cost curve would be composed solely of productive costs. Even so, falling marginal costs are compatible with profit. For the point of equilibrium is determined by the point of intersection of the marginal cost curve and the increment of aggregate demand curve. A halt is called to production [i.e. a halt is called to (conceptual) *increase* of production, or *output is settled*] at the point at which the net increment of cost rises above the net increment of receipts due to it. But if the demand curve is falling [i.e. is downward-sloping] the increment of net receipts due to an extra unit is less than the price per unit. If y_1 is the price per unit and η the elasticity of demand at the point of equilibrium, the increment of receipts falls short of the price by y_1/η... The increment of aggregate receipts is

$$\frac{d(xy)}{dx} = y + x\frac{dy}{dx} = y - \frac{y}{\eta}.$$

Except that Harrod has elected to regard the elasticity of a downward-sloping demand curve as positive, and has therefore used a minus sign before the term containing η, this formula is the same as the one we quoted from Yntema.

Cournot had shown that at the monopolist's most profitable price (and hence also, of course, at his most profitable output, since it is these mutually dependent variables in combination which determine profitability), price would exceed marginal cost. Yntema and Harrod showed that the size of the gap between price and marginal cost varies inversely with the *elasticity* of demand for the firm's product. Harrod in the passage we have quoted answered at one stroke our questions (ii) and (iii).

The famous and familiar diagram, which, by analogy with many a notational summing-up, we might call the 'fundamental diagram' of imperfect or monopolistic competition, was attempted, but not quite achieved, by Harrod in this article. He shows the five curves which express the association between output and, respectively, unit price or average revenue, marginal revenue, unit or average prime cost, marginal cost and lastly the result of adding to unit prime cost the quotient, by output, of a constant K representing 'overheads plus a normal return to capital invested.' Harrod had referred in his 'Notes on Supply' to the difficulties of the concept of supplementary or overhead costs, and we must give this matter a brief independent consideration before studying his diagram. A firm in perfectly competitive factor markets is conceived to face given prices for its factors of production; in imperfect factor markets we suppose it, for the purpose of analysis, to face given price-quantity schedules for its factors. In both cases there is, for any given quantity which it elects to hire, a given market price per unit. Once a contract has been signed, engaging such and such a number of units for such and such a period, the firm must pay the hire of these units willynilly, and the only question into which they enter is whether the firm will *renew* their hire when the period is over. If, then, we elect to study the firm at a moment when it has committed itself to the hire of some factors for a term of years, but is still free to decide, at the beginning of each week or month, how much of other factors it shall combine with these already engaged 'fixed' factors, we must divide the firm's problems into two kinds. In deciding how much to engage of the factors hired weekly, it will ignore the amount of its payments for the fixed factors. But in deciding whether or not it will, when the time comes, *renew* its contracts for the fixed factors, it will of course compare their prices with the returns which, on the basis of its present trading experience, they seem likely to earn. These present earnings of factors whose quantity in the firm is for the time being fixed, Marshall called quasi-rents. But the difference between such factors, and those engaged by the week, lies in the different lengths and terminal dates of the intervals at which a fresh choice can be made concerning the quantities to be employed, and not, as some of Harrod's words unintentionally suggest, in their having no market price. In short, factors are fixed, on the payroll and in the list of resources of the firm, for shorter or longer periods. Frequently, therefore, the firm will find itself free to alter the quantities it employs of some factors but not able for the time being to alter those of others. At such moments, nonetheless, the firm must look forward to a date when these others, through the expiry of a contract or through physical dissolution, will ceased to be fixed in quantity and in associated outgoings. Its intention to maintain, reduce or increase the quantity employed of the factors whose quantity is at present fixed, when it shall next be free to do so, will be governed, our model assumes, by the firm's present experience in using the present fixed quantities to the best advantage, that is, in combining them in optimal proportions with those factors which it can already vary. Our formulation does not exclude a possible asymmetry: a firm may sometimes be free to increase, when it cannot diminish, the fixed factors.

Harrod in his 'Notes on Supply' wishes to provide the entrepreneur with some simple test by which to know whether his commitment to his existing quantities of fixed factors was justified and whether and on what scale he should renew his commitment when the time comes. This is the interpretation which we suggest for his term 'normal' profit or return, which he himself puts in inverted commas:

There is no pre-determined supplementary cost, the price payable to the fixed factors [i.e. the earnings attributable to them out of the sale-proceeds of the firm's output] being in the short run [i.e. after the firm has committed itself to purchase a given quantity of these factors] passively determined by the relation of demand price [of product] to prime costs. The consequence of this is that the concept of supplementary cost seems to be meaningless. To overcome this difficulty, it is convenient to suppose that the fixed factors should receive a 'normal' rate of return.

Elsewhere in the literature, *normal profit* has been defined as that return to combined capital and entrepreneurship which leads neither to the establishment of additional firms in the industry nor to the disappearance of existing ones from it. The profit earned by existing firms is assumed, in this conception, to be

regarded by potential entrants as indicating what they themselves would earn if they set up in the industry. Since the output
of the industry can be changed either by changes of output of
existing firms or by changes in the number of firms composing
the industry, normal profit serves to help define an equilibrium
of the industry. Harrod himself makes no such use of the idea,
and leaves its purpose vague. Nonetheless his diagram (Fig. 1 in
'The Law of Decreasing Costs') has become, save for one error,
the standard picture of the firm in long period equilibrium in a
monopolistically competitive market. In it he wishes to represent the firm as earning normal profit at that output, marked by
equality of marginal revenue and marginal cost, which makes
its profit as large as possible in those circumstances which are
for the time being outside its control. Where marginal cost and
marginal revenue are equal, total cost and total revenue are
increasing, each as a function of output, at one and the same
rate, and curves representing these total quantities would
therefore have, at this output, the same slope as each other. If,
at the output where their slopes are equal, their ordinates are
also equal, they will be tangent to each other at this output.
These equalities of slope and ordinate will be unaffected if we
divide total cost and total revenue each by output so as to get
curves of unit cost and unit revenue. Thus when Harrod shows
his firm's maximum attainable profit as precisely equal to
normal profit, so that the relevant curves have their ordinates
equal, he ought also to show these curves as tangent to each
other at the best output and not, as he does, intersecting each
other. Such an oversight is surely a most natural thing in the
midst of an exploration of so much uncharted ground. The
classic diagram in its correct form appears and is described in
Mrs Joan Robinson's article on 'Imperfect Competition and
Falling Supply Price' (*Economic Journal*, vol. XLII, December
1932, pp. 547–9) where she acknowledges her debt for the
tangency proposition to Mr R. F. Kahn.

Had Harrod perceived the tangency proposition, his final
question and brilliant answer could have been launched with
even more *éclat* than they were. He asks:

If a source is subject to decreasing costs, it must be producing at what
is, from the productive point of view, less than the optimum rate. Is
this consistent with long-period equilibrium?

His argument had not allowed him to add 'Moreover, a monopolistic firm in equilibrium *necessarily is* subject to decreasing cost' yet this also is true. For the particular demand curve for the product of the monopolistic firm is downward-sloping, and a curve which is tangent to it must, at the point of tangency (that is, at the firm's equilibrium output) also be downward-sloping.

Is there, then, a paradox in supposing that in the long period, when by definition all things have had time for mutual adjustment and the ultimate economies which the state of knowledge allows should have been achieved throughout the 'industry' and the whole economy, a firm can deliberately have elected a scale of plant which, at equilibrium, will be working at less than its own optimum capacity, that is to say, at less than the output which enables a plant of this scale to produce at lowest unit cost? The resolution of this paradox was the concluding triumph of an article now long neglected:

If a firm is considering the desirability of reconstruction and the proper scale of operations, the question which it asks is, not—What is the plant the optimum output of which the normal demand will absorb? but—what is the plant with which the normal demand can be met most cheaply? If an increase of scale provides substantial economies, such an increase may be desirable, even if full advantage of the economies cannot be taken.

The firm is about to build a new plant, for which it can choose any scale it likes. The larger the scale, over some range, the lower, we assume, will be the minimum possible unit cost of production. We also assume that any plant will have a smooth U-shaped unit cost curve. Choosing some particular output, the firm will find that this is the output which gives minimum unit cost in some particular scale of plant. But this output could also be produced in a plant of larger scale, and, moreover, it could be produced *more cheaply* in some such plant. For the unit cost in the larger plant, considered as a function of output, will be found sweeping down towards its own minimum on a path passing below the minimum of the first plant. In sum, the lowest of all possible unit costs of production of a *given* output will be found in a plant whose own minimum cost of production requires a *larger* output. There is here a superficial air of paradox, but it dissolves as soon as the proposition is clearly understood. In our Fig. 4.1, the unit cost curves of two plants of different scale are shown, and the unit cost of producing a given output is seen to be higher in the smaller plant, although in that plant it gives minimum unit cost.

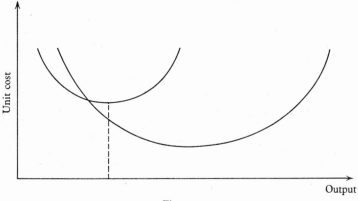

Fig. 4.1

Harrod's own diagram (*Economic Journal*, vol. XLI, p. 575) shows a selection of unit cost curves, one for each of a few plants differing from each other in scale by finite intervals. Since we suppose our firm to be free to choose any scale out of a continuous range of different scales, we must suppose the unit cost curves shown in the diagram to be merely specimens out of a family of infinitely many such curves. A curve tangent to every one of this infinity of curves would be called the *envelope*, and this is the locus of points showing, for each output that might be named, the lowest cost per unit at which that output could be produced. Harrod speaks of the U-shaped unit cost curve of each individual firm as a 'parabola', though of course it need by no means be a parabola in the strict sense, and lets x stand for output:

Plot a curve the ordinate of which is equal to the lowest of the ordinates of all the parabolas for each value of x. Such a curve (the envelope) may be called the long-period productive cost-curve, for it shows the cost of producing the normally required output x_1, if that is properly foreseen. If, as we suppose, the equilibrium firm has its plant constructed on less [a needless qualification] than the optimum scale, the long-period productive cost curve is falling in the neighbourhood of equilibrium. The long-period productive cost-curve must never intersect any parabola of the family, for if it did, it would for some value of x stand above the lowest value of one of the family. It follows that the long-period productive cost curve is for every value of x tangential to the parabola of the appropriate plant. But the long-period productive cost curve has a downward gradient. The parabola of the appropriate plant has, therefore, also a downward gradient at the point of normal output. This means that when the demand for the output of a firm is precisely that which the firm had in mind in constructing its plant, the parabola showing the costs of that plant has a downward gradient for that output, and the plant is being worked at less than its optimum capacity. Consequently in normal times the output of this firm may be subject to decreasing costs in response to a short-period rise in demand, and the rate at which costs decrease in the neighbourhood of normal is precisely equal to the rate at which costs decrease in response to a long-period rise in demand.

Harrod had shown that 'competitive equilibrium' is consistent with decreasing costs in both the short and the long period. To show this was to solve what we have called Sraffa's or Marshall's dilemma. Harrod may have felt that he had thus restored order and tranquillity. It was only in later years that the full loss of the great simplicities became apparent and was given by Hicks the dramatic expression we have quoted. Harrod had been concerned throughout with some notion of equilibrium. But this was a Marshallian evolutionary equilibrium and not a timeless abstract solution of unchanging forces:

If technical improvements of a kind that involve a larger optimum source of supply are occurring, the rate of expansion of the optimum source of supply [may exceed] the rate of increase of the demand... We may think of industries in which technical inventions make the optimum size of the source of supply increase rapidly as likely to be increasing returns industries.

Even in those early years of his professional life, Harrod was already concerned with 'dynamics'.

Marginal revenue was an idea instantly accessible to anyone who cared to make the simplest application of the differential calculus to the situation of the monopolist. It was formally obtained by Cournot, and only missed by him as a separate notion through his being careless in stating one of his results. It was written down in calculus notation, and the relative numerical importance of its positive and negative term was discussed in note xiv of Marshall's Mathematical Appendix to the *Principles*, where Marshall says:

The margin which [a monopolist] chose for his production would certainly be one for which the negative quantity $\beta\Delta p$ [β being output, p being price] is less than $p\Delta\beta$, but not necessarily so much less that it may be neglected in comparison. This is a dominant fact in the theory of monopolies discussed in Book v, chapter xiv.

Chapter xiv itself, however, uses a technique which quite avoids any explicit concept of marginal revenue, while in chapter xii of the same Book, as we have seen, Marshall points to a dilemma without at all indicating its solution. In his Appendix H he mixes static and evolutionary analysis so confusingly that we cannot tell whether he saw clearly the nature of the case or not.

Who, then, discovered marginal revenue? We could wish that Cournot had carried things a very little further or made one particular statement with more care. Then at least there need have been no dispute amongst the moderns. Our answer must be that marginal revenue was discovered by Marshall, not as an economist working in his own medium, but by the automatic reflex of a mathematician confronted by a certain preliminary statement in his own language. Having written down marginal revenue in this language as an immediate inference from that statement, he scarcely used it; apparently thought nothing of it, for he failed to coin it into a distinct concept by giving it a name, and left it lying hidden in the remotest corner of his book.

Once we define the firm as the maximizer of total revenue minus total cost, and the former as price times output, the formal condition for this maximum instantly declares that the firm's equilibrium consists in choosing that output (or, as with Cournot, that price) which equalizes marginal revenue and marginal cost; while marginal revenue itself appears automatically as the sum of two terms, viz. marginal output times price plus (negative) marginal price times output. It is not surprising that mathematically trained economists should have hit upon marginal revenue the moment they needed it. The interesting question is why, after Marshall, had nobody wanted it sooner?

When the demand curve for the particular firm's product is perfectly elastic, the marginal price, i.e. the difference of price due to a marginal change of output, becomes zero, and marginal revenue reduces to a single term, viz. marginal output times price. If, for marginal output, we choose one unit of output, marginal revenue is *equal* to price. Perfectly elastic demand for the firm's product implies that it is selling in perfect competition, and the perfectly competitive assumption came, during the forty years after the first publication of the *Principles*, to exert with good reason an almost unbreakable ascendancy over the minds of theoreticians. Nobody in those days wanted the *general* concept of marginal revenue because they thought of marginal revenue in the special form of *price*.

CHAPTER 5

THE NEW ESTABLISHMENT IN VALUE THEORY: (I) MRS JOAN ROBINSON

The value-theory revolution of the early 1930s produced no harsh polemics or violent opposition of views. It was a struggle, not of man against man, but of the whole body of trained economists against the tremendous grip of received doctrine, the established image of the economic world. This image showed a smooth sea of perfectly competitive firms in equilibrium, interrupted here and there by a few monopolist whirlpools obeying a different law. The monopolist was a thing apart. He did not fit in with the rest of the system. He must be studied in isolation, then was best forgotten. In a perfectly competitive world the laws of value would have approached the universal validity and beautiful simplicity of the law of gravity. Perfect competition was the great unifier binding the whole economic world into one market where, if the character of income distribution were treated as irrelevant or beyond human control, resources were allocated to the best general advantage. The thought of giving up perfect competition as the main and normal assumption was, quite literally, an unthinkable thought. The degree to which this is true can be appreciated only by reading the debate amongst some of the most eminent members of the English school, that is, the Marshallian or Cambridge school, in the pages of the *Economic Journal*. In March 1930, in that number of the *Journal* which immediately preceded the one containing Mr Harrod's 'Notes on Supply', there appeared a symposium on 'Increasing Returns and the Representative Firm' with main contributions by Sir Dennis Robertson (as he later became) and Mr G. F. Shove, with a brief interpolated protest by Mr Sraffa. Here Sir Dennis and Mr Shove performed astonishing gymnastic contortions in showing that, while tightly bound by the rope of perfect competition, their hands were quite free to juggle with increasing returns. Their chief recourse was to

Marshall's Representative Firm and Marshall's Trees of the Forest. The Representative Firm, they concluded, is not some actual, living firm but an idea. Each actual firm whom the finger of promised increasing returns might beckon towards expansion will refuse, well knowing that its management will have grown old and inefficient before it can reap the benefits which an increase in scale promises in principle. But by then another firm will occupy a position of representativeness, and this firm, still in the pride of its youth, will be on a larger scale and correspondingly able to produce more cheaply. Still it will expand no further itself for, like the earlier firm which enjoyed a monetary representativeness, it will foresee its own decline. Thus each *actual* firm is held in equilibrium by the knowledge of the individual life cycle, despite its awareness of the abstract potentialities of expansion. But that disembodied soul the Representative Firm nonetheless goes marching on down the curve of decreasing unit cost and economies of large scale.

Mr Shove and Sir Dennis Robertson could write nothing which was not full of deep insights and delightful images. Their contributions to the Symposium are models of persuasive writing and of the courtesies of genuine, truth-seeking dialogue. Their ostensible purpose was to rehabilitate the Representative Firm after its condemnation by Lord Robbins (as he now is), and it is this rather split minded purpose which, I think, accounts for the fantasies of their argument. Marshall's self-imposed endeavour was an intensely difficult one. He sought to describe a mechanism of evolution of the firm and industry; to derive the principles of this mechanism from the detailed and wide observation of a segment of British economic and industrial history, that of later Victorian England, which was being enacted before his eyes; and to make his account of this observable productive evolution the vehicle of laws which should be in some degree general and permanent. Yet he sought also to avoid the drily abstract, and was at his very best in explaining his propositions by means of realistic examples. To understand the evolution of the firm we must think, he seems to say, not of the whole diverse collection of firms making up the economy at any time, nor even of a composite picture which averages each characteristic of all these firms, nor of the most advanced nor the least advanced firm in the collection, but of some specimen firm which should illustrate the sort of thing that, at a particular date, has happened and is promising to happen to an unexceptional firm. I doubt whether Marshall meant anything much more precise than this. Marshall's occasional appearance of imprecision is the price of his extraordinary efforts, directed to binding together in one conception of economic society the permanent forces and their transient effects, like the gravity which accounts at once for tides and for waterfalls and so for all the stages in the history of a water drop from the clouds to the sea. The Representative Firm is an expository, not an analytic device.

When confronted with the dilemma of increasing returns in a supposedly competitive economy, Mr Shove and Sir Dennis Robertson turned quite naturally for an explanation to the 'dynamic' or evolutionary aspects of Marshall's theory. Two enemies could be killed at a blow. The threat to the Representative Firm could be repulsed by showing its relevance for resolving the dilemma, the dilemma could be resolved by appealing to the essential nature of Marshall's thought. The one thing that could not be contemplated, save by Mr Shove in two paragraphs only, with obvious distaste and nervousness, was the abandonment or the infringement of the competitive assumption. For the symposiasts, except Mr Sraffa, the problem was not how to account for a world full of increasing returns industries and also of monopolies, but how to reconcile increasing returns with (inviolable, indispensable, analytically essential, axiomatic) perfect competition. To have said 'Let us give up the supposition of perfect competition' would have been, for them, simple surrender and admission of defeat.

The strength and ubiquity of this conviction is shown in Professor Sir Roy Allen's 'Decreasing Costs: a Mathematical Note' which he contributed to the *Journal* two years later. This note was 'an attempt to interpret...some points made by Mr Sraffa and Mr Harrod [in the *Economic Journal* of December 1926, June 1930 and December 1931] on the question of the consistence of competitive equilibrium with decreasing costs'. In listing his premises Sir Roy Allen said: 'It is further assumed that the number of sources of production is so large that no one source can have any direct effect on the uniform selling price p...it is assumed that the conditions for a perfect market are satisfied.' Yet 'in addition to the actual cost of production, each source of production must take into account its marketing expenses'. Thus, he concluded, there can be competitive equilibrium with decreasing costs, provided their decrease is more than counteracted by rising marketing costs: 'Notice that costs cannot decrease at all rapidly unless the rate of increase of marketing expenses is large.' In a footnote Sir Roy Allen says that by marketing expenses he does not mean advertising, which would disturb 'the conditions for a perfect market on which the analysis is based'. What kind of marketing expenses, and what kind of need for them, we have to ask, can possibly fail to break up the market or can possibly leave untouched the uniformity of price? The competition which can only thus be made compatible with decreasing costs is not the competition which simplifies and unifies the economy. When marketing expenses have to be invoked the battle is already lost. And once the market for the single, uniform commodity has dissolved into separate markets, one for each firm, the type of action which has first claim on the analyst's attention is action via price. The firm has become a monopolist and must be analysed as such. All this had been said, in effect, by Mr Sraffa in 1926, but even in 1932 his commentators were heedless of his warning and advice.

Until the very end of 1932 the advance, as seen in print, was confused, vacillating and nostalgic. Yntema's discussion of pure monopoly had defined marginal revenue but had made no suggestion of analysing by its means a new kind or degree of competition. Harrod, independently reinventing marginal revenue, had burst through all the major entanglements on the path from perfect to imperfect competition but was still interrupting his clear stages of advance by diversions concerned with marketing costs. In two particulars his scheme fell short of what, by hindsight, we should now regard as a complete statement of the basic theory. First, his version of the 'fundamental diagram' was at fault in not showing the unit, or 'average' curves as having equal slopes at that output which gave the marginal curves equal ordinates. And, secondly, despite his reference to 'normal' profit, he had expressed his conclusions solely in terms of the individual firm, without explicitly discussing changes in the group, as such, of firms which compete with it and influence its market. Yet the question what is an 'industry' when competition is not perfect, what constitutes an equilibrium of the industry and how this equilibrium is approached and how it is to be recognized, are all part of the path from the theory of perfect to that of imperfect competition. In the *Economic Journal* of December, 1932, however, there appeared in the field a new participant of ruthless and incisive temper, determined to formulate everything in the new language and to follow the Sraffian path without distraction. Imperfect competition, as a branch of economic theory in its own right with its own freely chosen premises, begins with Mrs Joan Robinson's article on 'Imperfect Competition and Falling Supply Price'.

Between Mrs Robinson's article and those we have previously discussed, there is in the first place a sharp and striking difference in style of attack. The authors we have been considering were Marshallians. They examined the existing world in a spirit of respect, they brought as much of it intact into their discourse as they could, they valued the contours and features of the landscape they beheld and tried to mould their argument upon them rather than cut a path direct to rigorous conclusions. Mrs Robinson did the opposite. Clear and definite questions cannot be asked about a vague, richly detailed, fluid and living world. This world must therefore be exchanged for a *model*, a set of precise assumptions collectively simple enough to allow the play of logic and mathematics. The designer of a model works backwards and forwards, considering, when he has made some inferences from a given set of assumptions, whether a different set would yield a total scheme, of premises, reasoning and results, more interesting and generally illuminating as a whole than the former set. The model is a work of art, freely composed within the constraints of a particular art-form, namely the logical binding together of propositions. In this bounded freedom it resembles any other art form, the sonnet, the symphony, the cabinet-maker's or architect's conception:

It is only with imperfect competition that I wish to deal. If the problems arising from the passage of time are ignored, the question which remains to be answered is this: Is the existence of imperfect competition sufficient by itself to account for falling supply price? In order to isolate this one question and to reduce it to manageable terms, certain severe assumptions must be made.

To eliminate the problems connected with time I will assume first that the efficiency and the costs of individual firms do not alter with the passage of time, but only with changes in the scale of output; and, secondly, that each firm is always in individual equilibrium, in the sense that it is always able to produce that output at which its marginal gains are equal to its marginal costs.

To isolate the effect of imperfect competition upon supply price it is necessary to assume that every other possible source of changing supply price is eliminated. I will therefore assume that every factor of production is homogeneous; that every factor is in perfectly elastic supply to the industry; and that there are no economies of large scale industry... By these assumptions conditions are postulated in which, if competition were perfect, the industry would be producing at constant supply price.

Finally, to simplify the problem, I will assume that all firms are alike in respect of their costs and the conditions of demand for their individual outputs.

Discussion of the individual demand curve shows the need for one further assumption:

We assume that the imperfection of the market arises solely from... such differences between customers in their preferences for particular firms as cannot be altered by the action of the firms themselves.*

What a contrast is made by this complete, concise and exact preliminary statement with the bland unstated presumption of the earlier writers that the whole debate would be conducted within the four walls of Marshall's study, where the furniture was so familiar to everyone that there could be no need to describe it. 'To eliminate the problems connected with time...' Marshall's most famous concepts, the main goal of his labours and the heart of his method are thus swept aside: the model is a purely static one, concerned with timeless choice amongst strict alternatives. Selling costs are banished, and

In order to increase its sales, the firm must lower the price at which it sells. Every decrease in the price charged by a firm will lead to some increase in its sales, but not to the indefinitely large increase which would occur if competition were perfect and the individual demand curve perfectly elastic. From the individual demand curve of each firm can be derived its individual marginal revenue curve... The profits of the firm are maximized when marginal revenue is equal to cost... When [an output thus determined] is being pro-

* Joan Robinson: 'Imperfect Competition and Falling Supply Price', *Economic Journal*, vol. XLII, pp. 544–6.

duced, the firm is in equilibrium, in the sense that in the given situation it has no motive to increase or to reduce its output. Since we have assumed that all firms are alike, each must be supposed to act in the same way, so that a single price always rules throughout the whole market.

'All firms are alike...' This assumption, flatly set down without any statement of its implications or the mode in which it serves the argument, except that it is intended 'to simplify the problem', performs in fact a subtle and most noteworthy function: it preserves by a sleight of hand the concept of the industry. So long as all potential buyers of some physically and technologically uniform type of objects are perfectly indifferent amongst the firms which can supply these objects, these objects form a commodity and the firms supplying them form an industry. But how can the industry be defined when the *economic* uniformity of the goods is lost through consumers' preference amongst firms? Imperfect competition is that state of affairs where every firm's product, in the eyes of some buyers, is different from that of every other firm. A 'commodity' then is simply the product of a single firm, every firm is a monopolist of its own commodity and the industry and the firm are one. But now if we suppose that although some buyers prefer one firm and some another, yet every firm in regard to such preferences is in exactly the same position as every other, so that firm A's group of loyal customers is exactly matched, in numbers, wealth, tastes and strength of loyalty by firm B's group, the preferences amongst firms make no difference, and we are back with the old situation where all the technologically similar objects *behave like* an economically uniform commodity, preserving a single price throughout what will now still *look like* a single, unified market. And so the firms producing these objects can still be spoken of as an industry. Thus the analysis can concern itself with something larger than the firm, yet still small enough, by comparison with the economy as a whole, to leave demand for the product unaffected by conditions and amount of supply, so that the traditional analysis in terms of mutually independent demand and supply conditions can be pursued.

When all the firms, which supply some physically uniform type of objects, are alike in respect of both cost conditions and demand conditions, and when they are so placed in relation to buyers with various tastes and incomes that all changes in demand affect all these firms in exactly the same way, we can represent the situation of the industry (an 'industry' which this symmetry amongst firms allows us, despite the market imperfection which it conceals, to define) merely by showing the state of affairs in a single firm. Every firm will be always exactly as prosperous as every other, and this prosperity can be measured by the excess, in each firm, of total revenue (that is, annual or weekly, etc., sales proceeds of output) over total outgoings for the hire of all factors except the entrepreneur's own services. Some level of this excess, that is, this total *net* revenue or profit, will be just sufficient to keep the entrepreneur in his present technological line of production, and some level of this profit, observed by other entrepreneurs, will be just *in*sufficient to induce them to enter this line of production. Let us suppose these two levels of profit are one and the same, and then, dividing a firm's total profit, when the profit stands at this level, by the firm's output (which by the assumption that all firms are alike, is equal for all firms) let us call the resulting profit per unit of output 'normal profit'. When normal profit is added to the cost, per unit of output, of the hire of other factors, the result is an inclusive cost per unit of output, which has to be just and only just covered by revenue per unit of output if the number of firms in the industry is to remain constant. By this construction Mrs Robinson can define the conditions for equilibrium (that is, absence of inducement to alter the size of output) of the industry as a whole. The conditions are two. First, each firm must have no inducement to increase or reduce its output, and this will be the case at that output where its marginal revenue curve cuts its marginal cost curve from above. Secondly, there must be no inducement for existing firms to leave, or new firms to enter, the industry. This will be the case when, in each existing firm at its most profitable output, average cost including normal profit is just equal to average revenue or price. We saw that an output where the marginal curves intersect each other is an output where the average curves are parallel to each other. If at that same output the average curves happen to equal each other in their ordinates, it follows that these average curves will at that output be tangent to each other. Thus Mrs Robinson's double condition for equilibrium of the industry can be expressed by a single geometrical feature: the tangency, in each firm, of the average cost curve, including normal profit, with the average revenue curve.

It is the fulfilment, or the incentive to fulfilment, of this double condition which is illustrated by the fundamental diagram, as we called it, of imperfect competition. When, at the firm's most profitable output, the 'average' curves of that diagram are parallel but not tangent to each other, the firm and every firm is earning supernormal or subnormal profit, and in that case by assumption other entrepreneurs will set up additional firms in the industry or some of those already in it (though nothing is said as to how these will select themselves) will leave it. By the resulting gain or loss of output, price will be lowered or raised to a position of equilibrium, where the two average curves are tangent to each other in each of the identical firms whose identical similarity is the means of defining the 'industry'. From this point Mrs Robinson proceeds to the main purpose of her article, the study of how, in this sort of industry, output will re-act to a change in demand.

In imperfect competition, the curve which can be variously called the particular demand curve for the firm's product, or the firm's sales curve, or the price curve, or the firm's average revenue curve, will be downward-sloping. Any curve which is tangent to it will therefore also, at the point of tangency, be downward-sloping. If, therefore, the firm moves from such a point of former equilibrium towards a larger output, its cost of production per unit of output will become less. Does this mean that if the buyers of the industry's product become willing to pay a larger total annual sum than before for each annual number of physical units that might be supplied, the effect will necessarily be that they will find themselves buying a larger output than before at a lower price per unit? In other words, does a falling average cost curve of the firm imply a decreasing supply price in the industry? In showing that it does not, Mrs Robinson was the first to explain why imperfect competition does away with the supply curve. Harrod had considered how selling costs would affect the supply curve; that is, how the supply curve would be affected by active expenditure intended to *alter* demand conditions. Mrs Robinson appealed only to the firm's output response to *given* demand conditions. When competition is imperfect, she said in effect, it is not price but marginal revenue which the firm should consult in choosing its output; but marginal revenue involves elasticity, and, in any one point of a demand curve, any price can be combined with any elasticity. Thus the simple link, which prevails under perfect competition, between price and the output of the firm and of the industry, is broken when competition becomes monopolistic. Then a supply curve can no longer be meaningfully or usefully drawn, and cannot be drawn at all, save on the most restricted and artificial types of assumption.

Before we turn to Mrs Robinson's *Economics of Imperfect Competition* and her detailed discussion there of the fate of the supply curve, it is appropriate to consider whether she judged well in deciding to preserve the concept of the industry. In the analysis of perfect competition, a commodity can be un-equivocally defined by physical, objective characteristics which are the same for all its buyers. An industry is then composed of all the firms which produce such a commodity. To say that competition is imperfect is to say that buyers distinguish amongst products on grounds other than physical dissimilarity of the things themselves. Only when physically similar objects are all supplied from the same source can they then be regarded as one commodity. If the industry is that which produces a commodity, we have then to declare that the industry is nothing else than the single firm and that the effective competing environment of the firm, both in product and factor markets, is sometimes the entire economy. This is the direction in which we are led by Dr Robert Triffin in his *Monopolistic Competition and General Equilibrium Theory* (Cambridge, Mass.: Harvard University Press, 1940).

All that may be involved is a question of degree: every firm competes with all other firms in the economy, but with different degrees of closeness. Is anything gained by limiting the investigation to a group of close competitors, which we would call a group or industry? In an empirical, statistical study, yes: we can, in this way, reduce to a manageable size the research work involved, without any serious loss in precision or exhaustiveness. In the general statement of value theory, no: when competition is discussed in general abstract terms, we may just as well make the group (or industry) co-extensive with the whole economic collectivity. The problems are the same, and the complexity is no greater.

The complexity, however, is greater. Dr Triffin is recommending the abandonment of particular equilibrium analysis. But it is particular equilibrium analysis, the study of so small a part of the economy that the influence of this part on the rest of the economy results in no significant reflected effects upon itself, that enables us to suppose without illogic that, in the small part we are studying, demand and supply are mutually independent. The originators of general equilibrium analysis were unconcerned with the problems that we now call macro-economic, where the general demand of the population for goods is the general demand for the population's own factor services and thus determines their income and exercises a feed-back effect on their demand for goods. Particular equilibrium analysis is not pointless, even though other considerations may outweigh its claims.

Mrs Joan Robinson's *Economics of Imperfect Competition* (London, Macmillan, 1933) follows 'the argument where it leads' from the point of breakthrough which her own article in December 1932 had marked. The care and thoroughness of her statement of definitions and assumptions, the candour of her declaration about the abstract character of her analysis, the systematic organization which lets us know these things at the beginning and offers a formal explanation and training in the pure technique of average and marginal curves without, at that stage, giving these curves any specific content or interpretation, were at that date something new in economic reasoning. Mrs Robinson was a navigator, not a mere groping breaker of the jungle. Yet this radicalism is full of piety. To gain the ear of an audience, a teacher must refer to what they already know, must start from the ground laid out by a great predecessor. Moreover, a writer must start from what he or she knows. Continuity, tradition, are inevitable. The great disciples or successors of Knut Wicksell have always referred to their development of his work as 'immanent' criticism, a critical examination and improvement which remains within the frame of ideas set out by Wicksell himself. Yet Myrdal made a very great innovation, the formal recognition of the need to distinguish explicitly the expected from the realized.

Mrs Robinson, analysing the profit-maximizing firm's reaction to its circumstances (the simplicity of this analytic purpose is the indispensable basis of its detailed rigour) is conscious of the need to state just what are the immovable conditions that face the firm and what are the variables under its control:

The problem [of the firm's choice of output] may be considered either from the point of view of the short period, or the quasi-long period. In the short period the productive equipment of the firm is fixed, and part of the cost of production is fixed irrespective of output...In the quasi-long period the productive equipment is conceived to be adapted to changes of output, and all costs except the minimum reward of the entrepreneur may vary with output. In the true long period the firm itself may be created or may disappear.

The cost curve which will be relevant to this inquiry is the curve of marginal cost to the individual firm.

The curve of marginal cost may be adapted to deal with short period or quasi-long period problems...

Thus Marshall's great innovation, the taking into account of the extent of adaptation which technical facts make possible and the firm's expectations of demand make profitable, is adopted at the outset of the main analysis without any mention of Marshall's name. This adoption was natural, necessary, automatic. Its very anonymity paid Marshall tribute.

The Economics of Imperfect Competition can be mastered in detail only by close and sustained attention, severe efforts of memory in holding the long, complex and subtle train of argument in mind, and repeated readings. This very complexity and difficulty are the clue to what had happened to the theory of value. It had turned from mechanics into taxonomy. So far as there was anything which could still be called an industry, the demand for its output could take an infinite variety of forms and could change in an infinite variety of ways. On the cost side a similar case prevailed. The output and prices of the commodity were the upshot of an interaction between these two sets of conditions or changes of conditions, and only a card-index would suffice to give a truly comprehensive picture of the main sorts of things that could happen. This destruction of the old simplicity of value theory, a simplicity which makes the idea of perfect competition, which effected it, seem a miraculous inspiration, comes to a focus in the dissolution of the supply curve:

[The difficulty] that...the same commodity may be sold at different prices by different producers...could be disposed of if we assumed that the cost curves of all firms are exactly alike, that the individual demand curves all move in the same way when the total demand increases. But a more fundamental difficulty would remain. When competition is not perfect...marginal revenue will not be equal to price; it is marginal revenue, not price, which determines the output of the individual producer, and any number of different prices are compatible with the same marginal revenue. The relationship between marginal revenue and price will depend upon the shapes of the individual demand curves, and the effect of a given increase in the total demand for the commodity upon output will depend on the manner in which it affects the individual demand curves. [Even if] the individual demand curves all move in the same way...there are many possible ways in which they might move, and before we can say what effect an increase in the total demand will have upon output it is further necessary to postulate the particular way, out of all the possible ways, in which the individual demand curves will move.

The alternative assumptions which make it possible to preserve the appearance of a supply curve on which a given output is associated with a given price are all equally unplausible. There is no reason to choose one rather than another, and in fact a given increase in the total demand for a commodity is unlikely to be associated with any one of them.*

In Fig. 5.1, identical similarity amongst the demand curves facing all firms is represented by the identical similarity of all the curves in any one row. Their moving all in the same way is illustrated by the several forms of curve, each form common to all columns but varying between rows. The fact that there are many possible ways in which the demand curve, common to all firms, might move is illustrated by the variation of forms between rows.

To deserve to be called *a theory*, a body of ideas must have some oneness of theme or principle, must answer some set of closely related questions or else must answer questions which, despite a superficial independence and diversity, can really be shown to involve one and the same principle of explanation. A book which sets out to offer a theory, in this sense, necessarily shows in its own structure some reflection of the unity of its subject-matter, and this reflection seems often to take one special form, namely the presence of a chapter which is, as it were, the 'engine-room' or, if you like, the control room of the book as a whole. Mrs Robinson's book has such a chapter, and it is chapter 7 on 'Competitive Equilibrium'. Here we find,

* Joan Robinson, *The Economics of Imperfect Competition*, chapter 6.

first, the definition of *full equilibrium* of the industry, 'when there is no tendency for the number of firms to alter'. It is assumed that each entrepreneur has in mind some annual lump sum of fixed size, one and the same for all entrepreneurs, which is a

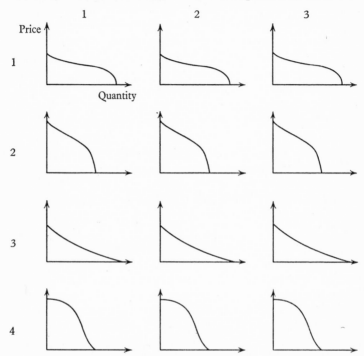

Fig. 5.1. Even if we suppose the demand curve facing a firm to be identical with that facing every other firm (identity of all demand curves in any one *row*), the supposition of a one-one correspondence between aggregate quantity demanded from all firms taken together, and a price common to them all, is destroyed by the variety of forms which the demand curve common to all firms could take (variation *between* rows).

just sufficient prospective reward to induce him to stay in the industry if he is in but not sufficient to make him enter it if he is not yet in. This 'normal profit' is then treated as a cost and included in the total cost of a given output of the firm, which, when divided by that output, gives the firm's 'average' or 'unit' cost for that output. Full equilibrium of the industry thus requires, for one thing, that in each firm price be equal to average cost. Equilibrium of the firm individually, however, requires only that marginal revenue be equal to marginal cost. Full equilibrium of the industry requires, for a second thing, that each firm should be in its own kind of equilibrium. Thus full equilibrium of the industry means that in each of its existing firms the average revenue curve should have a point of tangency with the average cost curve, the latter lying elsewhere above the former; and that the firm should be producing the output corresponding to that point of tangency.

What do these conditions imply for an industry which faces perfect, and for one which faces imperfect, competition?

Now when competition is perfect, marginal revenue is equal to price. Marginal cost must therefore be equal to price. But for full equilibrium price must be equal to average cost. Full equilibrium can therefore only be attained, under perfect competition, when marginal cost is equal to average cost. Marginal and average cost are equal at the minimum point on the average cost curve. It follows that under perfect competition there must be a minimum point on the average cost curve, that is to say, there must be a certain output beyond which the average costs of the firm begin to rise (p. 95).

The argument tacitly and justifiably assumes that in all relevant situations the average cost curve will be concave upwards. This granted, Mrs Robinson has brought her argument to the point where Marshall's, or Sraffa's, dilemma emerges: decreasing average costs are not compatible with perfect competition. She does not refer at this point to the fact that the whole subject and branch of economics, which her book sets forth, arose as an answer to this dilemma. The inference, that if in the real world we find an industry in equilibrium in perfect competition, we must be faced with increasing average cost, is not (as Mrs Robinson seems to suppose it) a case of 'deducing a fact about the nature of the costs of a firm from a purely geometrical argument.' The inference by itself tells us nothing about any firm in the real world. It only points out a set of statements which, if made about one and the same situation, would not be logically coherent.

Now Mrs Robinson tries to make clear a point which has given trouble to every fresh generation of students:

In a perfectly competitive industry each firm, in full equilibrium, will produce that output at which its average costs are a minimum. Each firm will then be of *optimum size*. It is sometimes supposed that the optimum size of the firm is that which is most profitable to the entrepreneur, so that the entrepreneur has a motive for wishing his firm to be of optimum size. But this view is mistaken. It is no disadvantage to the entrepreneur to produce more than the optimum output. Indeed it is when profits are abnormally high (because new firms are failing to enter the industry to a sufficient extent to keep profits at the normal level) that the firms are of more than optimum size. The entrepreneur will have no desire to return to the situation in which his profits are reduced to normal, and the fact that, at the optimum size, his average costs would be at a minimum will not influence his conduct.

In an industry which continues to be perfectly competitive, changes in demand are identical for all firms. They consist in a simple raising of the price without any departure from that infinite elasticity of demand for the individual firm's product which enables it (or expresses its ability) to sell any practicable output at the price set by the market. If the marginal cost curve of every firm in the industry, whether these firms are few or many, is identical with that of every other firm, and if each entrepreneur's minimum inducement to be in the industry is the same as that of every other, the condition for full equilibrium of the industry is easily conceived. There must be enough firms in the industry to satisfy that total demand for the commodity, which corresponds to a price equal to the minimum average cost of every firm.

Now when we relax the assumption of perfect competition, we have (in pursuance of Mrs Robinson's construction) to specify that, besides identity of marginal cost curves amongst all firms (which implies identity also of their average cost curves) there is at all times and in all circumstances an identity amongst them of the respective demand curves for their individual products. Thus when there is tangency between average cost curve and average revenue curve in one firm, there will be such tangency in every firm. And there *will* be such tangency provided there are just enough, and not too many, firms in the industry.

There is, of course, an important difference between full equilibrium in a perfectly competitive, and in an imperfectly competitive, industry, for in the latter the firms will not be of optimum size. Under perfect competition the tangency is between a horizontal particular demand curve (average revenue curve) and a U-shaped average cost curve, necessarily

at the minimum point of the latter. Under imperfect competition the tangency is between a downward-sloping average
revenue curve and a necessarily downward-sloping segment of
the average cost curve, necessarily *not* at the minimum point of
the latter. Firms in equilibrium under imperfect competition
are not of optimum size.

The argument we have sketched gives rise to a number of
reflections. There is the question of the role of time in such an
argument. In tracing its development from Marshall through
Harrod to Mrs Robinson, we can clearly perceive an increasing
awareness of the ambiguities to which any inclusion of time-
effects gives rise. Marshall was never willing to do more than
impose expository delay on the ineluctable change and evolution of things. No argument could be more against the spirit of
Marshall than one which explicitly, ruthlessly and finally
abstracts from the influence of time. Harrod found a content
for the phrase 'increasing returns industries' in the idea that
certain industries might so lend themselves to continuing rapid
technological advance as to have an optimal scale of plant
growing faster than the demand for the product, so that any given
output now required could always be produced more cheaply
in a larger plant than in the one for which this output occupied
the minimum point of the unit cost curve (see p. 40 above
and Harrod, 'The Law of Decreasing Costs', *Economic Journal*,
vol. XLI, p. 575). Mrs Robinson sets out to be more austere:

The technique set out in this book is a technique for studying equilibrium positions. No reference is made to the effects of the passage of
time. Short-period and long-period equilibria are introduced...but
no study is made of the process of moving from one position of
equilibrium to another...

An astounding statement, when we consider her analysis of the
effect of super-normal profit in *bringing about* an equilibrium
where before there was disequilibrium. The paragraph which
begins 'Now, starting from a position in which the industry is
in equilibrium, suppose total demand...is increased', and
ends 'A new position of long-period equilibrium will be established' seems a flat contradiction of her own words. A pure and
strict comparative statics is a hard goal: so many insights and
suggestive clues must be neglected.

Mrs Robinson's book consummately illustrates the virtue and

necessity of the particular equilibrium method. It offers no comprehensive and omnicompetent model from which all questions about her subject-matter can be answered. No such model is practicable. The theories of general equilibrium do not answer questions of detailed structure or response. The particular equilibrium method, holding, at each differently angled attack, nearly everything constant, drastically simplifying, and showing the related movements of, perhaps, only two things at a time, vitally requires the reader's or user's co-operation. He is presented with a series of separate and almost independent reasonings, separate models, *incapable* of being logically brought into one, incapable of being even roughly amalgamated in any formal manner, save by way of a complexity so grotesque that any account of it would be gibberish. When the mind requires a distillation of several of these 'partial' reasonings at once, it must compound them non-logically or informally, by getting the feel or general drift of their combined working. This oblique approach is part of the nature of economic analysis. Yet Mrs Robinson does sum up the heart of her matter, the central idea of which all else can be deemed an elaboration, in her very brief chapter 19, 'Relationship of Monopsony and Monopoly to Perfect Competition':

The monopolist takes into account the fact that when he increases his purchases of one or other of the factors of production, he raises the supply-price of the factor against himself...In short, when we say that a monopolist regulates his output by the marginal cost to him of the output, we have already implied that he is a monopsonist in respect of the factors of production which he uses. The principle of monopoly thus involves the principle of monopsony and we were implicitly introducing the principle of monopsony when we were engaged in the analysis of monopoly. Thus the common-sense rule that the individual will equate marginal gains (whether of utility or of revenue) with marginal cost, applies equally to monopsony, to monopoly and to perfect competition.

Perfect competition is a special case. But the endless virtuosity, the extraordinary tactical flexibility, the masterly and repeated recensions of her arguments and regrouping of her forces, which her task has exacted from her, show with overwhelming effect why the perfectly competitive assumption, and the usability of a theory of value, are almost inseparable conditions.

CHAPTER 6

THE NEW ESTABLISHMENT IN VALUE THEORY: (II) EDWARD CHAMBERLIN

The Theory of Monopolistic Competition was first published in 1933. The Preface to its first edition, and the Foreword to Mrs Joan Robinson's *Economics of Imperfection Competition*, are both dated October 1932. In her Foreword Mrs Robinson says: 'Professor Chamberlin's [book] provides a plentiful crop of coincidences, but it appeared too late for me to notice them in detail.' Professor Chamberlin says:

This study first took form in the two years preceding April 1, 1927, at which date it was submitted as a doctor's thesis in Harvard University. Since that time it has been completely re-written.

Not even Mr Sraffa's article can have played any part in starting Professor Chamberlin's train of ideas, and it is plain that two movements to reform the theory of prices and outputs began at the two Cambridges quite independently. We need not, for once, debate priorities: there was simultaneity.

The two books are very different in scope. Mrs Robinson's central concern is with the effect of supposing the demand for each firm's output to be less than perfectly elastic, so that each firm, though only one among a multitude of firms producing substitutes of varying closeness for each other's products, can exploit the essential position, powers and policies of a monopolist. She eschews discussion of those markets where each firm reckons on other firms' active retaliation to its moves, and of expenditure on selling effort. Oligopoly is quite alien, in its essential demands upon theory, to the spirit of static or equilibrium analysis; unlike the conscious and exact blending of monopolistic and competitive ideas, it is an old story going back to Cournot, and thus does not belong to our theme. Its best solutions depend upon tools later than our period. Professor Chamberlin includes selling expenditure in his analysis with a most ingenious formal precision. He also duplicates many arguments about price behaviour in order to point out that the entrepreneur should consider the profit possibilities of all products and choose in the end that output of that product which, with the optimal selling expenditure, yields the biggest total profit. With these ostensibly large extensions of the field, compared with Mrs Robinson's; with different emphases and a chief reliance on different diagrammatic tools; and especially with a personal interpretation of such words as 'supply' and with impalpable distinctions between his own and Mrs Robinson's use of the expressions 'monopoly', 'imperfect competition' and others, Professor Chamberlin is at great pains to insist that the two approaches are essentially different. Almost all other students of the matter have agreed with each other that in describing the structure and mechanism of equilibrium in firms and groups of firms when oligopoly and selling expenditure are absent, the two books present identical theories.

The marginal revenue curve appears in only four of Professor Chamberlin's forty diagrams, and even in those four places it is evidently a late and by no means indispensable arrival. We may surmise that he originally worked out his whole book with no such tool in mind. In section 2 of chapter v, for example, the equilibrium of the individual firm is defined as that choice of price, or of output, which gives it, in its supposedly given environment of the conduct of other firms, the greatest attainable profit. This profit is represented in Professor Chamberlin's Figures 9 and 10 as the area of a rectangle fitted between the 'average' or 'unit' cost and revenue curves with the abscissa of output as its horizontal side. After this complete account he refers, in a separate paragraph, to the marginal curves which also appear in these Figures: 'The point of maximum profit may also be defined with reference to curves of marginal costs and of marginal revenue.' In the last chapter of his main text, devoted to 'some mistaken notions in the general field of "monopolistic" and imperfect competition', he pillories first of all the notion of any essential importance of the marginal revenue curve in that field:

The first of these [misconceptions] is that 'imperfect' and monopolistic competition are in some special way related to the marginal revenue curve. The association might be described as an historical accident...Mrs Robinson states 'This piece of apparatus plays a great part in my work, and my book arose out of the attempt to apply it to various problems...Whilst many pieces of technical apparatus have no intrinsic merit, and are used merely for convenience, the use of marginal curves for the analysis of monopoly output contains within itself the heart of the whole matter'. It is, to be sure, an 'intrinsic merit' of the marginal curves that their intersection reveals monopoly *output* more neatly than does the fitting of areas between curves of average cost and average revenue. At the same time, it is an intrinsic demerit that they do not indicate the *price* at all [and] that they do not really indicate *profits*, either per unit or in the aggregate...Furthermore, when we get beyond equilibrium for the single firm in isolation, the marginal curves do not contain 'the heart of the whole matter' even for output, [for] in Mrs Robinson's own description of 'competitive equilibrium'...we find that full equilibrium requires a double condition, that marginal revenue is equal to marginal cost, and that average revenue is equal to average cost'.

The state of affairs whose structure both writers wish to display is that in which there is no tendency for the output of any of the firms in the group under study, nor for the list of those individual firms, to change. This state of affairs requires the fulfilment of two conditions. Each firm must be unable, given its circumstances of demand and costs and the posture of other firms, to increase its profit by altering its price or its output. And the profit thus attained must be, for every firm, sufficient to induce it to stay in production but insufficient to tempt any new entrant to produce a close enough substitute to affect the profit of any firm already in the group. Any geometrical symbolism which can properly represent this double condition must itself be separable into two elements, and this separability is in fact found in either of the two constructions which our authors respectively adopt. Equilibrium of the firm is represented in Mrs Robinson's language by the output at which the marginal cost curve cuts the marginal revenue curve from below; in Professor Chamberlin's language, by the output at which the average cost curve has the same slope as the average revenue curve and does not lie above it. Equilibrium of the group (the 'industry') is represented in both languages by equality of the *ordinates* of the two average curves; but in both languages, this equality of the ordinates is accompanied by equality of the slopes, in Chamberlin's case because we are directly assuming it, in Mrs Robinson's case because it is implied by what we *are* directly assuming, viz. the equality of the ordinates of the marginal curves. Thus in both languages, equilibrium of the group is represented by the *tangency*, for every firm, of the average revenue and average cost curves. Tangency, however, though one word, is two conditions. It is the equality of two functions of output and also equality of their first derivatives. Professor Chamberlin's last stricture, in the passage we have quoted, is thus unjustified. Profit can be shown in total either by the area under the marginal revenue curve less that under the marginal cost curve, or by the area of the rectangle inscribed between the two average curves at the given output, and having the abscissa of that output as its horizontal side. Mrs Robinson can avail herself of both methods. Price, of course, requires the average revenue curve, and no one would claim that the marginal curves give a complete picture by themselves. The marginal revenue curve is, indeed, that *completing* element of the picture which would have eliminated Marshall's dilemma, had he thought of it. Moreover it is latent in the familiar diagram of the firm in perfect competition, for then it coincides with the (horizontal) average revenue curve.

For the Cambridge (England) economists, the explicit formulation of marginal revenue was the clue and the catalyst that transformed everything. A principle of order had been introduced by its discovery and the events of 1928 to 1933 were simply the vast process of tidying-up which the application of this principle made possible. It is natural that Mrs Robinson, the chief administrator of this exercise, and those who had been concerned at earlier stages, should look upon marginal revenue as the key idea of the theory of imperfect or monopolistic competition. It is natural also that Professor Chamberlin should point to the role of this idea as an historical one. In the structure of completed theory, it is no more dominant and essential than the average revenue curve or any other of those pieces of notation by which we articulate our thoughts about firm and industry profit-equilibrium.

For the Cambridge economists,* imperfect competition was merely an improvement and refinement of Marshall. It was far from apparent to them at first that they had written a new theory

* Perhaps Sir Roy Harrod will allow himself to be covered by this name.

in a new language. Yet not only the answers, but the questions, were new. The whole notion of what value theory sought to do and the way its aim should be accomplished had been changed. Mrs Robinson starts her first chapter with a strangely revealing sentence: 'The purpose of this book is to demonstrate that the analysis of the output and price of a single commodity can be conducted by a technique based upon the study of individual decisions.' The individual decisions were those of the entrepreneur or his firm, and each of the commodities whose prices and outputs were in question was defined, not as a stuff having given physical characteristics, but as the product of a particular firm. Primacy had passed from the autonomously self-subsisting technical commodity to the firm considered as a profit-maximizing policy maker. The central theoretical concern was no longer with the means of life and how to produce and distribute it, but the actions and interactions of producers each with a product in some degree special to him. The *firm* was an entity which, being free to choose the character of its product, the means of producing it, and either the size of the output or else the price to be charged per unit, made all these choices as one, with the sole aim of making as large as possible the excess of sale-proceeds of product over outgoings necessitated by production. In making these choices each firm had to reckon with an environment composed of other firms as well as of demanders of its goods. And this environment of other firms was not constant in composition or conduct, but might press in upon a highly profitable firm and soak away some of its custom, or recede and leave breathing space for a firm which had been making losses. In the end, so long as demand, technology and the supply conditions of factors of production remained unchanged, everything would settle down and each firm would be making its best attainable unthreatened profit. But when this picture had taken shape, what importance was left to the *commodity*? Between the beginning and the end of Mrs Robinson's first sentence, the focus of interest has changed. Marshall began with the commodity and called the list of firms which produced it an industry. Mrs Robinson still speaks of the industry, and Professor Chamberlin of the group. These concepts at first are real and subjectively important to them, for each goes to the length of explicitly assuming, as an expository measure, that every firm in any one industry remains at all times identical, as to cost and demand conditions, with every other. Yet what can the industry be, in a theory whose *raison d'être* is the *distinctness* of the goods produced by the various firms?

The logical need to abandon the notions of industry and commodity is the chief theme of the last of the books we shall consider, Professor Robert Triffin's *Monopolistic Competition and General Equilibrium Theory*, published at Harvard in 1940. Half his book is a careful summary and criticism of Mrs Robinson's and Professor Chamberlin's work. He shows that even they have not followed wholeheartedly where the argument led. In a perfectly competitive industry the similarity of demand conditions for all firms was absolute, and the similarity of cost conditions was a highly reasonable assumption rather than a wholly arbitrary device for preserving the facade of 'particular' equilibrium. From these two similarities followed the similarity of profit for all the firms, and it was possible to speak of the level of profit in the industry as a whole and to make the entry or exodus of firms depend upon it. Under monopolistic competition, all this unity and uniformity is in the nature of things lost, the 'industry' dissolves and the concept of firms entering or leaving it becomes meaningless. There is no longer any natural boundary at which a relatively small portion of the economy can be cut off and isolated for study, other than the boundary of the individual firm itself. Yet for reasons which Professor Triffin overlooks, it is necessary for the sake of the coherence of value theory either to cut off such a small portion, or to build a model embracing macro-economic effects. For if we deem a number of firms, which together bulk large in the economy as a whole, to change their outputs together, we are in danger of destroying the mutual independence of the supply and demand sides of the market. We cannot allow the earnings of the factors who supply the goods to provide any large proportion of the spendings which demand it. In her chapter 1 Mrs Robinson opts for the preservation of the concept of industry even at the cost of imprecision and illogic:

A *commodity* is a consumable good, arbitrarily demarcated from other kinds of goods, but which may be regarded for practical purposes as homogeneous within itself...An industry is a group of firms producing a single commodity. The correspondence of such an industry to the industries of the real world is perhaps not very close. But in some cases, where a commodity in the real world is bounded on all sides by a marked gap between itself and its closest substitutes, the real-world firms producing this real-world commodity will conform to the definition of an industry sufficiently closely to make the discussion of industries in this technical sense of some interest.*

Professor Triffin is not satisfied:

Since the bulk of the Robinsonian analysis has to do with what is, in fact, the *heterogeneity* of that so-called *homogeneous* commodity, this wording seems, to say the least, unfortunate.†

But does Mrs Robinson really set much store by the notions of an industry and its correlative commodity? If we may hazard a guess that her Introduction was written later than her chapter 1, she seems to have recognized the dilemma and easily solved it according to her real intention, which was to plough the rich field of the *theory of the firm* with the new-found tool of the marginal revenue curve:

Every individual producer has the monopoly of his own output— that is sufficiently obvious—and if a large number of them are selling in a perfect market the state of affairs exists which we are accustomed to describe as perfect competition. We have only to take the word monopoly in its literal sense, a single seller, and the analysis of monopoly immediately swallows up the analysis of competition.‡

What is to be studied is the single firm in widely diverse environments, sometimes clamped in perfect competition, sometimes alone in supplying some technologically defined need, sometimes surrounded by variously imperfect substitutes for its own product. The 'industry' has vanished along with the supply curve, and not a reconstruction but a total replacement of the older economics has emerged.

Professor Chamberlin has a similarly ambiguous and changing attitude to the concept of industry or group:

These variations [amongst firms] will give no real difficulty in the end. Exposition of the group theory is facilitated, however, by

* Mrs Joan Robinson, *The Economics of Imperfect Competition*, p. 17.
† *Monopolistic Competition and General Equilibrium Theory*, p. 82.
‡ *Economics of Imperfect Competition*, p. 5.

ignoring them for the present. We therefore proceed under the heroic assumption that both demand and cost curves for all the 'products' are uniform throughout the group.*

A little later (as in Chamberlin, p. 110) it becomes evident that this notion of a group of identical firms is entirely needless and does nothing to advance the argument. We are told to look upon the diagrams as *illustrative* of the situation of a firm in monopolistic competition. Each firm can be conceived to have its own diagram, and these can differ in actual measurements to any extent. One reason for their differing will be differences amongst the products, and there is no basic need, and no basic test, for classifying such differences as important or unimportant, as leaving firms within an industry or carrying them outside of it. In the end Chamberlin throws away the concept of industry with the merest lip-service to its usefulness:

> In the matter of entry, all that we need say is that wherever in the economic system there are profit possibilities they will be exploited as far as possible...The results may be very simply described without any concept of freedom or restriction of entry—without even the concept of an industry.†

Not even lip service is paid by Triffin:

> It is now evident that monopolistic competition robs the old concept of industry (and also the Chamberlinian group) of any theoretical significance. As soon as the elasticity of substitution between two products is recognized as imperfect, their sellers can pursue independent price policies...The theoretical problem is the problem of general competitiveness between goods. Only in the case of pure competition does the grouping of firms into one industry reduce to a more simple and more definite type the behaviour and reactions of the sellers. Outside that simple case, groupings of firms do not in the least reduce the complexity and variety of competitive patterns.

In the middle 1920s the time, in some sense, was ripe for a new theory of competitive supply. A new theory, and, astonishingly, the same one, was worked out simultaneously and independently in two places widely distant from each other in geographical space, though intellectually close in their common inheritance from Marshall. It would be fascinating to discover in what precise way the time was ripe, what hint or stimulus

---

* *The Theory of Monopolistic Competition*, p. 82.   † *Ibid.* pp. 201, 202.

there was in the previous run of published ideas or in history at large, which could stir these unknowingly concerted reactions. Professor Chamberlin tells us nothing of the origin of his work. In the other Cambridge, Mr Sraffa propounded the dilemma that increasing returns are incompatible with perfect competition. This dilemma had been expressed by Cournot and by Marshall. Ninety years after Cournot and forty after Marshall, it now suddenly gave rise to Mr Harrod's intense and brilliant struggle to break out of the perfectly competitive prison, and to Mrs Robinson's and Mr Kahn's swift and splendid exploitation of the break. And the end result of all these efforts on both sides of the Atlantic was not so much to build up as to destroy. The prison was laid in ruins, but nothing was put in its place. Perfect competition had made supply a simple, monotonically increasing function of price, while demand was a monotonically decreasing function. Both supply and demand referred to a self-subsisting commodity, something directly recognizable in the real world by its physical properties, something called up in the mind of everyone by merely naming it. The price and the output of this commodity were settled by the tendency for supply and demand to be equalized and the market thus to be cleared. Such was the simple, satisfying account which perfect competition gave of the value of commodities. It showed also that, given time for full adjustment after any change in the basic circumstances of taste or technical knowledge, each commodity would be produced at the lowest possible unit cost, given the outputs of other commodities also being so produced. And it showed lastly that each employed unit of each factor of production, with the exception of the entrepreneur himself whose pay would be some fixed minimum just sufficient to induce him to be an entrepreneur, would receive the value of its marginal physical product. This account of industries and their mutual relations, and of the factors of production and their pay, a general account applying to the whole economy and answering all questions about prices, outputs and incomes, had now been left behind, not without many a backward glance. In its place had been put a *theory of the firm*. Realism had been served, but elegance, simplicity and generality had been lost to a degree which was at first scarcely realized. At the very end of our period, in 1939, Professor Hicks described the result of all the new work as 'the wreckage of the greater part of economic theory'. Yet when we look back at Cournot, we find that he took as his starting-point the theory of the single seller, the individual firm, and only then proceeded through that of a few firms to that of many firms selling in perfect competition. There is a sense in which theory during a precise century from 1838 had been travelling in a circle.

CHAPTER 7

THE INDIFFERENCE-CURVE

Let P, the utility of one party, $= F(x,y)$, and Π, the utility of the other party $= \Phi(x,y)$. If now it is inquired at what point they will reach equilibrium, one or both refusing to move further, to what *settlement* they will consent, the answer is in general that contract by itself does not supply sufficient conditions to determine the solution... Consider $P - F(x,y) = 0$ as a surface, P denoting the length of the ordinate drawn from any point on the plane of x, y (say the plane of the paper) to the surface. Consider $\Pi - \Phi(x,y)$ similarly. It is required to find a point (x,y) such that, in whatever direction we take an infinitely small step, P and Π do not increase together, but that, while one increases, the other decreases. It may be shown from a variety of points of view that the locus of the required point is

$$\frac{dP}{dx}\frac{d\Pi}{dy} - \frac{dP}{dy}\frac{d\Pi}{dx} = 0$$

which it is here proposed to call the *contract-curve*. Consider first in what directions X can take an indefinitely small step from any point (x,y). It is evident that X will step only on one side of a certain line, the *line of indifference* as it might be called; its equation being

$$(\zeta - x)\left(\frac{dP}{dx}\right) + (\eta - y)\left(\frac{dP}{dy}\right) = 0.$$

Thus Francis Ysidro Edgeworth, in his *Mathematical Psychics* of 1881, p. 21, made the first proposal of the notion of *indifference-curve*, which has proved itself applicable to every branch and almost every problem of economic theory, the most universally efficient visualizer that economists possess.

Edgeworth's equation of the line of indifference is to be understood as follows. A step, which we are to think of as numerically smaller than any pre-assigned size but still greater than zero, carries us from a point with co-ordinates (x, y) to one with co-ordinates (ζ, η). The difference between ζ and x, and that between η and y, being thus limitingly small, we can treat the corresponding differences $P(\zeta, y) - P(x, y)$ and $P(x, \eta) - P(x, y)$ as proportional to $(\zeta - x)$ and $(\eta - y)$, the proportions being respectively dP/dx (the slope of the surface $P = F(x,y)$ in the direction x) and dP/dy (the slope of the surface in the direction

y). A *line of indifference* is that direction, if there is one, in which the increase of P due to increase of x is precisely cancelled by the decrease of P due to increase of y, or vice versa. The lines of indifference being limitingly short, we can think of them as segments of a curve in the ordinary meaning of that word. At each point from which such a line of indifference starts, this line indicates the direction in which we shall find another, or other, points of the same utility, each of them no more nor less desired by our particular individual, in his particular circumstances, than the first one.

Edgeworth's use of his idea is not the one nowadays familiar, of the single consumer or producer choosing amongst pairs of quantities of goods in a perfect market. It is that of exchange between two people, where what one gives and the other receives is measured on one axis, and what the other gives and the first receives is measured on the other. A curve of indifference for either of them must slope upwards from left to right, for the constancy of his utility requires an increase of what he gives to be associated with an increase of what he receives. Thus instead of a region densely covered by downward-sloping indifference-curves, Edgeworth's diagram, reproduced in essentials in our Fig. 7. 1, shows a region bounded by just two indifference-curves, one for each of the exchangers, springing from the origin and sloping divergently upward:

To gather up and fix our thoughts, let us imagine a simple case— Robinson Crusoe contracting with Friday. Represent y, the labour given by Friday, by a line measured northward from an assumed point, and measure x, the remuneration given by Crusoe, from the same point along an eastward line. Then any point between these lines represents a contract. It will very generally be the interest of both parties to vary the articles of any contract taken at random. But there is a class of contracts to the variation of which the consent of *both* parties cannot be obtained. These are represented by a locus, the *contract-curve* CC', or rather, a certain portion of it trending from south-east to north-west between two points, say $\eta_0 x_0$ north-west and $y_0 \xi_0$ south-east; which are respectively the intersections with the contract-curve of the *curves of indifference* for each party drawn through the origin. Thus the utility of the contract represented by $\eta_0 x_0$ is for Friday zero, or rather, the same as if there was no contract. At that point he would as soon be off with the bargain.*

* *Mathematical Psychics*, pp. 28, 29.

To be 'off with the bargain' is of course to be at the origin, where zero pay is exchanged for zero work. Friday's indifference-curve (like Crusoe's) passes through the origin, and so every point on it represents a hypothetical contract which he would deem neither more nor less desirable than no bargain at

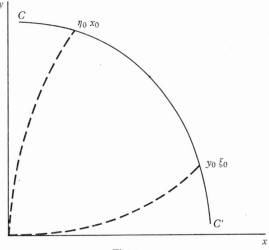

Fig. 7.1

all. From any interior point of the region bounded by the two indifference-curves and the contract-curve, a move north-eastward (indeed, infinitely many such moves) can be found which will be agreeable to both parties. But as Friday's hypothetical daily minutes of work increase, his distaste for an extra minute increases also, and will only be acceptable if compensated by larger and larger amounts of extra pay. Moreover, as Crusoe is supplied, in supposition, with more and more daily minutes of Friday's work, the urgency and usefulness of each extra minute declines, and will only be worth having at lower and lower prices. Thus a frontier exists, namely, the contract-curve, bounding the region to the north-east; a frontier where every point is a prison, since every direction of escape is unacceptable to one party or both. A move to the interior of the region is undesired by both; a move beyond the contract-curve involves a conflict between Friday's lowest acceptable, and

Crusoe's highest acceptable, price for yet more work; and a move *along* the contract-curve represents either a larger total number of daily minutes for a *smaller* total daily pay, or fewer total minutes for larger total pay, and is thus least acceptable of all to one or other party.

Edgeworth uses his construction to show the indeterminacy of contract between a pair of bargainers each isolated from all competitors (the indeterminacy of what has come to be called bilateral monopoly). The demonstration lies in the fact that, whatever point on the contract-curve chances to be tentatively tabled between the bargainers, there is from this position no escape route acceptable to both. We shall not pursue Edgeworth's construction, or our interpretation of it, further, but turn to the other primal source of the indifference-curve method, Vilfredo Pareto in his *Manuel d'Économie Politique*.

For the indifference-map conception fully explicated in the form which expresses the tastes of one individual, the *locus classicus* is chapter III, section 52, p. 168 and following of the *Manuel* (2nd edn, 1927, to which we everywhere refer).

Soit un homme qui se laisse conduire uniquement par ses goûts et qui possède 1 kilog. de pain et 1 kilog. de vin. Etant donnés ses goûts, il est disposé à avoir un peu moins de pain et un peu plus de vin, ou inversement. Il consent, par example, à n'avoir que 0·9 kilog. de pain pourvu qu'il ait 1.2 de vin. Ces deux combinaisons, à savoir 1 kilog. de pain et 1 kilog. de vin, 0.9 kilog. de pain et 1.2 kilog. de vin sont égales pour lui; il ne préfère pas la seconde à la première, ni la première à la seconde; il ne saurait laquelle choisir, il lui est *indifférent* de jouir de l'une ou de l'autre de ces combinaisons. En partant de cette combinaison: 1 kilog. de pain et 1 kilog. de vin, nous en trouvons un grand nombre d'autres, entre lesquelles le choix est indifférent, et nous avons par exemple

Pain	1.6	1.4	1.2	1.0	0.8	0.6
Vin	0.7	0.8	0.9	1.0	1.4	1.8

Nous appelons cette série, qu'on pourrait prolonger indéfiniment, une *serie d'indifférence*.

Série d'indifférence is immediately interpreted as *courbe d'indifférence* in a diagram with two specimen indifference-curves, downward-sloping from left to right and convex to the origin. Pareto explains that the whole region between the positive directions of the axes will be covered by an infinity of such curves, and refers to the term 'courbe d'indifférence' in a footnote as follows:

Cette expression est due au professeur F. Y. Edgeworth. Il supposait l'existence de l'utilité (ophelimité) et il en deduisait les courbes d'indifférence; je considère au contraire comme une donnée de fait les courbes d'indifférence, et j'en déduis tout ce qui m'est necessaire pour la théorie de l'équilibre, sans avoir recours à l'ophelimité.*

Edgeworth recognizes Pareto's use of the indifference-curve concept as something distinct from Edgeworth's own applications of his invention:

Professor Pareto is therefore in very good company [i.e. that of Jules Henri Poincaré the great mathematician] when, scrupling to designate utility as a function (say U) of quantities of commodities (say $x,y,\ldots$), he contemplates a family of successive *indifference-curves* (or generally surfaces in space of many dimensions) in the plane x, y (or corresponding hyper-surface); such that the advance from any one indifference-locus to the next in succession affords an *index*, rather than a measure, of the advance in satisfaction.†

And, with a splendid generosity:

Among Professor Pareto's original contributions to the subject we may notice his study on the quantitative data with which the mathematical economist has to deal. As we understand Professor Pareto, these data do not comprise measurements of utility: psychical quantities, unlike physical, cannot be expressed as the sum of so many units. The exercise of *choice*, the preference of the economic man for one combination of goods to another, results in a system of *indifference-curves* which are comparable with the isobars or isotherms of physical science in that each successive curve denotes a greater intensity of the attribute under consideration, but differ in that the economic, unlike the physical, curves cannot each be labelled with a number.‡

Edgeworth invented the name indifference-curve and gave it a formal mathematical definition. But it was Pareto who saw in this tool the possibility of dispensing with a concept of ophelimity or utility as something measurable on a cardinal scale, something whose portions could be added together and described,

---

* *Manuel*, p. 169.
† F. Y. Edgeworth, *Papers relating to Political Economy* (Macmillan, 1925), vol. II, p. 473.   ‡ *Ibid.* vol. III, p. 44.

for example, as being twice as large, or half as large, as one another. This is the vital step, and it is by Pareto that the seeds of a utility-free theory of consumer's behaviour were sown. Pareto was anxious nonetheless to make things easy for his reader, and he goes on to consider in what sense indifference-curves can be deemed to be contours of the individual's 'hill of pleasure'.

Every pair of quantities of the two goods will be assigned a number or *index*. Two pairs between which the individual is indifferent will have the same index, but a preferred pair will have a greater index. Subject to these conditions the indices are arbitrary, and any one of an infinity of such systems of indices could equally well represent one and the same preference-ranking of pairs of quantities of the two goods. However, if the person could compare not merely the utilities afforded him by this and that pair of goods so as to say which pair he prefers, but also the *difference* of utility between pairs A and B with the difference of utility between pairs B and C, and so on, he could find a succession of pairs A, B, E, F, G, ..., between successive members of which the differences were *equal* and thus com-posed an additive scale on which the utility of any randomly occurring pair of goods could be located. Such a scale would be private and peculiar to the individual concerned for Pareto rejects entirely the inter-personal comparison of utility:

L'ophélimité, ou son indice, pour un individu, et l'ophélimité, ou son indice, pour un autre individu, sont des quantités hétérogènes. On ne peut ni les sommer ensemble, ni les comparer. Une somme d'ophélimité dont jouiraient des individus différents n'existe pas: c'est une expression qui n'a aucun de sens.*

The method suggested for constructing a private scale of utility is the same as that proposed, independently of each other, by Ragnar Frisch (1926) and W. E. Armstrong ('The Determinate-ness of the Utility Function', *Economic Journal*, vol. XLIX). Pareto disbelieves in its practicability, but is chiefly concerned to show its needlessness.

The indifference-map, in Pareto's words, is 'a photograph of the consumer's tastes'. To find out what he will do, we must confront these tastes with the 'obstacles' which circumscribe

* *Manuel*, 2nd edn, p. 265.

their possibility of fulfilment. These obstacles, the scarcities and competing demands for goods, the circumstances which compel choice, are in the modern analysis epitomized with beautiful economy and simplicity in the budget-line, which shows both the consumer's income and the relative prices of the two goods. Pareto's efforts are less satisfactory. Throughout chapters III, IV, V and VI of the *Manuel* there are scattered many diagrams which, at a first glance, suggest the use of a budget-line in the modern manner. But it is only by taking several of Pareto's indications and arguments side by side and interpreting their total effect that we reach the modern statement. Pareto speaks of paths which the individual may be constrained to follow, but does not clearly explain in general what it is that shapes and locates these paths and sometimes, in his account of matters, brings them to an end in the interior of the quadrant rather than on the axes. He does explain, however, that a path which winds across his indifference-map from north-west to south-east (*Manuel*, chapter III, fig. 7, our Fig. 7.2) will reach its highest point where it is tangent to an indifference-curve:

Considérons un sentier *mn* tangent en *c* à une courbe d'indifférence *t''*, et que le sentier aille en montant de *m* jusqu'à *c*, pour descendre ensuite de *c* en *n*. Un point *a* qui, en partant de *m*, précède le point *c*, et au delà duquel les obstacles ne permettent pas à l'individu d'aller, sera appelé un point terminal. Le point terminal et le point de tangence ont une propriété commune, à savoir d'être le point le plus haut auquel puisse atteindre l'individu en parcourant le sentier *mn*. Le point *c* est le point le plus haut de tout le sentier, le point *a* le point le plus haut de la portion du sentier *ma* qu'il est permis à l'individu de parcourir.*

When the traveller on such a path passes in imagination from one indifference-curve to another he is evidently climbing or descending the hill of pleasure which these indifference-curves can be supposed to define. But when he is merely skirting, without crossing, one such curve, where his path is tangent to it, he has finished climbing but is not yet descending; he is therefore at the highest point which his path attains on the hill. In following such a path, Pareto's individual is deemed to be transforming one kind of good into another, either by some physical and technical process, or by exchange. He starts from

* *Manuel*, ch. III, section 64.

the eastward-pointing axis at a point whose distance from the origin represents the quantity he initially possesses of good *A*. According to the more westerly or more northerly direction of the path in this segment or that, he gets a larger or smaller

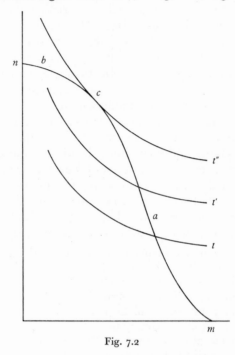

Fig. 7.2

further quantity of good *B* by the sacrifice of a given further quantity of good *A*. To represent a perfect market of a scale which renders the individual's operations insignificant, so that the relative prices or exchange ratio of the two goods remain constant at all points of the path, or to represent the technical production of one good from another, where again the ratio is constant, the path should of course be straight. In section 96 of chapter III Pareto declares his intention henceforth to consider only straight paths, 'because in reality they are more frequent' but he gives no interpretation of their straightness. Pareto's fig. 12 in his next section reminds us at once of the construction which Hicks and Allen made familiar in their *Economica* article of 1934. Here the path is specified as straight though still no meaning or reason is assigned for this straightness. Fig. 44 at the beginning of chapter VI shows a path not merely straight but at 45°, and these features are accounted for by the nature of the transformation of one good into the other, which is that of wine into vinegar at a ratio of one to one.

The idea of the indifference-map and of its uses is made more detailed and complete in the 133-page mathematical Appendix of the *Manuel*. In section 44 we find suggested the properties which 'everyday experience' tells us to expect in indifference-curves:

$$\text{Soit } \phi(x,y)$$

l'equation d'une courbe d'indifférence.

1° D'abord nous savons qu'une diminution de x doit être compensée par une augmentation de y, et vice-versa. On devra donc avoir

$$\frac{dy}{dx} < 0$$

2° En général, et si nous laissons à part certains faits exceptionnels, le quantité variable dy que l'on est disposé a donner le long d'une ligne d'indifférence, pour une quantité constante dx diminue à mesure que x augmente; on a ainsi le second caractère des courbes d'indifférence, exprimé par

$$\frac{d^2y}{dx^2} > 0$$

Pareto thus makes explicit the rule of convexity of indifference-curves to the origin. This convexity is, of course, that feature in the indifference-map analysis of consumer's behaviour which corresponds to diminishing marginal utility in the older analysis. On the page preceding the above passage, Pareto has proposed a method for determining an individual's indifference-map by experiment. This consumer is to be given some particular quantity of one good and allowed to exchange whatever proportion of it he likes for the other good at a given price. Then the experiment is to be repeated with a different initial quantity, and so on. From his choices under this range of conditions, his preferences and even his indifferences will eventually be discernible. The method is a solution of that theoretical difficulty which began to trouble writers forty years after Pareto's book was published, namely, that it is *preference*, not *indifference*, that reveals itself in conduct. These modern theorists adopted the language of the physicist P. W. Bridgeman, who had declared in 1927 that in science a concept should be defined by stating the operation by which we measure it, so that, for example, the length of an object is that characteristic of it which we determine by comparing it with a foot rule. In order to dispense with the 'non-operational' concept of indifference, the modern theorists of consumer's behaviour speak of 'revealed preference', and mean by it a procedure essentially like Pareto's.

Nous avons jusqu'ici raisonné en général et en nous efforçant de ne pas faire usage des prix; mais cependant nous avons du en parler quand nous avons imaginé des examples concrets, et même dans les théories générales nous avons dû en faire usage plus ou moins implicitement: nous nous en sommes servis sans en parlé nommément. Il était utile de montrer que les théories de l'économie ne dérivent pas directement de la considération d'un marché ou existent certains prix, mais bien de la consideration de l'equilibre, qui nâit de l'apposition des gouts et des obstacles.

This passage is a summary of Pareto's economic faith: the whole nature of the economic world, the key to its understanding, resides in the notion of equilibrium, where the strength of desires and of obstacles is equal at the margin and reason has been fulfilled. Powerful objections could be raised against his view that prices are no more than 'useful auxiliaries, to be finally eliminated, leaving us in the presence of tastes and obstacles alone'. Price, in a market economy, is the effective form which obstacles take, and here, as elsewhere, form and content are one. Price generalizes the obstacles, giving to each participant of the market, in effect, a knowledge of the whole field of possibilities and enabling him to profit by the desires and consequent potential conduct of every one else. Without the market, the obstacles would be those of barter; they would be random and chaotic, and knowable only, as it were, by casual and isolated collisions. Price provides the general chart of economic opportunities. Pareto meant that behind the mechanism of the equilibrium solution, behind the means of a general concert of action, there lay the circumstances determining the specific character of that solution. But his deliberate relegation of price to a secondary role prevented him from applying his indifference-curves in the most efficient way, so as to demonstrate what constitutes, and what is implied by, rational conduct on the part of the consumer in his real circumstances, those of the impersonal, ineluctable market. Pareto refers in several places to the *budget* of the individual as consisting in the equality of his receipts and expenditures, but he does not use the budget-line as a general means of stating diagrammatically the individual's ascribed income and the market prices facing him, and of epitomizing the whole range of pairs of quantities of the two goods which, with that income and those prices, are open to him to choose amongst. This use, however, was immediately made by others.

In 1912 in the *Giornale degli Economisti* Barone published his 'Studi di economia finanziaria'* where the comparison of direct and indirect taxes, in respect of the sacrifice imposed on the consumer by the taking from him of a given annual sum, is illustrated by the now classic diagram combining the individual's indifference-map with his straight budget-line. Barone's diagram shows, in fact, two specimen indifference-curves and three positions of the budget-line. One pair of these positions represents a parallel shift resulting from diminution of the consumer's disposable income by a direct tax, and another pair represents a pivoting of the budget-line from its initial position because a commodity tax on good *B* has reduced the amount of *B* purchasable for a given sum. Each kind of shift carries the consumer down from the higher to the lower of the two indifference-curves, and thus subjects him to equal sacrifice, but the revenue yielded by the indirect tax is less than that of the direct tax.

Barone's diagram (our Fig. 7.3) thus contains all the elements essential to Hicks's treatment of consumer's behaviour in Part I of *Value and Capital*: indifference-curves downward-sloping from the left and convex to the origin, supposedly covering the entire positive-positive (north-eastern) quadrant of the two commodity plane, combined with straight budget-lines representing both income and prices, able to show changes of money income by parallel shifts and changes of relative prices by pivoting shifts. The family of indifference-curves states com-

---

* Barone's argument and diagram are reproduced by Mauro Fasiani in his article 'On a Particular Aspect of Consumption Taxes' translated by J. M. Buchanan for *International Economic Papers No. 6* from the Italian original published in *La Riforma Sociale*, vol. xli (January/February 1930).

pletely, in a two-commodity world, the consumer's tastes; the budget-line states completely, in such a world, his relevant circumstances. The indifference-curve analysis of consumer's behaviour is thus a perfect example of that supposition, basic to the greater part of value theory, that a man's 'choice' of

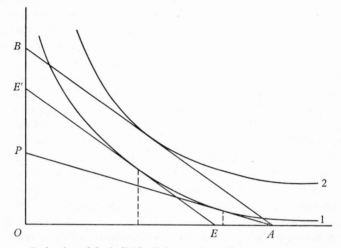

Fig. 7.3. Reduction of the individual's income by a direct tax is represented by a shift from budget-line *AB* to budget-line *EE'*. Increase of price of good *B* by a commodity tax is represented by pivoting the budget-line from *AB* to *AP*.

action is the completely determinate outcome of the confrontation of given tastes with given, and supposedly completely known, relevant circumstances. Hicks makes no reference to Barone. In writing their article 'A Reconsideration of the Theory of Value' (*Economica*, New Series, vol. I, 1934) he and R. G. D. Allen drew directly upon Pareto. After writing it, they discovered the article by Eugen Slutsky 'Sulla Teoria del bilancio del consumatore' in the *Giornale degli Economisti* of July 1915, of which Hicks says in Value and Capital, p. 19: 'The theory to be set out in this chapter and the two following is essentially Slutsky's; although the exposition is modified by the fact that I never saw Slutsky's work until my own was very far advanced, and some time after the substance of these chapters had been published in *Economica* by R. G. D. Allen and myself.'

Let us consider briefly the origins and the upshot of the new theory of consumer's demand. Pareto offered evidence that such a theory could be based upon the notion of indifference-curve, but he did not show what would be gained thereby. For the gain does not lie in ridding ourselves of a non-observational, non-operational concept called 'utility'. The role of 'utility' in Marshall's theory is purely nominal. Marshall's argument rests in fact, not on diminishing marginal utility, but on *diminishing money prices that the consumer will pay* for successively envisaged increments of supply. This is as perfectly operational, observable and measurable a concept as could be wished. Its drawback is that it makes the consumer's demand for a good independent of his income. The new theory's achievement is to throw out utility without paralysing income. This is the possibility which Slutsky in algebra, Hicks and Allen by the use of indifference-curves themselves in their visual and veritable form, perceived and brought to consummation. If Edgeworth invented indifference-curves and Pareto invented a demand theory based upon them, it was Slutsky on one hand, Hicks and Allen on the other, who independently of each other exploited the opening and secured the fruits of innovation. Hicks in this matter as in others has been the great technologist. In the next chapter we shall try to show evidence for this assessment of the record.

CHAPTER 8

TWO THEORIES OF DEMAND

The advantages which Hicks claims for the method of preference over the method of utility, in the theory of demand, are found to be two. There is first that of economy of assumptions:

The quantitative concept of utility is not necessary in order to explain market phenomena. Therefore, on the principle of Occam's razor, it is better to do without it. For it is not, in practice, a matter of indifference if a theory contains unnecessary entities. Such entities are irrelevant to the problem in hand, and their presence is likely to obscure the vision.*

Likewise appealing to methodology on behalf of the preference method, Pareto had claimed that indifference-curves were data of observation:

[Edgeworth] partait de la notion de l'*utilité* qu'il supposait être une quantité connue, et il en déduisait la définition [des lignes d'indifférence]. Nous avons inverti le problème. Nous avons fait voir qu'en partant de la notion des lignes d'indifférence, notion donnée directement par l'expérience, on peut arriver à la determination de l'equilibre économique.†

But Marshall himself had called for an observational or, as it would nowadays be called by some, an operational concept:

It has already been agreed that desires cannot be measured directly, but only indirectly by the outward phenomena to which they give rise: and that in those cases with which economics is chiefly concerned the measure is found in the price which a person is willing to pay for the fulfilment or satisfaction of his desire.‡

Satisfaction or utility is to be measured by the price that a person will pay for it. But if so, the money unit in which price is expressed must evidently be treated as something absolute and not subject to variations arising from the circumstances of purchase. That is to say, the marginal utility of *money* must be

---

* J. R. Hicks, *Value and Capital*, p. 18.   † *Manuel*, Appendice, p. 540.
‡ *Principles*, II, iii, § 1.

treated as a constant. Later, in explaining consumer's surplus, Marshall makes this assumption explicit:

The substance of our argument would not be affected if we took account of the fact that, the more a person spends on anything the less power he retains of purchasing more of it or of other things, and the greater is the value of money to him (in the technical language every fresh expenditure increases the marginal value of money to him). But though its substance would not be altered, its form would be made more intricate without any corresponding gain; for there are very few practical problems, in which the corrections to be made under this head would be of any practical importance.

Marshall asserts the law of diminishing [marginal] utility as a 'familiar and fundamental tendency of human nature' (*Principles*, III, iii § 1). Hicks says

We need the principle of diminishing marginal rate of substitution for the same reason as Marshall's theory needed the principle of diminishing marginal utility. Unless, at the point of equilibrium, the marginal rate of substitution is diminishing, equilibrium will not be stable. Since we know from experience that some points of possible equilibrium do exist, it follows that the principle must sometimes be true. We have to assume that the condition holds at all intermediate points; that there is regularity in the system of wants. This assumption may be wrong; but, being the simplest assumption possible, it is a good [one] to start with.*

Both writers appeal to experience, both of them also to a theory's need for simplicity. Marshall, having asserted the law, translates it into 'operational' terms by taking the various money prices, that a consumer will pay for a given marginal difference in his supply of something, as a measure of the utility of this difference at various sizes of the supply. Hicks makes his principle effective by expressing it as the convexity of the indifference-curves to the origin. Marshall's method involves him in assuming that the marginal utility of money is constant. Hicks requires no corresponding assumption, and is by that fact made free to study 'income effects'. Thus Hicks's method has only one, and not two, advantages over Marshall's. Both are 'operational', but Hicks can resolve the total effect of a price-change of some good into two parts. This is the second of the two advantages claimed by Hicks, and the only one we can concede.

* *Value and Capital*, pp. 21–4.

There is then one general *law of demand*: the greater the amount to be sold, the smaller must be the price at which it is offered in order that it may find purchasers. The one universal rule to which the demand curve conforms is that it is *inclined negatively* throughout the whole of its length.*

To give this 'law of demand' some reasoned position in our store of ideas, to find other propositions which can be exhibited as the premises from which it flows or as consequences which flow from it, to build under it an explanatory argument; this sort of purpose is, for Marshall and Hicks alike, the central if not almost the sole concern of the theory of consumer's demand. Chapter II of *Value and Capital* is called The Law of Demand, and the last sentence of Part I of that book contains this same phrase. Marshall starts from the idea that marginal utility, manifested and measured by money, diminishes as supply increases. Hicks starts from the assumption that all can be explained by the in-difference-curve, then asks what character the indifference-curve must have in order to provide positions which the consumer will prefer to neighbouring positions, and lastly proceeds to show that an indifference-map whose curves have this character leads to the law of demand. Marshall's argument leads to the result that '[The consumer's] demand for any commodity is independent of his income' (Hicks, *Value and Capital*, p. 26). To escape with ease and elegance from this position unquestionably shows the preference theory at a great advantage, and Hicks is perhaps too modest in his claims in this respect on its behalf.

At any and every position, representing, that is to say, any and every combination of money income and of respective market prices of the two commodities, the straight budget-line necessarily has some point of tangency with some one of the consumer's indifference-curves, the latter being all smoothly convex to the origin and sloping down everywhere from left to right. From this construction there arises without any special provision whatever the possibility of looking at a movement from one such point of tangency to another, when these points correspond to the beginning and end of a pivoting of the budget-line around one of its original intercepts on one or other axis, as composed of a *parallel* shift of the budget-line to become

* Marshall, *Principles*, III, iii, § 5.

tangent to the new indifference-curve, and of a movement
along that indifference-curve to the new final point of tangency.
The pivoting of the budget-line represents a change of price of
one good, the other price remaining unchanged. This change of
price enables the consumer to buy a larger quantity than before
of the now cheaper good while buying an unchanged quantity
of the other, or to buy more of both. This increase in his real
income is registered on the indifference-diagram by a shift to a
preferred indifference-curve. There remains for the consumer
to choose how precisely he will take advantage of this improvement of his situation, that is to say, how will he divide his now
greater purchasing power between the two goods. This choice is
shown by the new point of tangency on the newly attainable
indifference-curve.

The generalness and efficiency of the Hicksian construction
compared with Marshall's method may be seen by representing
the latter in indifference-curve form. If the good measured on
the vertical axis is taken to represent 'money' or 'general purchasing power', then Marshall's assumption of constant
marginal utility of money will require all the indifference-curves
to have the same slope at every point of a straight line parallel
to the vertical axis, and a similar statement must be true of every
such parallel line. Thus when the good, say B, on the horizontal axis is cheapened, the whole change in the quantity
bought of good B will be due to the substitution effect, since
every *parallel* shift of the original budget line will yield a new
point of tangency vertically above the original one, and thus
represent an unchanged quantity of good B. The indifference
map which interprets Marshall's assumption is thus a highly
special one incorporating an artificial restriction of its shape.
Such a map is illustrated in Fig. 8.1.

It was to the English-speaking world of economists that Hicks
and Allen rendered so great a service. Until their work appeared
in *Economica* in 1934, that world was unaware of the indifference-
curve. It was then already more than fifty years since *Mathematical Psychics*, twenty-five years, with a foreign language and
the Great War intervening, since Pareto's *Manuel*. To Italian
readers of Pareto and Barone, to mathematically capable
readers of Slutsky, the matter was available and even familiar.
The vast use that has been made of the indifference-curve in

88   THE YEARS OF HIGH THEORY

Anglo-Saxon work since 1934 is tribute enough to what Hicks and Allen achieved. They gave an incomparable tool of exact thought and assured insight to economists to whom algebra

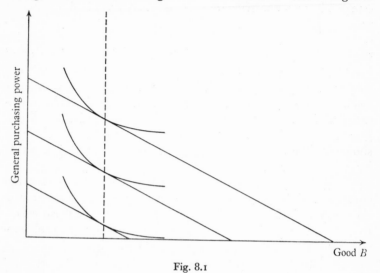

Fig. 8.1

is uncongenial and verbal argument intractable. They developed and exploited Pareto's suggestions independently of Slutsky and even (it appears) of Barone. They began that demonstration, which has since advanced by giant strides, of the indifference-curve as one of those remarkable notational inventions that can nearly think for itself.

CHAPTER 9

MONETARY EQUILIBRIUM

When total demand expressed in money for goods of all sorts produced today is equal to the total money value placed on those goods by those who offer them, nothing is visible at this level of description such as to call for any change either in the general level of prices or in the size of general output and the employment its production gives. If, for example, employment is full, it can, so far as this equation can penetrate the matter, go on being full. The statement we have given of 'monetary equilibrium' raises a long list of questions, as to meaning and interpretation, and as to how such equilibrium is to be brought about. It was a monetary equilibrium with something of the above meaning that Knut Wicksell had in mind as the central notion of his monetary theory, and that Erik Lindahl and Gunnar Myrdal, by their separate but mutually illuminating contributions, succeeded thirty-five years later in perfecting as a main tool of analysis. The whole theory which thus emerged has been stated and explained, its origins and evolution traced and credit for its ideas assigned, with the utmost clarity and exactness, and with generosity, modesty and piety of a very impressive kind, by Gunnar Myrdal himself, whose role in creating this theory was as important as that of Wicksell, and who produced, in his *Monetary Equilibrium* in its original Swedish and German versions, as remarkable and in some respects as successful an explanation of the variations of general output as Keynes's own. Indeed, the two theories have very much in common, though Keynes's work was known to Myrdal only in the form of the *Treatise on Money* whose theoretical framework is utterly different from that of Myrdal or Keynes's *General Theory*, while Myrdal's work is not referred to by Keynes (though Wicksell's is).

The first question to be asked about equilibrium of total demand and supply is whether the equality of these two things is not identical, that is, arising from their meaning, and so quite precluding treatment as a condition logically capable of non-fulfilment.

The demand and the supply of a single kind of product, studied in particular equilibrium analysis, are only held to be equal at an appropriate price. This price has somehow to be discovered. The market, operating in a manner idealized by Walras's *tâtonnements* or Edgeworth's re-contract, is the practical means of solving the system of simultaneous equations by which, in principle, the conditional intentions of the participants can be expressed. The quantity, per time unit, that each will buy or offer is a function of the price; is conditional upon the price; and when a unique price-condition is found, for which the corresponding total of individual demands and the total of individual supplies are equal, we have equilibrium and the clearing of the market. Equilibrium pre-supposes the solution of a problem. In the case of a single commodity the market mechanism can be imagined to work successfully. What of the parallel problem when all products are taken together, and the question concerns the demand and supply of general output?

In particular equilibrium analysis we do not ask why the individual consumer's income is what it is, but simply assign him some stated income and discuss his disposal of it. In general equilibrium analysis we value all goods in terms of a unit of account, and the equilibrium solution assigns to each good a price, in terms of this unit, at which its demand and supply are equal. A condition included amongst those satisfied by this solution is that prices and quantities shall be such that the total number of value-units (units of account) offered is equalled by the total number demanded, and so the question of where the needful income for purchase of the goods arises, and the question whether it is sufficient, is answered at the same time as the quantities and prices are determined. In both particular and general *equilibrium* analysis, choice of action is supposed to be based on sufficient knowledge, and it is the role of the equilibrating mechanism (whether this be a realistic market or a computer programmed with conditional promises) to achieve the paradoxal result of simultaneous choices based upon knowledge of each other. General equilibrium analysis assumes that the only thing acceptable in exchange for today's products is, in effect, other of today's products. Units of account are merely what their name implies. Now when, instead of an equilibrium model, we suppose one where each producer must decide what size of output to produce and offer, of his own kind of product, on the basis of his mere *conjecture* of the demand curve facing him, there is nothing to ensure that the revenue (price times output) resulting from this offer will be, in the event, the amount which his decision assumed. Nonetheless if all today's conjectural income is intended, by those who expect it, to be spent on today's products, the total of revenue will necessarily, in the event, equal the total of these conjectural incomes, and a short fall of one person's revenue below his expectation will be exactly compensated by an excess of others' revenue above their expectations. Thus in the model or assumed system where the only acceptable means of purchasing today's products is other of today's products, *total* demand and supply in value-unit terms are necessarily equal. It is only when we introduce a *substantive* means of purchase, one which does not merely *represent* today's products but exists or arises in its own right, *outside* the list of products, that total demand and total supply can be unequal. It is *money* which destroys the necessary, inevitable equality which they have in a barter or virtual barter system. Money, of course, could not do so in the general *equilibrium* system, where indeed its independent existence would be meaningless and any role beyond that of unit of account non-existent. If we cared to construct a general equilibrium system where 'money' entered on the same footing as current products, the system of simultaneous equations determining this equilibrium would have to specify the conditional intentions in respect of spending or accepting money, and the enlarged system would still show an equality of that total of demand and supply which included offers and demands for money. For in a general equilibrium system we suppose that each action-chooser has full relevant knowledge, provided for him by the equilibrating mechanism whatever its precise nature and mode of working. Inequality of total demand and total supply, to be logically possible, requires the presence and the play of both *ignorance* and *money*. Ignorance, in the real world, there is indeed: ignorance of the future. And money is that institution which permits *deferment* of specialized, fully detailed choice.

A general equilibrium* is the outcome of simultaneous

---

* G. L. S. Shackle, 'L'équilibre: étude de sa signification et de ses limites', *Cahiers de l'Institut de Science Economique Appliquée. Les Cahiers Franco-Italiens* (2).

choices of action (one effective choice per person) by all members of the society, these choices being made in two stages. In the first stage we suppose each person to formulate his personal action-function, wherein for each conceivable set of actions on the part of others, he says what his own action would be. If the resulting system of conditional promises is solvable, the second stage consists in the finding (by some means) of a solution which indicates for each person the act he would prefer, given the acts similarly prescribed for all others. Actions in this context can be complex, but must be chosen as wholes, each act being a plan which the individual commits himself to carry out completely without alteration if it shall form part of the equilibrium solution. This notion of equilibrium thus reconciles itself to that of Hayek for whom equilibrium meant mutual compatibility of plans of individuals.* In this conception of equilibrium, there can be choice only once, and nothing can be said, at the time when the choices composing this equilibrium are made, about the detailed specific character of any new and later equilibrium which might be called for when circumstances beyond the control of the choosers may have changed. The life of a society where goods were consumed almost as soon as they were produced could be roughly pictured as a series of such equilibria, the mechanism of solution being provided by the market, which continually digests the information of fresh demands and offers, and reports the price or constellation of prices which will equalize demand and supply.

It is evident that equilibrium thus conceived provides no framework for the analysis of actions chosen *without* full relevant knowledge of the simultaneous choices being made by other persons. It does not in itself offer any account of, or means of describing, a process of trial and error or of step-by-step approach to a complete mutual adjustment and reconciliation of the actions of different persons, an approach to an equilibrium solution. It cannot link together in a logical dependence the choices of action made at one moment with those made at an earlier moment, it provides no dynamic scheme. And when exchanges are mediated by money, which exists, and can be increased in existing quantity, with virtually no use of productive resources, and which is not desired for its own sake but, in

* F. A. von Hayek, 'Economics and Knowledge', *Economica*, N.S. vol. II (1935).

the last resort, only because it will exchange for other things, not only is the identical equality broken between the total of expected production earnings and the total of intended expenditures on the product, but there is introduced the possibility of exchanging *money now*, spot cash, for promises of money to be paid later. The ratio of exchange of differently dated sums of money, or the interest-rate, can affect the mutual exchange-ratios of present goods. Money, indeed, has no existence in such an equilibrium model as we have defined, for it is only when all the choices embraced by the model are made simultaneously in a unique moment lacking any subsequent history, that each choice can be made in complete knowledge of all the other choices. Money being ultimately valued only because it can be exchanged for something useful in itself, something wanted for its own sake, would not be acceptable if no further opportunity of exchange were going to be available. Money's presence, when that presence is part of the theoretical essence of a model, implies the presence also of uncertainty, which is expressly alien to the meaning of equilibrium; for money is a means of *deferring decision*, and decisions which are deferred cannot be known by anyone, yet are going to affect future situations and events. Money's presence destroys Say's Law of the identical equality of total demand and total supply of all current products taken together. In a model, therefore, where money in its full nature (not merely in its role of unit of account) plays an essential role, the equality of total demand and total supply is a condition or special circumstance which is logically capable of non-fulfilment. The monetary theory which Wicksell evolved from suggestions of Ricardo, and which Lindahl clarified and to which Myrdal gave the vital spark by his distinction of the two temporal viewpoints *ex ante* and *ex post*, and to which he gave a brilliant elegance and logical rigour, was devised with the very purpose of analysing the *conditions* of equality of total monetary demand and supply of the general output of goods of all sorts. It had also, of course, the purpose of studying the implications of non-fulfilment of these conditions.

CHAPTER 10

MYRDAL'S ANALYSIS

Decisions to produce are made by the business men; decisions to demand goods for consumption are made by the whole body of income-receivers, including the business men in their private capacity; decisions to demand goods for net investment, that is, for positively improving (as distinct from merely maintaining) the society's equipment, are made by the business men. Is there, then, any guarantee that the value set by the business men on all that they have decided to produce is exactly equal to the total intended demand, for consumption and net investment taken together, which the income-receivers as such, and the business men in their capacity as such, have in mind? There is no mechanism which can supply any such guarantee. Let us, however, turn from what is decided to what is recorded as having occurred. If incomes in total are the value of what has been produced, must not any net addition which has been made to the society's stock of equipment, being necessarily equal to the excess of the value of production over the value which has been consumed, be thus identically equal to the excess of income over spending on consumption? If the answer here is yes, we appear to have two contradictory answers to the question whether or not saving and net investment are necessarily equal. But in fact there is not one question but two. Is *intended* net investment necessarily equal to *intended* non-consumption of income? No. Is *recorded* net investment necessarily equal to *recorded* non-consumption of income? Yes. The whole subject of economic dynamics, as Myrdal in 1933 conceived it, consists in explaining how intentions which in general will be disparate are transformed into recorded totals which are identically equal. To throw this problem into relief and provide a frame for its solution, Myrdal made a suggestion of utter simplicity yet of transforming power. He said that the events of any named time-interval must be considered from each of two temporal viewpoints: the threshold of the interval, when all that can be assigned to it is action decided on and intended; and the final date of the interval, when its events have uniquely occurred and been recorded as fact. By formulating in language the *ex ante ex post* distinction, Myrdal provided a theoretical scheme which recognizes that the future is qualitatively, fundamentally and essentially different from the past.

In one respect only it may seem that Myrdal's formulation of the relation between net investment and saving was not quite complete. He omitted to point out that the two distinct groups of people, one including but not the same as the other, the business men in their capacity as such and the income-receivers as a whole, would in spite of their distinctness reckon the same total of expected incomes for any named interval seen *ex ante*. Incomes can be divided into the two classes, profit or the excess of sale proceeds of product over contractual outgoings of the firm, and these contractual outgoings themselves viewed as incomes for the factor-suppliers of the firms. Aggregate expected profits will be one and the same whether the business men think of them as something they will pay out to themselves or as something they will receive from themselves. Contractual incomes in aggregate will be one and the same whether viewed by the business men as sums promised to be paid or by the factor-suppliers as sums due to be received. Thus we can write five equations, four of them identities and one expressing a condition, the equality of total demand and total supply. All of them refer to aggregates over society as a whole, and all of them consist of *ex ante* quantities:

Expected income is identically equal to value of intended production (i)

Expected income is identically equal to intended consumption-spending plus intended saving (ii)

Value of intended production is identically equal to intended consumption-spending plus intended saving (iii)

Intended demand is identically equal to intended consumption-spending plus intended net investment (iv)

Intended demand can be equal to value of intended production (v)

Identity (iii) follows from the combination of (i) and (ii). When we subtract from each side of (v) the term consumption-spending, we are left with the fallible equality: Intended net investment can be equal to intended saving (vi). The fulfilment of this condition is that state of intentions which constitutes *monetary equilibrium*, and this equilibrium, which might be more illuminatingly called equilibrium of general output and general demand, is nonetheless justifiably linked with the notion of money because only the presence of money in the full sense makes possible any divorce, *in the aggregate*, between production intentions and demand intentions. The analysis of monetary equilibrium consists in seeking the influences which bear on the sizes of the two aggregates: value of intended production and value of total demand; or, what is for some purposes equivalent, in asking what influences bear on the sizes of intended net investment and intended saving. Having thus marked out the region to be mapped, we may turn to see how Myrdal, starting from Wicksell's outline survey, filled in a self-consistent picture.

One has to divide income into *saving* and *consumption demand*, and similarly production into *investments* of real capital and *production of consumption goods*. In the combination of those four quantities arises Wicksell's new statement of the problem of monetary theory. The underlying idea is that one cannot assume an identity between demand and supply of consumption goods except in a state of static equilibrium. This proposition should seem obvious to the unsophisticated mind, since decisions to buy and sell a commodity are made by quite different individuals. Similarly, one cannot assume that capital (investment) demand and capital (saving) supply are identically equal; for they, too, originate with non-identical groups of individuals. To treat supply and demand in these cases as being *identically*, rather than *conditionally* equal, would involve a highly unreal and abstract concept of equilibrium.*

This formulation differs only trivially from our own foregoing statement. In the latter we have elected to ignore the question of how intended production is divided between goods expected to be sold to consumers as such, and goods expected to be sold to those who mean to add them (over and above maintenance) to the stock of equipment. All that is essential is the single comparison of total intended production, measured by the values set on its items by their producers, and the total of intended demand reached by adding intentions to buy goods as a net increment of

* Gunnar Myrdal, *Monetary Equilibrium* (William Hodge and Co. Ltd, 1939), pp. 22, 23. Translated from 'Der Gleichgewichtsbegriff als Instrument der Geldtheoretischen Analyse', included in *Beiträge zur Geldtheorie*, ed. F. A. von Hayek (Vienna, 1933).

equipment to the intentions to buy and consume goods. Even when, *ex post*, it is possible to look back and see that what has been added to stock is simply what was produced over and above the equivalent of what was consumed, there is nothing to guarantee that these *ex post* additions to stock will consist of goods which, *ex ante*, were expected by their producers to be devoted to that purpose. In our own statement, we do not say that intended consumption expenditure will, or will not, be equal in total amount to the value of goods intended for consumption within the interval, since the category 'goods intended for consumption' has no place in our formula. It is not really essential to Myrdal's. It is the last fifty words of the paragraph we have quoted from Myrdal which contains the essence of the Wicksell-Myrdal theory, viz. that there is nothing to ensure that capital demand and capital supply are identically equal. Myrdal's theme, which despite his piety is his own and not Wicksell's, has three strands: first, to state rigorously the meaning of the basic proposition that saving and net investment can be un-equal; secondly, to show the consequences of their happening to be unequal; and thirdly to describe the mechanism of their separate, mutually independent determination and to state in terms of the factors which influence them the condition for their equality, that is, for what Myrdal calls monetary equilibrium and we would prefer to call equilibrium of general demand and output. All of these purposes depend on Myrdal's central contri-bution, the express distinction and emphatic contrast between the two temporal viewpoints:

At a point [of time] there are only *tendencies* which must be studied as a preparatory step to the dynamic analysis proper which refers to the *causal development in time* up to the next point studied. This essay is mainly confined to the study of the tendencies existing at a point of time. Such a study defines the quantities to be used in the further analysis of the dynamic problem. Some of these quantities refer directly to a point of time. That is true of 'capital value' and of demand and supply price. Other terms, [for example] 'income', 'revenue', 'return', 'expenses', 'savings', 'investments' imply, however, a time period *for* which they are reckoned. But in order to be unambiguous they must also refer to a point of time *at* which they are calculated. An important distinction exists between prospective and retrospective methods of calculating [such] economic quantities. Quantities defined in terms of measurements made at the end of the period in question are referred to as *ex post*; quantities defined in terms of action planned at the beginning of the period in question are referred to as *ex ante*. Probably the chief contribution of this essay, if any, is to have originated the concepts *ex ante* and *ex post*.*

This rather flat and formal statement gives little hint of the radical novelty of Myrdal's venture. For the first time, an economic theory was to be based on men's imaginative construction of an unknown future. Myrdal himself did not thus express it, being content to refer to anticipations and their uncertainty. But the dramatic, uncompromising shift of ground ought to be seen in its full meaning. The view of economics as a human counterpart of celestial mechanics was being abandoned. The difference in nature and essence between any moment's past and that moment's future, the non-determination of the latter by the former except, at most, via men's thoughts ill-based on only partly relevant and greatly insufficient knowledge, contrasted wholly with a model of *pre-reconciled* individual actions, a model of general equilibrium where the market brings men's actions into rational coherence as the sea brings ships to the same level. Myrdal did more than perceive the basic role of expectations and the radical effect of their uncertainty. He worked out with exact logic a theory where subtle and elusive difficulties are recognized and coped with, where Wicksell's dimly visualized goal is brought sharply and completely into view. In all but its assignments of emphasis, *Monetary Equilibrium* anticipated Keynes's *General Theory*, though not conveying Keynes's sense of revolutionary achievement and conviction of power.

The meaning of *monetary equilibrium* for Wicksell was the absence of a cumulative process. When the state of affairs tempted business men towards actions whose combined effect would renew a similar but stronger temptation; as when, for example, a price rise of consumer goods in general, by making production seem more profitable and leading to the competitive bidding-up of factor prices, the increase of factor-suppliers' money incomes, and a stronger demand for consumer-goods, itself generated a further price-rise of consumer goods; Wicksell called this initial state of affairs a monetary disequilibrium, and

* Gunnar Myrdal, *Monetary Equilibrium* (1939), pp. 45–7.

its sequel a cumulative process. This he regarded as a disorderly phenomenon and one which had bad social effects. He sought accordingly some rule by which the monetary authority might recognize at the outset, and correct, a monetary disequilibrium, and he, in fact, formulated three such rules.

If the owner of a forest cuts certain of his trees today, he can lend the money from their sale for a promise of repayment of $(1+r)$ times this money in a year's time. If he leaves the trees standing, he can expect to sell them in a year's time, with their then greater weight, for a price $(1+g)$ times what he could sell them for today. The fraction g is what Wicksell meant by the natural rate of interest. His first rule for monetary equilibrium was that the money rate of interest, r, must be kept equal to the natural rate. Myrdal's chapter IV is wholly concerned with examining the meaning of this rule and finding a satisfactory statement of it.

Much of Wicksell's theoretical system was evolved from the work of the Austrian school as it existed in the 1880s, and in especial from that of Böhm-Bawerk, the chief proponent of the idea that the stock of producers' goods existing at any moment manifests and embodies the productive role of time. Willingness to wait longer for the fruits of dated human and natural activities enables these forces to be more efficiently, because more complexly, deployed. To carry forward the work of one day to aid that of the next and make it more powerful, the work of the earlier day must be stored up in 'intermediate products', more and more of which must co-exist, the longer the average lapse of time between input of dated packets of human work or natural forces, and the emergence of the consumable goods ascribable to those packets. This average lapse of time, the 'average period of production' thus supplies a measure of the size of the industry's or the society's stock of producers' goods. This stock, with its immense technical diversity, may on these lines be considered a single and homogeneous factor of production, and a marginal productivity calculated for it as the ratio of the increase in output from *given* quantities of labour and land, to the increase in the average period of production with which this increase in output is associated. By waiting 40 years instead of 35 between his annual planting of a fresh acre of ground with trees and his cutting of that same acre, the forest-owner has at all times a forest of greater average maturity and also is able *each* year to cut a greater weight of timber. When he makes the transition from a 35-year to a 40-year cycle, the forest owner must forgo for five years the cutting of any timber. Thus he both saves and invests. The result of his investment is a *permanent* increase in the annual output of timber from his now effectively larger capital stock.

The Austrian theory of capital, which we have thus sought briefly to explain, was the work chiefly of Eugen von Böhm-Bawerk (1851–1914) and Knut Wicksell (1851–1926) at its beginning, and in the 1930s of F. A. von Hayek (1899–   ). Its brilliant and arresting central idea, that 'capital is time', has proved under close scrutiny somewhat disappointing to those theorists who wish economics to show the precision, rigour and self-contained completeness of classical mechanics. The objections which, on such a level, it seems exposed to are certainly no worse than those which afflict the notion of a general price level or the Quantity Theory of money. Its chief difficulty is in passing from the notion of a capital stock composed solely of 'goods in process' to one which involves durable instruments which are used, almost without physical change, over and over again. Despite all, it provided Wicksell with a concept of the physical or technical productivity of a stock of capital goods, and on this he sought to base that of the 'natural rate of interest'. Myrdal's first concern is to examine (and in the event, to reject) the interpretation of the natural rate as a purely physical or technical phenomenon.

Evidently the forest owner, in asking himself whether it will pay him to borrow money (or forgo lending it) in order to keep his trees growing one more year, must have regard not only to their physical increase in weight but to the ratio he expects between the price of timber a year hence and its price today. Myrdal, however, does not resort to this direct argument but seeks a more general insight, and is, in fact, groping after the notions of liquidity and liquidity preference without naming or clearly conceiving them:

If, therefore, one wants to make the Wicksellian construction of the natural rate of interest really useful for monetary analysis, one has in contradiction to Wicksell to replace the concept of a physical productivity by that of an *exchange value productivity*. This latter can [only] be derived by calculations which assume some sort of uniform abstract unit of account. If we assume that the economic subjects replace some of their loan transactions *in natura* [i.e. in goods useful in themselves] by credit contracts which they make in that calculating unit, then this unit acquires the other properties of a monetary unit too, for the process of price formation is then influenced by *changes* in the exchange value of the monetary unit with respect to other commodities.*

The goods whose rates of exchange for *each other* are altered by an alteration in the rate of exchange of money now for money deferred (that is, in the interest rate) are those which each represent some series of expected and deferred instalments, e.g. of net profit. For when two non-identical such series, discounted at some one interest rate, have equal present values, their present values at a different interest-rate will in general be unequal. It is in a world of uncertainty, one which therefore can be in a state other than that of perfectly informed rational adjustment of all acts to each other, that money gains freedom and a life of its own, and so a value of its own as the means of *deferring decisions* and avoiding commitment to technically specialized, hazardous types of asset. In his search for these notions, Myrdal is handicapped by his avoidance, in the Austrian tradition, of any mention of durable tools or equipment. For it is such durable producers' goods which above all depend for their value on series of expected and deferred instalments of profit. Nonetheless through these pages of chapter IV Myrdal's book dimly foreshadowed the notion and influence of liquidity.

The natural rate of interest must thus be expressed in value terms. But what is far more important, it must be conceived as an expectation, a statement about an imagined future, in strictness a figment despite the careful study of data which may guide its selection. Myrdal's chief originality and greatest contribution was his invention of a scheme which sharply separates the book-keeping record serving as a basis for expectations from the expectations themselves which alone are relevant for decision:

Any calculation of a yield must evidently be related to a point of time at which the calculation is made and to a period of time for which the yield is reckoned. Two different methods of calculation

* *Monetary Equilibrium*, pp. 51, 52.

are possible. The yield can be regarded either *ex post* or *ex ante*. The first method is 'book-keeping' about what has actually happened during a completed period, the second is an estimation of what will happen in the future. Both ways of calculating revenues and costs have a very real meaning in actual business practice. It is the latter method, based on discounted anticipations, i.e. the *expected profitability* of an undertaking, which, of course, is decisive for entrepreneurs' programs, not the profitability actually experienced during a past period. The latter profitability in principle has importance in the calculations only indirectly as evidence of future profitability. As basis for the *ex ante* calculations, the *ex post* recorded experiences may regularly be decisive. But that does not mean that the two concepts should not be kept separate in theory.

In appearance, Myrdal's proposed reform of economists' ways of thought was simplicity itself, but it was vital and indispensable.

Myrdal believed that in general structure Wicksell's insight and scheme were true: equality of the cost and the profitability of borrowing money was a state of things, a condition, which had a high significance for society's affairs; and equality of the demand and supply of saving was another such condition. These two conditions, in Wicksell's view, were equivalent in the sense that either of them was sufficient to ensure the absence of a cumulative rise or fall of money prices in general. Myrdal, however, believed that the relation between these two conditions needed to be further studied, and that to this end Wicksell's measure or meaning for the profitability of borrowing money for investment, namely the 'natural rate of interest', needed to be replaced by a new concept. The concept he arrived at, by a difficult and circuitous route, turns out to be none other than what Keynes later called the marginal efficiency of capital, and what Irving Fisher had long since called the rate of return over cost. We shall show that there is no equivalence between the two conditions even when the first is reformulated with the new concept. Equality of the marginal efficiency of capital and the rate of interest at which money can be lent or borrowed is a roughly effective condition in the short period, *ceteris paribus*, for a *constant* flow of net investment: we shall call it *investment equilibrium*. There is no guarantee whatever that when the flow of intended net investment has been brought to a level where the marginal efficiency of capital is equal to the money rate of interest, the aggregate of expected incomes will at once be such as to match that flow by the flow of intended saving; and therefore no guarantee that general output (whose value is what we mean by aggregate income) will not tend to rise or fall, either in real terms or by a price-change or both. When it does change it is likely to affect expectations and thus undermine any approach to equilibrium.

Myrdal's final notion of the inducement to invest was precisely Keynes's notion in the *General Theory*, and it was expressed in the same two forms. The first of these forms was the comparison of two discounting rates, one measuring the supposed earning power of investments and the other their displacement cost in sacrificed interest. The second was the comparison of the demand price with the supply price of equipment. Except for one analytical insight which the latter method can give and the former cannot, the two methods are equivalent. Myrdal called that discounting-rate which measures the supposed profit-earning power of investments, the *yield of planned investments* (meaning by investments, of course, the ordering and purchase of equipment). Keynes called it the *marginal efficiency of capital*. Myrdal only found his solution after a long and devious search, openly conducted in the pages of his book. The first stage of this search, as we have seen, was the rejection of a purely physical or technological notion of the 'natural rate of interest'. Next, however, he allowed himself to be turned aside by a feature of his own scheme of the *ex ante* and *ex post* viewpoints, so that for many pages he assumes it necessary to concentrate on the business man's immediately future unit interval and derive a profit-rate which has, as it were, two components, first the expectations of sale-proceeds of product and factor costs of *operating* the plant in the interval, and secondly an allowance for 'value change' of the plant during the interval, that is, in the main, for its depreciation. This way of looking at things can, as we shall see, be made illuminating by interpreting it into a compact formula, but in this formula the two components take on quite different meanings from those which Myrdal had in mind. The formula comes down in the end simply to the marginal efficiency of capital. Thirdly Myrdal shows that we are concerned, not with the historical cost of already existing equipment but with the supply price for which equipment which might now be ordered could be obtained. This we might express by pointing out that *investment* must mean what it says, the decision or action of devoting freely disposable resources to a fresh improvement of productive facilities.

Myrdal thus defines the net return of real capital:

The net return e' for an individual firm for a unit period, calculated *ex ante*, at a given point of time is:

The discounted sum of all anticipations of gross returns in the next unit period, b'; *minus*

The discounted sum of all anticipations of gross cost in the form of operating cost of the co-operating means of production in the next period, m'; *minus*

The anticipations of the value-change, d', calculated for the period by taking into consideration all expectations of income and cost for the *whole* remaining life of the capital goods and also the interest rates which actually rule in the existing situation and are expected to rule in future. The anticipated value change is here given a positive sign when the change is a depreciation in value. Thus we get

$$e' = b' - (m' + d').*$$

By gross returns Myrdal means here sale proceeds of product, and by gross operating cost he means the outlay for labour, materials and power to run the equipment or 'capital goods'. The calculation is concerned ostensibly with what is expected to happen within the immediately future unit interval, and these expected happenings comprise, first, the purchase of means to operate the equipment, its operation and the sale of its product; and secondly the decrease or increase in the value placed on the equipment, which will occur between the beginning and the end of the interval. However, this division of the future life of the equipment into a single immediate unit interval, on one hand, and on the other hand all the rest of its life, and the corresponding division of its economic performance into operation and depreciation, is quite needless and beside the point. Despite the ostensible confining of attention to the single immediate unit interval, the reckoning in of depreciation means that the whole expected life of the equipment is being taken into account, for the value which will be assigned to it at the end of the immediate unit interval will merely and solely reflect the assumed power of the equipment to produce goods,

* *Monetary Equilibrium*, p. 58.

in the further future beyond the immediate interval, which will sell for more than the cost of operating the equipment in producing them. In short, the notion of depreciation, or value-change, is needless and out of place in the sort of calculation that Myrdal really seeks. The future life of the equipment can be viewed as a whole from the business man's present moment, and the significance, for his decision whether to invest in it or not, of all its expected net earnings during that life, no matter what their date, whether in the immediate or remote future, can be derived by a treatment which will be the same in character for all of those earnings.

The relation of Myrdal's formula for the net return of real capital, to the concept of the marginal efficiency of capital, can most conveniently be shown by supposing the intervals, into which we conceive expected time to be divided up, to become limitingly short, so that expected sale-proceeds and operating costs, and their difference, net operating profit, can technically each be treated as a continuous function of the lapse of time. Let us define our notation as follows:

x the time-distance separating some variable date from some fixed earlier date $x = 0$.

t the time-distance of the business man's present moment from the earlier date $x = 0$.

g the sale proceeds of product, or gross receipts, expressed as a time-rate of flow, which, at date t, the business man expects for date x from operating the equipment.

h the operating cost of the equipment per time-unit expected for date x.

$f(x) = g - h \geqslant 0$.

v the value placed on the equipment by the business man at time t.

$r(t, x)$ the rate of interest at which money can be borrowed at date t for repayment of the amount of the debt accumulated at compound interest r at date x. For simplicity, however, we shall assume that r is the same for all t and all x.

$\rho = \log_e (1 + r)$.

Then we have

$$v \equiv \int_t^\infty f(x) \, e^{-\rho(x-t)} dx,$$

where the sign of identical equality is appropriate because this equation is a mere definition of the left-hand member, in which respect it stands in contrast with the superficially similar conditional equation whose solution is the marginal efficiency of capital. Myrdal's *value-change* associated with the movement of the business man's present moment along the calendar axis will be

$$\frac{dv}{dt} = \rho \int_t^\infty f(x) \, e^{-\rho(x-t)} dx - f(t)$$
$$= \rho v - f(t).$$

To this, according to Myrdal's formula for the net return of real capital, we have to add the excess of expected sale proceeds over operating costs for the immediately future interval. In our 'continuous' model, that interval is made limitingly small, and so the operating profit of this interval is simply $f(t)$, and we have for the net return, say $\mathcal{J}$, of the equipment, in Myrdal's sense

$$\mathcal{J} = f(t) + \frac{dv}{dt}$$
$$= f(t) + \rho v - f(t)$$
$$= \rho v.$$

Now ρ, or r, being given (it is well known that for ordinary levels of r, say $r \leqslant 7$ per cent for annual compounding, ρ approximates r and does so the more closely the shorter the compounding interval and the smaller, correspondingly, the numerical value of r) ρv is proportional to v the capital value of the equipment, which in turn depends on the whole series of expected profit instalments or what, in our 'continuous' model, we can call the whole *time-shape* of expected profits indefinitely far into the future. But it is precisely upon this time-shape that, on the demand side, Keynes's reckoning of the inducement to invest also depends. His two methods of expressing the strength of this inducement are to compare either the capitalized value v of all expected profits with the supply price, say s, which would have to be paid for the equipment if the investment were decided on, or else the rate of interest obtainable for money lent, r or ρ, with the marginal efficiency of capital, namely that discounting rate z which satisfies the equation

$$s = \int_t^\infty f(x) \, e^{-z(x-t)} dx.$$

This, in contrast with our expression defining the capitalized value of expected profits, expresses a *condition*, namely that the rate z used for discounting shall be such as to make equal, on one hand, the value of profits capitalized *at this rate*, and on the other the construction-cost or 'first cost', s, of the equipment. Investment equilibrium; the absence, in the short period before the equipment now being decided on has time to affect productive capacity, of any inducement to alter the size of the aggregate intended investment flow; will prevail when either $v = s$ or, equivalently, when $z = \rho$.

Myrdal, as we have seen, did not go directly to these conclusions, but explored every detour which offered itself upon the route. His concept of net return was cumbersome, but it had the essential clue, that the inducement to invest depends upon expectations. Having defined this net return, he proposed to form its ratio to the 'stock' which yielded it, for some such ratio, it must be supposed, would indicate the profitability to be hoped for from investing a fresh sum of money in buying or constructing equipment. Such a ratio he calls the yield, and says

The yield, y_1', is obtained by dividing the net return so calculated by the capital C_1', of the capital goods at the time of calculation. Thus

$$y_1' = \frac{e'}{C_1'}.*$$

Yet something is wrong:

We have analysed the net return, and defined the yield as the ratio between the net return so defined and the capital value. But, now, capital value is nothing else than the discounted sum of all future gross incomes minus operating costs. The capital value is in other words only a price reflection of the two magnitudes: Net return and 'market rate of interest'. This means that there is always and necessarily a conformity between the yield thus defined and the interest rate in the market; for capital value and net return are defined in such a way that they must constantly fulfil this equation.

This, indeed, is shown at once by our 'continuous' version of Myrdal's entities, for we saw that in this version the net return becomes ρv while the capital value of the equipment, or of its expected profits, is of course v itself, so that the yield is

$$y_1' = \frac{\rho v}{v} = \rho.$$

* *Monetary Equilibrium*, p. 59.

The mistake is not, as Myrdal supposes*, that he has been considering equipment which already exists instead of equipment whose construction is yet to be decided on, but quite simply that he is trying to compare capital value with itself instead of with the construction cost of the equipment; that same equipment which, when it has been constructed, possesses or will possess this capital value. For the equipment derives its capital value, on one hand, and its construction cost, on the other, from wholly different and unrelated circumstances. The capital value represents the profits which the equipment is expected to *earn*; the construction cost is the fund which its construction will require to be *spent*. Yet Myrdal's mistaken diagnosis leads him back to the proper path. Once planned rather than already existing equipment is in question, the idea of asking how much it is going to cost presents itself naturally and inevitably, and Myrdal transfers his attention to it almost, it would seem, without noticing what he has done:

Henceforth we shall mean by yield the *yield of planned investments*. It would evidently have to be defined as *the ratio between the net return on the projected real investments and the cost of their production.*†

This formula has still one fault. It uses the clumsy notion of Myrdalian net return, unnecessarily involving the division of the future into immediate and more remote, and the performance of the equipment into productive operation and change of value. Myrdal himself is dissatisfied with it, not on the ground of conceptual complexity but because of the difficulty of filling its empty boxes with statistics. He refers to the fact that there is not at any moment just one money rate of interest, but many different ones each belonging to a different time of maturity of the loan. The expectations held by different business men about the profitability of this or that projected investment are far more various still, and immeasurably more difficult for a detached observer to find out, even if we conceive the business man to imagine them clearly in his own mind. Myrdal therefore decides upon a final step of reformulation, and by this step he attains the ultimate simplicity of that statement which Keynes unconsciously matched in the *General Theory*. Wicksell's first condition for monetary equilibrium, that is, for the absence

* *Monetary Equilibrium*, p. 64.   † *Ibid.* p. 65.

of any incentive for business men to take action which would initiate a cumulative process, is to be interpreted as the equality, on one hand, of capital values, which summarize expectations of operating profit (and require no mention whatever of 'value-change'), and on the other hand of costs of construction of the equipment:

The equilibrium condition can, however, be put in another form which means the same but which does not encounter the same difficulties if applied in the analysis of an actual situation. We have according to our definition [writing i for the money rate of interest]

$$i = \frac{e'}{c_1'} = \frac{e''}{c_1''} \text{etc.}$$

[the successive right-hand members referring to different individual firms]

and
$$y_2' = \frac{e'}{r_1'} = \frac{e''}{r_1''}; \text{ etc.}$$

Therefore the equation $i = y_2$ [viz. equality of the money rate of interest and the yield of new investment] implies the equation $C_1 = r_1$ [viz the equality of the capital value and the cost of construction of equipment].*

Myrdal goes on to expound the practical and theoretical virtues of the new statement:

First of all, the magnitude 'money rate' is not explicitly contained in the equilibrium formula thus reformulated. But the whole complex of very different [i.e. very diverse] credit conditions which in Wicksell's theory are represented by the magnitude 'money rate' are nevertheless implicitly contained in the capital values. And, moreover, the capital value includes for each firm exactly those credit conditions in exactly those proportions which are important for the capitalization of future revenue and cost expectations in that par-ricular section of economic life. Similar statements are true about the yield. In the new formula the net return does not appear explicitly. But the capital values express exactly the very anticipations of future price and production conditions and the very attitude towards risk which present the real difficulties in a practical applica-tion of the concept of net return. We have avoided the whole com-plex of the money rate and its determination, and we have avoided the concept of the 'net return'. Both are adequately represented by the actual capital values.†

* *Monetary Equilibrium*, pp. 69, 70.   † *Ibid.* pp. 70, 71.

Myrdal's final version of the first Wicksellian condition for monetary equilibrium is thus the equality, for every item of equipment whose construction is imagined, of its total of dis-counted expected *operating profit* (its capital value) and its total discounted expected *costs of construction*, and this condition can be even more briefly expressed as the judgment of every business man that there is for him no possibility of *investment gain*. *Investment gain* has, indeed, already been defined by Myrdal on earlier pages. On p. 61 he has still not quite escaped from the notion that 'expected profits' have to belong to equipment which already exists or nearly exists, there is even a vestigial hint of seeking to *combine* the *ex ante* and the *ex post*:

Investment gains and losses arise if the capital goods just *being constructed* have, at the moment when they are ready for use, a capital value which is larger or smaller than the total cost of con-struction.*

But on p. 65 we have the ultimate liberation, the definition is stated wholly in *ex ante* terms, and we find that

the anticipated 'investment gain' in relation to the capital sum being invested [is] the rate of capital gain which the entrepreneur could make by buying means of production and transforming them into real capital [i.e. equipment] which, at its time of completion, is anticipated to have a higher value than the sum of its costs of production.

The investment gain is something the entrepreneur *could* make by constructing equipment which *is anticipated* to have, when it shall be ready for use, a higher value...Profit *hypotheses* and investment *decisions* are recognized to be something in a man's *mind*.

Like Myrdal, Keynes has two versions of the inducement to invest. In one of them the *marginal efficiency of capital* takes the place of the *yield of planned investments*. The marginal efficiency is superior because simpler. It treats all expected operating profits as on the same footing, discounts them all to the business man's moment of decision at a discounting rate which brings their total present (capital) value to equality with construction cost discounted to the same moment, and is then compared with the money or loan rate of interest with which, by variation

---

* Italics in the original.

in the size of the flow of orders for construction of equipment, it tends to be brought to equality. Equality of the marginal efficiency of capital and the loan rate of interest leaves business men with no incentive to *alter any further* the aggregate of their individual intended flows of investment in construction of equipment, and this equality may thus be called investment equilibrium. Keynes's second version is identical with Myrdal's final formulation:

When a man buys an investment or capital asset, he purchases the right to a series of prospective returns, which he expects to obtain from selling its output, after deducting the running expenses of obtaining that output during the life of the asset. This series of annuities $Q_1, Q_2, \ldots Q_n$, it is convenient to call the *prospective yield* of the investment. [Let us note Keynes's assignment of an entirely different meaning to the word *yield* from that which Myrdal gives it]. If Q_r is the prospective yield from an asset at time r, and d_r is the present value of £1 deferred r years at the current rate of interest, $\Sigma Q_r d_r$ is the demand-price of the investment; and investment will be carried to the point where $\Sigma Q_r d_r$ becomes equal to the supply price of the investment.*

'Investment will be carried to the point...' means here, of course, that the orders given *in unit time* for new installation of equipment will be pushed to the level which brings down the demand price for the marginal tool or instrument of each kind to equality with its supply price.

One aspect of Myrdal's conception which has somewhat escaped our effort to define its formal frame, is his insistence on the uncertainty inherent in a process of thinking and deciding, where the ultimately essential elements are suppositions about the future. Myrdal himself went no further, in making uncertainty an element in his analysis of investment, than to refer to probabilities and to attitudes toward risk:

Since there exists a whole series of probabilities for every single element of gross returns and costs, we have to multiply every expectation of incomes or costs by a coefficient before we can discount it. This coefficient gives the assumed degree of probability. The expression for the net return, calculated in this way, must subsequently be multiplied by a second coefficient which expresses as a valuation the

---

* John Maynard Keynes, *The General Theory of Employment, Interest and Money*, pp. 135–7.

attitude toward risk which is held by the entrepreneurs evaluating the probabilities of such future elements of returns and costs. In reality this calculation is naturally done only crudely and summarily. But this should not hinder us from keeping this theoretical pattern of calculation clearly in mind during our analysis.

Other references to the uncertainty or risk inherent in investment decisions are scattered through Myrdal's pages. In this respect the comparison with Keynes is exceedingly interesting. Keynes's whole essential explanation of the paradox that, in a world of basic universal scarcity, there can occur at times a massive refusal to make anything like full use even of those productive resources which are available, rested on the existence of an escape for the individual, by resort to liquidity, from the uncertainties of investment. At times, business men refuse to fill the saving gap, at the size it would have at full employment, with net investment because they are too uncertain what the outcome of investment would be. Uncertainty is the very bedrock of Keynes's theory of employment, as he makes clear with single-minded force in the article called 'The General Theory of Employment' with which, in the *Quarterly Journal of Economics* for February, 1937, he sought finally to drive his message home. We should expect, therefore, to find in his discussion of the marginal efficiency of capital a large space devoted to the formal analysis of uncertainty. But there is nothing of the kind. In the *General Theory of Employment, Interest and Money* the only scheme we find mooted for formally including uncertainty in the analysis of business men's decisions is in the third footnote to p. 24:

An entrepreneur, who has to reach a practical decision as to his scale of production, does not, of course, entertain a single undoubting expectation of what the sale-proceeds of a given output will be, but several hypothetical expectations held with varying degrees of probability and definiteness. By the expectation of proceeds I mean, therefore, that expectation of proceeds which, if it were held with certainty, would lead to the same behaviour as does the bundle of vague and more various possibilities which actually make up his state of expectation when he reaches his decision.

In line with this treatment of production decisions, we may perhaps understand the series of annuities Q, which the marginal efficiency of capital discounts to equality in total present value with the construction cost of the plant, as *certainty equivalents* wherein the 'objective' estimate of unsureness and the attitude towards it are both subsumed. For Keynes, the dependence of investment on expectations implies something beyond this, namely, the *fragility* of the inducement to invest. Expectations are mere soap-bubbles which can burst at the touch of an adverse or irreconcilable piece of news. This instability of the structure of thoughts on which investment depends can be brought into the analysis by supposing the schedule of the marginal efficiency of capital to be subject to abrupt, wide bodily shifts. The curve relating the number of units of a given kind of equipment ordered per time-unit, to the marginal efficiency of capital thus invested, must be imagined capable of sweeping bodily up or down, and thus intersecting the curve of the interest-rate at a different abscissa and so at a different number of orders per time unit. Keynes, about to rest the whole weight of his argument about employment on the uncertainty afflicting investment, was casual to the point of total neglect in his formal treatment of it. Myrdal, at least, explicitly recognized and many times insisted on the role and essential, ineluctable presence of uncertainty in all investment calculations.

In his chapter IV, Myrdal explores every line that suggests itself for interpreting Wicksell's first condition of *monetary* equilibrium, and comes eventually, as we have seen, to a statement identical with Keynes's statement of the condition of *investment* equilibrium. In the last sections, 15 and 16, of that chapter, Myrdal perceives that these two equilibria are not the same:

[Wicksell's] basic assumption is that when prospective investment-profits are zero [capital value equals construction cost for every imagined investment] the entrepreneurs are just exactly replacing the old outworn real capital but do not endeavour to make new investment. We now have, however, to ask why the zero-profit situation should mean monetary equilibrium. In a dynamic study [viz. that of a non-stationary economy], the assumption that lack of new investment is a necessary condition for monetary equilibrium is of doubtful validity.*

In the passages from which the above sentences are extracted, two questions seem to be confused, but again the confusion

* *Monetary Equilibrium*, pp. 80, 81.

supplies the essential clue which leads to a final true insight. One question is whether the so-called 'zero profit situation' implies that there will be zero net investment, the other is whether zero net investment is a necessary and sufficient condition for the absence of any impulse towards a process of cumulative price change. Myrdal's ultimate position is that zero investment profit (a zero difference between total discounted expected operating profits and discounted construction cost) does not mean zero net investment, and that zero net investment is not necessary for the avoidance of a cumulative process. But in seeking to explain the first of these propositions he entirely misses the one vital and simple point, that we have to distinguish between the profitability of investment in many units of equipment all ordered together, and the profitability of the *marginal* unit. Indeed the most familiar proposition in economics tells us to locate the maximum of a function (of a suitable kind) by finding the point where its derivative is zero. If, when attention is being confined to a single type of equipment, its operating profit per unit is judged to be a decreasing function of the number of units ordered per month or year (and this will be more probably the case the more imperfect is competition in the market for this equipment's output) then a zero *marginal* profit will signal the maximum *total* profit. It is the *marginal* efficiency of capital which, in Keynes's presentation of the matter, will tend to be brought to equality with the interest rate and so bring about what we have called investment equilibrium, the momentary absence of any incentive to change the size of the investment flow.

At the end of his long wrestle with Wicksell's first condition of monetary equilibrium, Myrdal has in effect achieved two insights which together constitute a full solution of the problem that Wicksell had intuitively and somewhat confusedly envisaged. The first of these insights is that when 'the equality of the natural and the money rate of interest' is satisfactorily reexpressed as the absence of marginal investment gain, this equality is the condition for *ceteris paribus* constancy, not of the general price level but of the size of the aggregate net investment flow. The second insight is that this first condition is nonetheless useful, for since it tells us how the size of the aggregate investment flow is determined, it shows us how to regulate that flow so as to satisfy Wicksell's second, and true, condition for monetary equilibrium. For reasons which we shall consider below, Myrdal prefers to express Wicksell's second condition of monetary equilibrium as the equality, not of *net* investment with saving, but of gross investment with the sum of saving and depreciation allowances. The difference between the two expressions is a purely formal one. In the final section of chapter IV Myrdal says at last:

In order to find the principle for the final re-modelling of Wicksell's first equilibrium equation, we have to make his second equilibrium condition our premise and infer the profit equilibrium [i.e. the investment equilibrium] from the requirements of equilibrium on the capital market. The equilibrium on the capital market means that total investment R_2 just balances total capital disposal available $(W = S+D)$ [R_2 is *gross* investment, S is the excess of income over consumption-spending, D is depreciation allowance, that is to say, the deduction from sale-proceeds of output necessary to reduce it to net income. Myrdal would naturally give to all these an *ex ante* meaning]. The profit margin which corresponds to monetary equilibrium is, therefore, the complex of profit margins in different firms which stimulates just the amount of total investment [$\equiv$ gross investment] which can be taken care of by the available capital disposal.*

This passage calls for one last emendation. Does Myrdal deem each firm in his 'complex' to have in mind a schedule relating investment gain per unit of equipment to the number of units about to be ordered within the impending unit time-interval, and does he thus suppose each firm to order that number of units of equipment which will reduce the *marginal* investment gain to zero, leaving the *average* gain, over the entire number of units presently ordered, at a level greater than zero? Such a conception would be in perfect accord with the wording of this passage, but is not suggested by it. On the other hand, Myrdal has repeatedly proposed a zero investment gain as the equivalent and appropriate gloss for Wicksell's condition of equality of the natural and the monetary interest-rate, and has at the same time been evidently puzzled as to how a zero gain can be supposed to induce a greater than zero investment flow. To regard a zero investment gain as applying to the marginal, not

* *Monetary Equilibrium*, pp. 82, 83.

the average, unit of equipment concurrently ordered seems to us the natural and plain solution of the dilemma, and a means of tracing an unbroken strand of thought from Wicksell through Myrdal to Keynes.

One single suggestion by itself, which he made, will be enough to earn Myrdal bright fame in the history of ideas. By insisting, in effect, that the future and the past are different sorts of things; that the image of a named particular month or year seen from its beginning can be quite different from its image seen from its end; Myrdal released economic theory from the tacit, imprisoning assumption that the economy moves like the planets, in paths each known as a whole irrespective of the point in it which a given planet happens to be at when we do our calculation of its orbit. The future is not known to those whose decisions, in their combined effect and interplay, determine it. Myrdal's innovation, radical and momentous as it was although in the backward perspective so natural and simple, was a by-product. No doubt the same is true of many great inventions. Myrdal set out, not to invent a new scheme of economic analysis, but to set his own mind at rest, I daresay, on the questions of what Wicksell's conditions meant and whether they were valid. Wicksell's first condition, he found, needed interpretation, a need which we can see to have arisen partly, indeed, from the conciseness of Wicksell's expressions, but partly also from the preconceived ideas which more orthodox writers had planted in Myrdal's mind. The first need and task of an innovator is self-release. He must twist and wrench the prison-bars as we can watch Myrdal doing, sentence by sentence, in the remarkable document of his book. Behind the words of this book we can read a tale of arduous and intense thought, intimately and essentially bound up with a great linguistic effort of expression. In the end he won through to a conclusion wholly reconcilable with a Keynesian view, though set in a different frame of assumptions.

Wicksell's concern is with the general level of money prices, Keynes's is with the size (according to some quasi-physical measure) of general output. For a fruitful comparison of their ideas it is essential to bear this in mind. Wicksell and Myrdal tacitly ignore the possibility, or at least the relevance, of any kind of under-employment equilibrium. We do not mean by this that they consider only those situations where no physical increase at all of general output is possible. A change in the price of labour or of land may elicit a larger (or smaller) market-supply, a smaller or larger quantity being withheld for leisure or direct enjoyment. But in the Wicksell–Myrdal theory the main response to a general strengthening of demand is a rise in prices; in Keynes's conception the main response is an increase of employment and of physical outputs. It follows that Keynes is describing a formally stable, and Wicksell a possibly unstable, system. For if, in Keynes, at a given level of monthly or annual orders for equipment, the demand prices (capitalized expected profits) of marginal units of these orders exceed their supply prices, the business men will increase their unit-time orders so as to raise supply prices and lower demand prices to a point where they are equal. Or if supply prices exceed demand prices, orders given per time-unit will be reduced. Keynes thus thinks of an investment equilibrium as tending always to be established. But when the flow of investment orders is thus determined and has settled to a given level, general output and its money measure, aggregate income, will according to Keynes rise or fall until the saving gap between this income and the flow of consumption-spending is equal to the self-determined net investment flow. And thus Wicksell's second condition, expressed in Keynesian terms, will be satisfied. Such adjustments can come about because Keynes considers in general an under-employment situation. For Wicksell, by contrast, an upward stimulus occurring when employment is already full must result mainly in price rises, these leading to action engendering further such rises and so on, so that there is no reason in general why a new equilibrium should be attainable.

Myrdal and Keynes both speak of the same two conditions: the first, the equality of the natural rate and the money rate of interest (as Wicksell expressed it) or the vanishing of the marginal investment gain (as we have glossed Myrdal's expression of it and as Keynes in effect expressed it); the second, the equality of the supply of and demand for saving (as Wicksell put it), or equality of saving and investment, as Myrdal himself, without any gloss, expresses it. Each of these is, for Wicksell, a sufficient condition for monetary equilibrium, that is, for the absence of any incentive to business men, considered in the aggregate, to take such action as would start a self-reinforcing movement of the general price level up or down. We must surely suppose, then, that for Wicksell himself these two conditions are, in relation to monetary equilibrium, equivalent. What is the relation of these two conditions for Myrdal?

In the passage we quoted above from pages 82, 83 of Myrdal's book it is 'the available capital disposal' which means different things for Myrdal and for the Keynes of the *General Theory*. Wicksell himself, and Myrdal in seeking to interpret him, tacitly take for granted that the economy will all the time be fully employed. This does not imply a strict constancy of the national income, for the 'full employment' offer of factors of production may be larger or smaller according to the prices offered for them. But it does imply a directing of attention to the division of some given aggregate of (assumed or expected) incomes between consumption-spending and saving, rather than to the possibility and genesis of large variations of this aggregate itself. When, therefore, Myrdal contemplates a situation where a former equality of 'total investment and capital disposal' has just been destroyed by a sudden brightening of profit hopes of business men, he sees the aggregate of their intended expenditures on equipment outstripping the aggregate of the society's intended saving plus depreciation allowance for the same immediately-future interval; that is to say, he sees the amount of money which is about to flow into the producers' goods market as *demand* as exceeding the money value, at current prices, of factors and goods available to supply that market; and he sees this, of course, as about to bring an increase of those prices. But will such an increase restore equilibrium? There is a very strong presumption that the 'first round' of such an increase will not do so; for any rise of prices of producers' goods raises the prospective incomes of their suppliers, and this in turn may well increase these suppliers' intended spending on consumption, and thus increase still further the expected profitability of enterprise and further strengthen the inducement to invest. A new equilibrium may eventually be reached; but who can tell? The mechanism of a self-reinforcing price rise in a condition of full employment is a *psychic* mechanism; no reasoning *in vacuo* can inform us of its character and course. If there is no restriction of the increase of the quantity of money, or if its velocity of circulation can increase without limit, there appears to be no mechanical limit to the cumulative process. The only thing that can stop it, other than a radical change of business men's expectations from a source other than observation of the price-rises themselves, is a raising of the *money rate of interest*, the terms on which enterprise, production and business operations generally can be financed, to a level which annihilates the investment gain on any investment flow larger than the intended saving flow, both reckoned at the prices which have been attained. What that money rate will have to be will evidently depend on the state of mind, the state of expectation, induced by the repeated rounds of price-rises which may already have taken place. And when such a rate does kill off the sequence of those price-rises, it will have changed expectation in a way which will doubtless bring about a reversal of the cumulative movement, unless the money rate is swiftly lowered again.

Wicksell and Myrdal take for granted full employment. On this assumption, any lowering of the money rate below the natural rate of interest, any emergence, that is, of a greater-than-zero marginal investment gain, will necessarily originate a self-reinforcing rise of the general price level. Provided the two rates are kept equal when no such cumulative process is in being, no such process will start. Such is the essence of Wicksell's thesis as interpreted by Myrdal, and we may accept it. But let us turn to the supposition of general under-employment. In this case an increase of the aggregate of net investment intentions might be followed, through a Keynesian Multiplier process, by an increase of general output and its money measure, aggregate income, sufficient to enlarge the saving gap between the latter and consumption-spending up to equality with the new size of intended net investment, and if that new size remained constant in spite of the enlargement of output and income, a new equilibrium of total demand and supply for goods of all sorts would be attained. The great question here is whether, and why, expected investment gains would not respond to an observed increase of general production and income. Nonetheless, if we assume general under-employment as the initial situation, it may be that the aggregate intended investment flow, after a change of profit expectations, could readjust itself to a *given* money rate of interest, and that general output (aggregate income) could then adjust itself to this new size of investment flow, and equality of total demand and supply for goods of all sorts be thus established at a new level, by a process not requiring any responsive action on the part of the monetary authority. We may conclude that there is some difference between the full-employment and the under-employment case, regarding the mode of application of Wicksell's theory to them. Only the former is a legitimate testing-ground for the theory as Wicksell himself conceived it.

Myrdal's own formulation still belongs tacitly to the full-employment frame of ideas. Yet even in a more general context it is very difficult to fault it. The passage we quoted from pp. 82, 83 of Myrdal's book can stand as a quite general statement, and affords just as good a description, in implicitly *ex ante–ex post* terms, of a Keynesian under-employment equilibrium as it does of a Wicksellian full-employment equilibrium. It makes no mention of the money rate of interest, but this is of course to be understood as governing the investment gains ('profit margins') which arise from given expectations of future trading-profit. In order to preserve a given level of employment and general output, the investment gains would have to be brought to the appropriate size by adjustment of the money rate of interest.

Myrdal's discussion has many elements and characteristics of great interest besides those we have considered. He insists that:

It must be our endeavour to formulate the condition of monetary equilibrium in such a way as to contain observable and measurable magnitudes. The theory ought to yield certain simple and definite formulas which are sufficiently amenable to observation to be useful in a statistical analysis. Whoever, like the present author, looks at abstract economic theory as a rational complex of questions to be put to the factual material will consider this demand self-evident.*

Whether, when he wrote this, Myrdal was acquainted with P. W. Bridgeman's now famous demand, published in 1927, that the concepts used in physics should be 'operational' we do not know. But Myrdal's plea is in essence an identical one. In pursuit of this principle, Myrdal finally expresses the inducement to invest, the functional link between investment gain, as the independent variable, and the number of money units which, in the aggregate, business men decide to spend in a

* *Monetary Equilibrium*, pp. 47, 48.

forthcoming unit interval on equipment, as a weighted sum of the decisions of individual men or firms, the weights being an expression of the individual elasticities of investment expenditure with respect to individual expectations of investment gain:

Here we are up against the fundamental difficulty that we cannot assume the differences between c_1 and r_1 [c_1 is capitalized expected trading profits and r_1 is cost of construction of the equipment] to be the same over the whole economic system. Suppose that the profit margin, $c_1 - r_1$, could be obtained for individual firms. What principle is there for grouping and weighting [such] differences [i.e. margins] in different branches of the economy to compose a general index? The combination in a uniform expression $\Sigma_w (c_1 - r_1)$ of the differences of c_1 and r_1 which are found in different branches of the economy, has to be made by a method which weights each such difference with regard to its effects on the amount of real investment, measured in cost of production. The weights must be different for different branches of the economy, and they must depend on the sign, the size and the direction of movement of the profit margin, and on the general business cycle situation of the economy as a whole. We define a firm's coefficient of investment-reaction as the ratio between the amount of net *new* investment—i.e. investment over and above the replacement of outworn old real capital—which it decides to undertake during a unit period and the amount of prospective investment-profit $(c_1 - r_1)$ necessary to induce this investment. These coefficients may be interpreted as average elasticities of investment with respect to profit. They are not constants, but depend on the size of the profit margin, among other things. They are, in fact, a mere symbol for an unsettled problem.

In not despising 'a mere symbol for an unsettled problem' Myrdal is wholly in tune with the method and outlook of Marshall, Keynes and the whole Cambridge school of their day. Such algebraic expressions as these writers used were, for them, mere capsules enclosing and identifying a content of private thought too complex and subtle by far to be made explicit, and manipulated, mathematically. This content could be indicated to the reader only verbally, and then largely by the *exposition* of difficulties rather than by their precise and definitive solution.

One final point in the above-quoted passage may be considered. That passage speaks of the investment coefficient as referring to new, i.e. *net*, investment. In the next chapter of his book, Myrdal is driven by a peculiar interpretation of monetary equilibrium, and of the part played in it by the money rate of interest, to insist that we must always work in terms of *gross* investment and 'free capital disposal', the latter being the sum of saving proper (viz. the excess of income over consumption-spending) and of amounts set aside, out of gross sale-proceeds of product, for depreciation of existing equipment. Myrdal himself points out, however, that gross investment can always be reduced to net investment, and free capital disposal to saving, by the subtraction from each of them of one and the same allowance for depreciation of existing capital; and we may add that it is always necessary to arrive at some figure for depreciation, since without it we cannot reckon income.

For the student of the origin of theories, no source could more deserve attention than Myrdal's book. He calls it an 'immanent criticism' of Wicksell. By this he means that he took from Wicksell a set of interrelated propositions about how to avoid the start of continuing self-regenerating change of the price-level, and sought to exchange the concepts, and the names of the concepts, used by Wicksell, for others whose referends in the observable word could be more easily pointed to. Terms and phrases with a sharper meaning being thus obtained, an argument could be constructed whose logic was more open to examination and whose conclusions could be more readily applied. To any reader who has experienced a writer's pains, Myrdal's book conveys overwhelmingly the sustained intensity of its author's effort. From the result, four lessons emerge which nothing could more plainly teach. First, this is a book avowedly and expressly designed as a continuation or development of the work of another writer. Here, then, if anywhere, there should appear the cramping limitations of starting with a foundation of ideas already laid down, and having to build within its purpose or general plan. Yet this book makes as great a theoretical advance as Wicksell himself, and yields an even greater innovation. There is in this no paradox. *Every* writer must start with an outfit, or even a scheme, of preconceived ideas. Indeed, it is obvious that to write *in vacuo*, to begin by inventing ideas that owe nothing to anything that has gone before, is inconceivable or could be the work only of a madman who, if he achieved it, would communicate nothing to the world outside himself. An idea may have an element of powerful novelty, but must also have aspects of familiarity, else it could mean nothing to us, it could find no place in our thought, could not attach itself to any conceptual structure of ours or even belong to language itself. Myrdal, therefore, was constrained in the purpose and direction of his thought, once he had elected to raise his structure on Wicksell's foundations, but he was not in the least constricted in the degree of originality he could exercise. But, secondly, it was the essence of Myrdal's self-imposed task to change, not Wicksell's broad purpose but the form and exact design of his concepts, the very characteristics upon which their logic and capacity for locking themselves together in a structure of reasoning depends. To decide which characteristics of which elements in the Wicksellian sketch (for in comparison with Myrdal's work it was no more than a bold plan) needed to be abandoned, and above all what to put in their place; to select new elements which would carry the argument beyond the immediate difficulty, whatever it was, and serve in a completed scheme; these were the steps of crucial difficulty calling for trial after trial of tentative ideas. A writer in the Cambridge tradition, after just such an exploratory struggle, would have thrown away the record of it, chosen a new starting point and shown us a short cut to the goal.* Myrdal implicitly gives us the whole course of his thought, and in the reading of it there is plainer and plainer to be seen the real source of his success: his having begun and been inspired throughout with an exacting semantic standard. Nothing would do that was not exact, clear and rigorous; or if the very nature of the economist's tools, as in the concept of index-number, involves imprecision and arbitrary choice of meaning, then this element of indeterminacy must be made public and explicit in the argument. It was a passion for exactly formulated, clear, quantifiable and well-identified ideas that enabled Myrdal, when he applied it to Wicksell's powerful suggestions, to say in Swedish in 1931 in very large measure what Keynes said in English in 1936.

Myrdal's long list of discarded formulations gives us a third insight into the process of invention of theory. A theoretician

* On the Cambridge method, see a brilliant commentary by Fouraker, *Journal of Political Economy*, vol. LXVI.

necessarily starts with some *given* ideas, conceptions which have somehow, in reading, talk or experience, been thrust upon him. These are his home base, his frame of reference. To abandon these ideas in any part is a wild sortie, a truancy and defiance, possible only in crisis and then only in sight of some replacement; possible, moreover, only to a natural intellectual adventurer. The grip of an idea, once understood and familiarized, is too strong for the majority of men. Invention of a new theory requires, first of all, a questioning and release from the old, and against such release all habit, instinct and indolence contend. Finally, there is in Myrdal's book an illustration of something occasionally to be seen in books which propose a novelty, the existence of a focal chapter or part, an 'engine room' which contains the power of the whole argument. In Marshall's *Principles* we have book v; in Keynes's *General Theory*, chapter 12; in Harrod's *Towards a Dynamic Economics*, lecture 3; and so on. In *Monetary Equilibrium* we have chapter iv. That chapter and its sequel are the battlefield where the decisive action occurs. We have examined their contents and effect in detail. But after them come passages of high interest, confirming and extending the conclusion that, had the *General Theory* never been written, Myrdal's work would eventually have supplied almost the same theory. This contention must be briefly made out before we turn to Keynes's own work.

We have suggested that Wicksell and Myrdal were not really concerned with unemployment of productive resources in the sense in which Keynes treats it. In regard to Myrdal's central discussion of the two first Wicksellian conditions, this suggestion rests mainly on Myrdal's constant reference to price and price relations, and his insistence that Wicksell's great achievement was to include the theory of absolute or money prices within that of relative prices. Myrdal's crucial chapter iv makes no reference, explicitly or, we would say, by implication, to under-employment or involuntary unemployment of resources. But in his illustrations of the practical meaning of his theory in subsequent chapters, he comes to a consideration of unemployment via that of business 'depression'. Even here, however, unemployment is in a sense voluntary, since it is ascribed to the monopolistic action of trade unions. Myrdal, however, lacks one vital Keynesian insight: he makes no mention of the *inability* of labour as a whole to reduce its *real* wage, an inability due to the fact that the demand for products comes largely from the incomes paid to their producers and that thus a reduction of money wages leads to a weakening of demand for goods and a lowering of the profits to be gained by employing a given number of men.

In a brief reference to what would nowadays be called the consumption-function, Myrdal indeed is far ahead of Keynes's unclear discussion, where the lack of an explicit *ex ante–ex post* distinction leads Keynes to confuse the *ex post* identity of saving and investment with their conditional and fallible *ex ante* equilibrium, and to rely quite fallaciously upon the former for proof of the quantitative dependence of income on investment. Myrdal says:

> The fact that the size of our current income available for purposes of consumption or saving is in this way ultimately dependent upon our own subjective calculations, relating the present to the future periods by imputation, deserves increased attention in the explanation of booms and slumps. Thus it comes about that in certain conditions a sudden fall or rise in people's available incomes and consequently their consumption and savings can occur, although the so-called objective circumstances do not justify the change.

Income is subjective. The size of a person's income depends upon his assumptions about the future, his expectations, what he can imagine as coming true; income is partly the direct creation of a man's own mind. This is how we must interpret Myrdal's passage just quoted, and this is only in small degree a gloss on his actual words. Myrdal indeed gives to income the character that Keynes gives to investment: something governed by elusive movements of the human psyche under the influence of 'the news' and thus in effect spontaneously and unpredictably mutable. Like Keynes, Myrdal in our quoted passage makes changes of income the source of changes of consumption-spending, but in Myrdal's case the income which governs consumption is an expectational variable. Lacking an explicit *ex ante–ex post* distinction, Keynes nowhere makes clear how, in his scheme, that income which governs consumption is to be conceived; but in discussing the propensity to consume he treats the relevant income as known. Myrdal lacks the notion of the Multiplier, but Keynes, in describing it, vacillates between a 'process' conception involving expectation and decision, and an 'instantaneous' conception which is in fact merely an alternative expression of the existence of the functional dependence called the propensity to consume. By the brief suggestive passage we have quoted, Myrdal thus anticipated Keynes in one further respect, besides those relating to profit and investment, namely that of the dependence of consumption on a variable income, and not merely on the inducement given by a variable interest-rate to divide a given income in various proportions between consumption and saving. Again Myrdal has the immense advantage in clarity given by his invention of explicitly *ex ante* concepts. He lacks only the Multiplier.

In Keynes and Myrdal, in the *General Theory* and *Monetary Equilibrium*, we see yet again two writers creating one and the same theory by mutually independent and simultaneous work. Even the mutually corresponding portions of their books can be pointed out. Myrdal's chapter II is Keynes's chapter 3: each deals with the relation of total general demand to total general supply. Myrdal's chapter IV is Keynes's book IV: each deals with the inducement to invest. Myrdal's chapter V is Keynes's book III: they deal with the consumption function and the saving gap. Myrdal's chapter VI has its affinities with Keynes's chapter 21, on prices; and Myrdal's chapter VIII, dealing with the policy implications of his theory, loosely parallels Keynes's book VI. The essential identity of their ideas on the inducement to invest has been argued in some detail in the foregoing. It is much more striking to find them in agreement, against the rest of the world, on the effects of a general strengthening of the desire to save. By a 'strengthening' we mean a bodily shift of the curve relating aggregate consumption-spending to aggregate income; and by income it seems to us appropriate to mean *expected* income; though at this stage of his book (chapter v) Myrdal has ceased to remind his reader, at each step, of the need to consider whether some quantity is an expected or recorded one:

We now turn briefly to a case often discussed in the literature and ask: What are the monetary effects of increased savings? [In a situation of equilibrium on the capital market] the curve of saving changes so that total saving increases. This is the only primary change. Since saving has increased, free capital disposal has increased too. Real investment is not directly stimulated (we shall see presently that the reverse will very soon be the case) [Thus] a downward Wicksellian process has been started. Furthermore, it is obvious that real investments not only do not increase but must even decrease. For increased savings, defined to mean decreased demand for consumption goods, necessarily brings about some decrease in the prices of consumption goods. This fall in prices must itself tend to lower capital values by influencing anticipations; with the consequence that the profit margin will move in the negative direction, which naturally means that real investments will decline.

A writer of today, using both Keynesian and Swedish insights, would suggest that an unheralded increase in the propensity to save would at first be reflected in the piling-up of unsold stocks of goods which producers had expected to sell to consumers, this accumulation of inventories representing, *ex post*, an unintended increment of investment matching the *ex post* increment of saving which, income being at first unchanged because producers could not foresee the need to reduce output, would be the short-period consequence of the greater propensity to save. But the next consequence would be a reduction of output and incomes, a probable reduction of consumer-goods prices, and the beginning of a process carrying income down to a level where net investment and saving might once more be equal *ex ante* at a size far smaller than where they had started. The whole Myrdalian passage we have quoted is wholly Keynesian in spirit, though written five years or more before the appearance of the *General Theory*. Kalecki, arriving in England in 1936, showed an immediate grasp and acceptance of the *General Theory*, for the reason that he had himself independently evolved a similar line of thought. His deep disappointment at having been forestalled ('For three days I felt ill' he said to the present writer) was, we think, largely healed by Keynes's very great admiration for the theoretical and statistical developments that Kalecki made on the basis of the insight they had in common, an admiration which Keynes expressed in print. How did it come about that three men, at least, almost at the same time and in ignorance of each other's work, all conceived what was virtually one and the same new theory? One plausible explanation is not far to seek. The depression of the 1920s and its drastic worsening in the early 1930s was not only a disaster in the real lives of millions but a profound intellectual shock. It exposed the established theoretical picture of the economic system as fallacious and helpless. Out of a stunning intellectual crisis there arose a sudden mental freedom to overturn all accepted systems of thought on the subject, to question and reject without limit and to start afresh. A handful of audacious and imaginative minds, who happened for this reason or that to be crouched upon the mark when the starting-gun was fired, outdistanced all pursuit. In the next chapters we shall try to show how Keynes came to be poised for his immense success.

CHAPTER 11

TO THE 'QJE' FROM CHAPTER 12 OF THE 'GENERAL THEORY': KEYNES'S ULTIMATE MEANING

Writers on Keynes's theory of investment incentive give all their attention to the concepts of the marginal efficiency of capital and the interaction of a quantity so named with the interest-rate on loans of money. To do so is to study the formal configuration of the engine without asking about its thermal source of power. The marginal efficiency of capital is nothing but a formal sum waiting for the insertion of numerical values in place of its algebraic symbols. The essential problem of why at any time the investment flow has the size it has is contained in the question what is the source of these numerical values, by what psychic alchemy is the list of incongruous ingredients chosen and fused into an answer to the unanswerable. Keynes's whole theory of unemployment is ultimately the simple statement that, rational expectation being unattainable, we substitute for it first one and then another kind of irrational expectation: and the shift from one arbitrary basis to another gives us from time to time a moment of truth, when our artificial confidence is for the time being dissolved, and we, as business men, are afraid to invest, and so fail to provide enough demand to match our society's desire to produce. Keynes in the *General Theory* attempted a rational theory of a field of conduct which by the nature of its terms could be only semi-rational. But sober economists gravely upholding a faith in the calculability of human affairs could not bring themselves to acknowledge that this could be his purpose. They sought to interpret the *General Theory* as just one more manual of political arithmetic. In so far as it failed this test, they found it wrong, or obscure, or perverse. The same fate had overtaken his Treatise on Probability.

The *General Theory of Employment, Interest and Money* has for this reason two entirely different natures or modes of being. It is for the most part a description of how society, in its economic parts and functions, fits together. This account, however heterodox its content, was in purpose quite orthodox. It was a piece of balance-sheet work, a piece of accountancy, an establishment of the detailed coherence of society's economic anatomy and physiology. It tells us what is composed of what; what adds up to what; what values are dependent on or to be compared with what. But at the heart of this system, which was itself only superficially strange, lay something totally different. Chapter 11 shows us the arithmetic of the marginal efficiency of capital and its relation with interest-rates, a matter for actuaries and slide-rules. Chapter 12 reveals the hollowness of all this. The material for the slide-rules is absent, or arbitrary. Investment is an *irrational* activity, or a non-rational one. Surmise and assumption about what is happening or about to happen are themselves the *source* of these happenings, men make history in seeking to apprehend it. This is the message of the *General Theory*, and that is the only part of it which Keynes troubled to reproduce when in the *Quarterly Journal of Economics* for February 1937 he brushed aside the painstaking detail of his critics' incomprehension and attempted a final penetration of their minds:

If the simple basic ideas can become familiar and acceptable, time and experience and the collaboration of a number of minds will discover the best way of expressing them. I would, therefore, prefer to occupy such further space, as the Editor of this *Journal* can allow me, in trying to re-express some of these ideas, than in detailed controversy which might prove barren.

[Ricardo, Marshall, Edgeworth, Pigou and more recent writers] were dealing with a system in which the amount of the factors employed was given and the other relevant facts were known more or less for certain. This does not mean that they were dealing with a system in which change was ruled out, or even one in which the disappointment of expectation was ruled out. But at any given time facts and expectations were assumed to be given in a definite and calculable form; and risks, of which, though admitted, not much notice was taken, were supposed to be capable of an exact actuarial computation. The calculus of probability, though mention of it was kept in the background, was supposed to be capable of reducing uncertainty to the same calculable status as that of certainty itself.

Actually, however, we have, as a rule, only the vaguest idea of any but the most direct consequences of our acts. Now the whole object of the accumulation of wealth is to produce results, or potential results, at a comparatively distant, and sometimes at an *indefinitely* distant, date. Thus the fact that our knowledge of the future is fluctuating, vague and uncertain, renders wealth a peculiarly unsuitable subject for the methods of the classical economic theory.

By 'uncertain' knowledge, let me explain, I do not mean merely to distinguish what is known for certain from what is merely probable. The game of roulette is not subject, in this sense, to uncertainty. Or, again, the expectation of life is only slightly uncertain. The sense in which I am using the term is that in which the price of copper and the rate of interest twenty years hence, or the obsolescence of a new invention are uncertain. About these matters there is no scientific basis on which to form any calculable probability whatever. We simply do not know. Nevertheless, the necessity for action and for decision compels us as practical men to overlook this awkward fact and to behave exactly as we should if we had behind us a good Benthamite calculation of a series of prospective advantages and disadvantages, each multiplied by its appropriate probability, waiting to be summed.

How do we manage in such circumstances to behave in a manner which saves our faces as rational economic men? We have devised for the purpose a variety of techniques, of which much the most important are the three following:

(1) We assume that the present is a much more serviceable guide to the future than a candid examination of past experience would show it to have been hitherto. In other words we largely ignore the prospect of future changes about the actual character of which we know nothing.

(2) We assume that the *existing* state of opinion as expressed in prices and the character of existing output is based on a *correct* summing up of future prospects, so that we can accept it as such unless and until something new and relevant comes into the picture.

(3) Knowing that our own individual judgement is worthless, we endeavour to fall back on the judgement of the rest of the world, which is perhaps better informed. That is, we endeavour to conform with the behaviour of the majority or the average. The psychology of a society of individuals each of whom is endeavouring to copy the others leads to what we may strictly term a *conventional* judgement.

Now a practical theory of the future based on these three principles has certain marked characteristics. In particular, being based on so flimsy a foundation, it is subject to sudden and violent changes. The practice of calmness and immobility, of certainty and security, suddenly breaks down. New fears and hopes will, without warning,

take charge of human conduct. The forces of disillusion may suddenly impose a new conventional basis of valuation. All these pretty,
polite techniques, made for a well-panelled board room and a nicely
regulated market, are liable to collapse. At all times the vague panic
fears and equally vague and unreasoned hopes are not really lulled
and lie but a little way below the surface.

The climax of contemptuous impatience to which this passage
rises may have made some readers understand that Keynes was
concerned only superficially with details of mechanism and
institutions, but really with the nature of things. They could
not have been expected to draw that message from chapter 12
of the book itself, where the scattered bones of the thesis which
we have quoted lie waiting for life to be breathed into them.
Chapter 12 is a curiously unsatisfying chapter. It loses sight of
what in the end Keynes saw as its profoundly important meaning, and spends many pages discussing the possible advantages
of abolishing the joint-stock company, or at any rate of greatly
reducing the marketability of its shares. A chapter called 'The
State of Long Term Expectation' turns out to assert that there
is virtually no such thing. This is confusing for the first-time
reader. In the *General Theory of Employment, Interest and Money*
Keynes was still exploring. In 'The General Theory of Employment' he had arrived.

The deliberate self-deception of business, in supposing its
investment decisions to be founded on knowledge and to be
rationally justifiable; the insecurity of its faith in its own judge-
ments, which the awareness of this self-deception engenders;
the paralysis of decision and enterprise which can result when
the structure of pretended knowledge is violently overthrown by
events; this central core of the *General Theory* is to be found in
chapter 12, but expressed with a relative diffuseness and buried
in an exposition of the nature of Stock Exchange speculation
and its consequences for the inducement to invest in newly
ordered and yet-to-be-constructed equipment. This latter
aspect is doubtless important. Low Stock Exchange prices of
ordinary shares in existing concerns may be a symptom rather
than an original source of despondency about the profitability
of contemplated enterprise; but it is also a signal, widely and
conspicuously spreading the suggestion that such despondency
is general amongst business men, and thus giving it a specious

plausibility. Nonetheless, Keynes may be thought, in his book itself, to have given this Stock Exchange influence excessive weight; it seems to unbalance the emphasis of chapter 12, which can in consequence appear at a first reading as a strange intruder into the main current of thought.

It is not only business men, but economists themselves, who ardently subscribe to the rationality, the objectivity, the scientific well-conductedness of business reasoning. Economic theory is the theory of an orderly and reasonable world, a world of a concerted interchange of knowledge, a world where actions are pre-reconciled by the great market computer, and a world where what we intend is what will happen. Such a conception of economic society had a measure of plausibility in the modern Antonine age, the second Victorian generation and its Edwardian sequel, where, after 1870, western Europe seemed to have turned its steps towards the liberal vision of free internal and international competition, of political liberty and of peace. *General equilibrium* is a state of general agreed consistency and public availability of knowledge of the economic situation, as it is being shaped by the actions of individuals and itself bears upon each individual's choice of his own action. General equilibrium consists in and depends upon the coherence and universal diffusion of relevant knowledge by means of a system of prices publicly determined and announced. If the ends which are being pursued by the participants in such an equilibrium consist in *altering* the existing measurable economic configuration of society; if these ends consist, that is to say, in what is nowadays comprehensively known as 'growth'; this makes no difference to the ultimate conception itself of the equilibrium as a mutual conformity of simultaneously prevailing plans. Economics is about order.

But unemployment is the consequence and reflection of disorder. A theory of unemployment is, necessarily, inescapably, a theory of disorder. The disorder in question is the basic disorder of uncertain expectation, the essential disorder of the real, as contrasted with the conventionally pretended, human condition. It is the disorder of adventurous decision, of 'enterprise'. The world in which *enterprise* is necessary and possible is a world of uncertainty. The notion of enterprise, so central in Marshall, the realist, had no proper or legitimate place in the conception of a *general equilibrium*, the equivalent of a general agreement on what is to be done and on the meaning of what is being done. Enterprise is risk, risk is ignorance, and equilibrium, by contrast, is the effective banishment of ignorance. It is not surprising that an *Economics of Disorder* was not intellectually acceptable to those trained in the Economics of Order, viz. in Value Theory, the theory of how to cope, by the best use of *all available* resources, with ineluctable scarcity, that gravitational principle of economics. It is not surprising that a theory of how *scarce* resources, known to be available, known to be scarce, come to be left unused, was puzzling and alien to the inheritors of Victorian value theory. In perceiving and in stating this ultimate ground of the possibility of massive general unemployment, Keynes, we may claim, had no predecessors. To state this ground was to deny the orderliness of economic society and economic life, and to deny this life the attribute of orderliness was to seem to deny the study of it the attributes of science.

CHAPTER 12

THE ANATOMY OF THE
'GENERAL THEORY'

The composition of this book has been for the author a long struggle of escape...from habitual modes of thought and expression. The ideas which are here expressed so laboriously are extremely simple and should be obvious. The difficulty lies, not in the new ideas, but in escaping from the old ones, which ramify, for those brought up as most of us have been, into every corner of our minds.*

'The fox knows many things, the hedgehog knows one big thing.' Sir Isaiah Berlin once made brilliant use of this line from Archilochus to distinguish two types of scientific approach. It has its application to Keynes's approach to his attempted destruction of the old conception of the economic system. In the early chapters of the *General Theory*, Keynes seeks mechanical defects in that conceived system, neglect of particular facts and of logical implications, failures of detailed design. In that apotheosis of his thought which he published just one year after the book, in the *Quarterly Journal of Economics*, he totally ignored such matters. He no longer troubled himself as to whether unemployment can be called 'voluntary' if a reduction of real wages would cure it, or even whether real wages can be reduced by reducing money wages. He was content to sum up in a sentence the arithmetic of total demand and supply. Something immeasurably more fundamental, more general, more completely beyond the reach of legislation or improvements of organization and technology, had emerged from his work and raised itself above the mists like a mountain from which we have retired. This was the fact of the existence of an uncertain, an unknown future. Every step is a step into the void. It is this which makes investment hazardous and therefore often insufficient to fill the saving gap. Of course the detailed structure of things is the necessary frame for the operation of uncertainty in producing its effects. But our ignorance of the future was the one big thing which the refinements of equilibrium eco-

---

* J. M. Keynes, Preface to *The General Theory of Employment, Interest and Money.*

nomics had allowed to slide into oblivion. The fatal defect of the older conception was its assumption that men possess adequate knowledge, that they can act in the light of reason fully supplied with its necessary data. But this assumption is contrary to all experience. It is the false analogy from celestial mechanics, the unconsciously wrong and misleading interpretation of the word 'equilibrium'. In the *General Theory* itself Keynes considered many things; in his 'third edition', the *QJE* article which finally focussed all the effort of the *Treatise on Money* and the *General Theory*, he attended exclusively to the one big thing, the nature of decision in general and therefore of the decision to invest.

In this chapter we wish to list and examine the 'many things' which Keynes found it necessary to eliminate, first from his own mind and then from others. These 'postulates of the classical economics' are summarized in his chapter 2, and at intervals throughout the book their consequences are contrasted with his own results.

Keynes's work on the Great Quantities, the general level of prices, the size of the flow of output as a whole, the proportion of available labour employed, began with a very long *Treatise on Money*, and ended with a brief, uncompromising thesis on the governance of human affairs by ineluctable ignorance of the future. The reader of all this work is bound to ask himself at the end whether the logical possibility of general, involuntary unemployment, of 'general overproduction', of a failure of the total demand for products of all kinds to match their total supply, arises from the presence in our system of *money* or from the presence, in the frame of human consciousness, of irreducible lack of knowledge. In a system without money, could there be these disparities? In a barter system, or its equivalent, does not Say's Law hold true? The answer which seems to me to impose itself is that money absolves those who seek to accumulate wealth out of current production, from necessarily themselves deciding what real form this wealth should take, placing the burden of this decision, and its consequences, on a few business men. It thus greatly multiplies, and offers extensive leverage to, the basic fact of ignorance of the future, and enables what might, in a barter system, be a large number of mostly unimportant discrepancies between the supply and demand of individual goods and the exertions and reward of individual persons to become a unified, measurable and very large gulf between what has been deemed worth producing in hope, and what, when market day comes at the end of a long period of speculative commitment of resources, actually proves to be exchangeable for money. Money enormously enlarges the hurtful power of uncertainty at the same time as it enormously facilitates the beneficent power of specialization. For the effects which Keynes is concerned with, in the character and scale they take in our world, the explanation must be sought, as he sought it, in both the finally inescapable uncertainty of things and in the dependence of our system on money.

These questions impose themselves as soon as we turn back, from an attempted synoptical survey of the whole Keynesian opus, to the beginning of chapter 2 of the *General Theory* and the statement there given of the classical theory of employment:

I   The wage is equal to the marginal product of labour.

That is to say, the wage of an employed person is equal to the value which would be lost if employment were to be reduced by one unit.

II   The utility of the wage when a given volume of labour is employed is equal to the marginal disutility of that amount of employment.

That is to say, the real wage of an employed person is that which is just sufficient (in the estimation of the employed persons themselves) to induce the volume of labour actually employed to be forthcoming. The volume of employed resources is determined, according to the classical theory, by the two postulates. The first gives us the demand schedule for employment, the second gives us the supply schedule; and the amount of employment is fixed at the point where the utility of the marginal product balances the disutility of the marginal employment.*

Keynes's logical (as distinct from a secondary, and factual) objection to this theory is that [according to the classical school themselves]

Prices are governed by marginal prime cost in terms of money and money wages largely govern marginal prime cost. Thus if money wages change, one would have expected the classical school to argue that prices would change in almost the same proportion, leaving the real wage and the level of employment practically the same as before. This argument would, indeed, contain, to my thinking, a large element of truth.

* *General Theory of Employment, Interest and Money*, p. 5.

The classical theory assumes, in effect, that factor-owners sell their productive services in direct exchange for *goods* whose usefulness to themselves they know, rather than for money whose purchasing power is outside of their control. If the factor-services were in fact bought with goods, the factor-owners would have to choose those goods, and if we conceive these goods to be valued in terms of each other on a comprehensive market where equilibrium would be established before final service-contracts of the factors were signed, it is plain that the marginal disutility of service would in those contracts be set equal to the marginal utility of the goods given as pay, and that by this procedure involuntary unemployment would be ruled out. In this light, what is the basic reason why it is significant that in fact productive services are paid for in money and not in goods selected by the owners of the factors? The question can be answered on two levels. On the more fundamental level, the institution of wage-payment in the form of general purchasing power rather than in the form of defined baskets of goods has the consequence that neither the earner knows what he will be able to buy nor the employer what he will be able, for a given price, to sell. By contrast, if wages and other incomes were paid in baskets of goods, all products would be automatically sold to their collaborating producers, and lack of knowledge would play no part; general overproduction (and even overproduction of particular goods) would indeed be impossible, and Say's Law would hold true.

Thus the first point at which Keynes attacked the old system of thought was its assumption that the payment of the factors' remuneration in money, and the expenditure of their incomes by the factor owners in the form of money, made no difference in comparison with a non-money economy. He showed that, on the contrary, the intervention of money prevented the factor-owners from adjusting their real pay to equality with their marginal disutility of provision of productive services. To this argument he devoted the first 18 pages of chapter 2. In its remaining three pages he advances quite separately a second proposition, simply putting it forward without supporting argument or demonstrated connection with what has gone before; the statement, namely, that saving on one hand and net invest-ment on the other are determined independently of each other:

It has been supposed that any individual act of abstaining from consumption necessarily leads to, and amounts to the same thing as, causing the labour and commodities thus released from supplying consumption to be invested in the production of capital wealth. Contemporary thought is still deeply steeped in the notion that if people do not spend their money in one way they will spend it in another. Those who think in this way are deceived, nevertheless, by an optical illusion, which makes two essentially different activities appear to be the same. They are fallaciously supposing that there is a nexus which unites decisions to abstain from present consumption with decisions to provide for future consumption; whereas the motives which determine the latter are not linked in any simple way with the motives which determine the former.*

Chapter 2 falls thus into two parts. In the first, Keynes shows that the owners of sources of productive service lack the power to adjust their real rates of pay to a level equal to their marginal disutility and thus elicit full employment. In the second, he says that there is no nexus binding net investment and saving into mutual equality. What is missing from this chapter, and from the whole *General Theory*, is an explanation of how these two propositions interlock. Yet such a link is vital to the completeness of Keynes's construction. In seeking to supply it, our first suggestion is the need to remember the dual capacity of business men in the economy. They are both income-payers and income-receivers. In the latter capacity their tastes, as to spending or saving income, enter into the general composition of the society's propensity to consume. In speaking of the 'owners of sources of productive service' we accordingly include the business men along with wage earners and other suppliers of productive service. Keynes's distinction between wage-goods and other products can be misleading if (quite contrary to any suggestion of his) we think of it as severing the mutual competition of the two classes of products for factors in the factor market. The production of each and every kind of good requires (in some set or other of proportions) all sorts of factors or productive services, and an increase in the production of those goods which can form the physical outcome of net investment will, in the short period as Keynes sees it, raise the prices of wage-goods and reduce the 'real' equivalent of a given money wage. What,

* *General Theory*, pp. 19, 20, 21.

then, connects the two propositions of chapter 2? The link consists in the fact that the real wage or other real pay, which the workers or other suppliers of productive service would be willing to accept at a higher level of employment, and the real wage or other pay which the employers in their capacity as such, bearing the hazards of enterprise, would be willing to pay at a higher level of employment, are *differently composed of consumption and non-consumption*. The suppliers of productive service, that is, the income-earners in their capacity as such, all taken together, would push their supply of productive service to a higher level than the existing one, despite the concomitant necessity of accepting a lower real wage or other real pay, provided that this lower real wage was composed of less consumption and more saving than the real wage which, at that higher level of employment, the employers in their entrepreneurial capacity would be willing to provide. And the unwillingness of the employer-enterprisers to provide a real wage of the composition desired by the suppliers of productive service arises from the fact that the *saved* part of that real wage would be paid to the suppliers of service, not *in natura* in the form of direct and responsible ownership of newly created equipment, but merely in the form of general purchasing power, leaving the hazards of equipment-ownership to be borne by the employers in their capacity as enterprisers. We must re-define for Keynes the notion of involuntary unemployment. It is that unemployment which is due to a conflict between the offered and the desired real aggregate reward, of all factors taken together, at full employment, in the matter of its saving–spending composition. Such unemployment occurs because our system provides no mechanism for sounding the 'conditional intentions' which income-earners and employers might be led to express, to pool and to solve as an equilibrium system so as to discover for each person, in each of his capacities of income-earner, income-disposer and perhaps employer, an action (in the matter of productive service offered or engaged, at this or that rate of real pay) which would make mutually equal for each of them his marginal disutility of service and the marginal utility of his real pay.

In this last paragraph we have suggested that unemployment is due to men's failure to secure, in good time, knowledge of each others' 'conditional intentions' or potential reactions. It is due, we are saying, to an implicit conflict of intentions, the intentions of income-receivers to save a large part of the incomes they would receive at full employment not being matched by an intention of the business men to buy a corresponding large part of their own general output for net improvement of their equipment. This, of course, is in essence pure Keynesian doctrine. We have merely expressed it, as Keynes did not do, in terms of intentions, that is to say, in *ex ante* language.

Chapter 2 of the *General Theory* raises many questions: What is it in human institutions or in the nature of things that makes possible involuntary unemployment? What is the connection of society's liability to involuntary unemployment with its anxiety for the future, conflictingly manifested in a desire to save and a reluctance to invest in specialized, committed equipment? Can these troubles be cured by re-organization? Can they be best analysed by Keynes's method of comparison of equilibria, or by Myrdal's method of step-by-step analysis of a disequilibrium process?

We have suggested above that involuntary unemployment is due to people's ignorance of each other's potential reactions to this situation and that. If attitudes in the matter of spending or saving income and in the matter of committing wealth to specialized durable and uncertainty-exposed equipment were able to be fully known by a system of pooling conditional promises and extracting from them a solution prescribing individual coherent actions, there could be an equalization for each person of his marginal disutility of work (etc.) and of the marginal utility of real earnings. In a system without money, such matching of desires would necessarily be much more nearly approached, since suppliers of productive service would have to specify *products* that they would accept as pay. Money in this statement means a full money serving as a store of value. The mere use of a *numéraire* in a computerized system of pooling conditional intentions would of course not loosen the equilibrium bond. It is lack of knowledge of the circumstances of one's own action, consisting chiefly of lack of knowledge of the intentions and potential reactions of others, which makes possible involuntary unemployment. This lack of knowledge arises far more readily and naturally in a system using money than in a barter system.

It need hardly be added that the practical disadvantages of barter must surely outweigh its virtue of binding together the actions of people in their capacity of producers with people in their capacity of income disposers.

Involuntary unemployment might be avoided by an equilibrium mechanism applying to each time-interval in turn. This does not mean that the employment so determined would be the highest possible. A given aggregate consumption function of Keynes's type, where higher aggregate income is associated with a desire for higher aggregate saving, would still enable general output to be increased on condition that it should contain an appropriately increased proportion of intended net investment.

The involuntary unemployment that arises in a money economy without a mechanism for rendering intentions coherent, is worsened in its effect by the institution of the firm, which tends to require people to be either fully employed or not employed at all. For those wholly unemployed, unemployment is 'involuntary' in the strictest sense, since they cannot increase their proportion of spending out of incomes which do not exist.

Let us lastly consider the contrast of methods. Keynes offers no discussion or justification of his own procedure, but appears to take for granted the sufficiency and inevitability of confining strict analysis to equilibrium situations, and treating the transitions between them as disorderly episodes which by their nature defy any detailed explanation. This method greatly aggravated the difficulty which early readers experienced in understanding the structure in which general output or income, consumption spending, saving and net investment are in his treatment bound together in dependence on one another. Saving and net investment, Keynes says, are determined independently of one another, yet they become equal. How? This question of *how* cannot be satisfactorily answered within Keynes's own construction, for it belongs to the disequilibrium phases that intervene between one equilibrium and another. Keynes's real difficulty, indeed, goes deeper than a refusal to concern himself with the *events* which carry the economy from one equilibrium to another. It arises from confusing the contingent and fallible equality of aggregate intended saving and aggregate intended net investment, an equality which, when it occurs, can properly be called an equilibrium, with the inevitable, definitional and identical equality of the saving and investment which have been realized in some past period and are both recorded in some self-consistent set of accounts. Saving and net investment in the latter sense are two measures of the same thing. The distinction between these two ideas, the equilibrium equality of desires or intentions and the definitional equality of a given thing under one name with itself under a different name or measured by a different procedure, can only be conveniently made by means of the explicit *ex ante–ex post* language. Keynes's own substitute for such a language involved him in many pages of irrelevant, confused and fallacious argument.

Nonetheless Keynes did make bold, brilliant and powerful innovations of method. By an incisive use of Marshall's principle of the short period (which is the principle of the vanishing of functions to a different order) he dispensed with all but two kinds of unit:

On *every* particular occasion, let it be remembered, an entrepreneur is concerned with decisions as to the scale on which to work a given capital equipment; and when we say that the expectation of an increased demand, i.e. a raising of the aggregate demand function, will lead to an increase in aggregate output, we really mean that the firms, which own the capital equipment, will be induced to associate with it a greater aggregate employment of labour. The concepts of output as a whole and its price-level are not required in this context, since we have no need of an absolute measure of current aggregate output, such as would enable us to compare its amount with the amount which would result from the association of a different capital equipment with a different quantity of employment. When we wish to speak of an increase of output, we must rely on the presumption that the amount of employment associated with a given capital equipment will be a satisfactory index of the amount of resultant output. In dealing with the theory of employment I propose, therefore, to make use of only two fundamental units of quantity, namely, quantities of money-value and quantities of employment.

The real innovation here is the abandonment of the pretence that economics can hope for unambiguous precision in the sense in which this was sought in nineteenth century physics. Keynes could have been even briefer in stating his case for reckless simplicity. For in fact, at any moment, there exists a collection of machines and a collection of men; each stock, when anchored to its moment in history, is given. Machines can be unemployed as well as men, and the starting-up of fresh streams of output probably draws in hitherto unemployed units from both stocks. There is no *formal* reason for treating one, rather than the other, as if it were a farmer's field always fully employed itself whether cultivated by few men or many. But it is perfectly just to say that except when a hard-pressed handful of men are trying to maintain and operate a grossly excessive indivisible piece of equipment, output will be an increasing function of the quantity employed of *each* factor of production. This is all that Keynes's argument needs.

Keynes's first constructive chapter, following his demolition work in chapter 2, is the statement of a macro-theory, a construction which treats aggregates as though they were simple variables of uniform composition. He was far from being the inventor of this idea, for the Quantity Theory of Money gathers every kind of object or service under the heading of 'transactions'. In Keynes, however, we have not merely the treating of diverse objects as units in a count, but the combining of many people's diverse feelings, reactions and intentions, or at least their resulting conduct, into a variable standing for the conduct of the society, or a large sector of it, as a whole. But again there are precedents. Wicksell had treated all business men as motivated together by an improved prospect of profit, and as to the operations of whole sectors of the economy each treated as one, we may go back to Quesnay's *Tableau Économique*. In *Banking Policy and the Price Level*, in 1926, Sir Dennis Robertson had used a supply curve of investment goods in general, and Professor J. E. Meade did the same in *The Rate of Interest in a Progressive State* in 1933. We have seen that Myrdal anticipated the *General Theory* in almost every respect except that of its huge impact on economics and the world. Yet Keynes has a claim as innovator even in this respect. The macro-model of the *General Theory* does not emerge gradually as a hard-won solution but is explicitly adopted from the outset as though natural and inevitable. This bold and assured imposition of a method is Keynes's claim to be an innovator in respect of macro-economics.

One more of the great changes in the outlook of economic theoreticians stands largely to Keynes's credit, and again it is a case where an idea or practice of Marshall's was radically deepened and enlarged. Marshall had compared the existing with the desired total stock of money, and proposed to regard the latter as proportional to the national income. This was perhaps the first turning of the tide against the neo-classical emphasis on flows in contrast with stocks. Keynes's theory of the interest-rate fused method and meaning inseparably in a purely 'stocks' analysis. It is of the essence of the liquidity-preference theory that stocks and not flows are in command, and in stating this theory Keynes showed a 'stocks' analysis at work. Its elegant power led Professor Kenneth Boulding to attempt to re-work the whole of economic theory in terms of stocks instead of flows.* His *tour de force* made no mass conversion, but all economists were compelled by the interest-rate controversy to take notice of the idea of *dimension* and even to recognize that stocks can be mentally re-valued by their owners, and by those who desire them, without passing through the market in a flow from one ownership to another. The liquidity-preference theory itself, though intimately necessary to the *General Theory*, can be considered in isolation, and stands as Keynes's most inalienable piece of original economic thought. And once more Keynes had dramatically illuminated and thrown into relief a method by no means new but currently neglected, the attribution to stocks (in this case, of money or bonds) and their owners' valuations of them, of a life of their own. Keynes's part in this reform (its propagation powerfully assisted by R. F. Kahn and Mrs Joan Robinson) lay once more in his investing the method with an air of effortless power, seeming the more dramatic for being the vehicle of genuine novelty.

Books I and II of the *General Theory* are by way of preparing the reader's mind for a revolution of thought and briefing him about the essential scheme of the demonstration which he is to witness. That scheme falls into the two natural divisions of the theory itself. The theory declares that employment will tend to settle at that level where desired annual saving out of the aggregate income corresponding to that employment is just matched by the annual net augmentation of equipment that

* Kenneth E. Boulding, *A Reconstruction of Economics* (John Wiley and Sons and Chapman and Hall, 1950).

business men are induced by their judgement of the prevailing circumstances to attempt. The things to be studied are thus, in book III, the manner in which saving depends on income; and in book IV the question what circumstances bear upon investment decision and how their influence works. One such circumstance, centrally involved in Keynes's conception, is said by him to be determined in a manner wholly different from what had been supposed, and thus within the second division of his argument a self-contained part is his theory of the interest-rate. We have now to consider what there was of apparent novelty in those two books, and how these ideas can be linked to what had gone before, in the literature and in affairs.

In order to conceive a theory of employment, a writer had at the very outset to reverse in his own mind the whole orientation, outlook and purpose of the existing core of economic theory. That core consisted of the theory of value and distribution, the theory, that is to say, of how a society, naturally driven (as was tacitly assumed) by a general scarcity of the means of life and enjoyment to use all its available productive resources to the full, could get the most out of those limited forces and how it would share the result among its members. The theory of value, the theory of allocation of resources, *assumes* full employment. How could it offer any hint or hope of a theory to explain unemployment? When Keynes had finally completed his work on the nature of unemployment, he came to resolve this strange intellectual situation by showing that in the accepted theory of value a whole dimension of affairs had been neglected. Value-theory had dealt in elaborate detail with the consequences of scarcity, and wholly ignored those of uncertainty. The practical problem of uncertainty, of how to make rational dispositions in face of a future which is unknown, is insoluble, and men choose therefore (very reasonably) in large part to ignore it. But this attitude shapes their conduct, and the history which arises from that conduct, in essential and dramatic ways. It makes them withdraw from enterprise when the possibility of losses is too plain, and the size or consequence of those losses too serious, and the weight of this menace outweighs the hope of gain. But enterprise, in a society organized like ours upon the autonomous firm, is the source of employment. Thus massive unemployment of resources can occur in a world where resources still, in the basic sense, are scarce.

If, as the theory of value assumes, available productive resources tend always to be fully employed, no great change of
general output can occur except as a consequence of a change
in the amounts of available resources. If the capacity of these,
in a broad sense, changes only slowly, so will general output
and its money value at constant prices, aggregate real income;
and so also, if the society's desired saving flow depends only
upon the size of its real income, will the size of that desired
saving flow. It was therefore natural for the theory of value to
pay no attention to the idea of the society's desired saving flow
as a function of its income. The society's saving flow could be
regarded as a function of the interest-rate (though Marshall
thought the latter's influence probably negligible), and gradual
changes in habits of thrift were evidently possible; but as a
short-period variable and a link in any short-period mechanism,
the desired saving-flow never entered the scheme of thought. In
a sense the great revolution of book III was the mere recognition
that, even in its shortest period, a theory of employment must
treat aggregate income as a variable. A variable dependent
upon what? Keynes's incomparable gift was his eye for the
efficient assumption, able to supply the needed effect with the
least air of being itself special and peculiar. What could be
more natural than the idea that the derivative of the society's
desired saving flow with respect to its income was greater than
zero and less than unity? It followed that in equilibrium, that is,
when desired net investment was equal to desired saving (each
being a flow), the society's general output measured in value, or
its aggregate income, could be treated as depending on two
things: first, the size of the net investment flow desired and
intended by business men; and, secondly, the society's desired
ratio of saving to income, which is equal to the difference between unity and the desired ratio of consumption spending to
income. The reciprocal of either of these evidently gave, *in
equilibrium*, the ratio of aggregate income to desired investment,
and that desired investment, because of the equilibrium, was
realizable and would (in a model assumed immune from outside
disturbances) actually occur. This conclusion being established
in book III, it remained for book IV to show how the size of the
desired investment flow was determined.

In the foregoing paragraph, we have given a conspicuous

place to the word *equilibrium*. In setting out the main structure of his argument, Keynes scarcely uses this word. The whole of chapter 7 is devoted to showing that saving and investment are necessarily and identically equal. The reader of that chapter will perceive that its reasoning refers to *ex post* quantities, and taking it by itself we therefore find it perfectly acceptable. But it leaves Keynes's general position highly ambiguous. Does he believe that by proving this identity he is saying something about a coherence of intentions or wishes? If not, what is the mechanism by which a possible (and exceedingly likely) disagreement between total intended saving and total intended investment is corrected into an *ex post* equality? Keynes's answer is that if we find saving and investment discrepant we are reckoning as a part of income something that is going to prove illusory. But this kind of argument is a botch. We need to be shown just how the interpretation of given conduct, by those who decide upon and perform it, alters as these acts pass from design to actuality in circumstances not successfully foreseen, and how the acts themselves are perhaps revised in the course of performance. Keynes appears to be assuming that if business men's intended output of consumers' goods, measured at the prices they intend to ask, is greater than the intended expenditure of income-disposers on them, the whole of the physical quantities will nevertheless be sold, but at appropriately reduced prices, so that all can be bought for income-disposers' originally intended expenditure. But this is far from being the only way in which the situation can resolve itself. Unsold goods can be carried over, perhaps at the original and perhaps at a reduced valuation. The problem is a matter for sequence analysis or, failing that, for a rigid and explicit limitation of the analysis to a comparison of *equilibrium* positions, where the question how *disequilibrium* positions are resolved does not arise. Keynes seems to claim that his *ex post* identity serves the purpose of 'dynamic' analysis. But it does not. In this respect the *Treatise on Money* had a clearer vision than the *General Theory*.

To invest is to exchange money for means of production. When this policy promises more profit than could be had by lending the money, there is an *inducement* to invest. The general investment flow will tend always to be of such a size that at the margin this difference of profitability vanishes, leaving a positive profit on the intra-marginal parts of the investment flows into particular types of equipment. Such is the theory of the inducement to invest put forward in the *General Theory*, and its detailed elaboration is the content of book IV.

The *General Theory* proceeds from the confrontation of two bodies of thought. On the one hand, Keynes was deeply seized of the *precariousness* of any effort at calculation of human affairs. For most of the time men's awareness of this is suppressed by certain schemes and conventions which give the illusion of rational foresight; but when from time to time they are suddenly driven by a too-obvious general breakdown of their plans to acknowledge it, it inhibits enterprise and the giving of employment, because there is for each individual decision-maker an apparent refuge for his reserves of wealth, namely, money itself. The possibility of massive general unemployment thus springs from the bearing of a human institution, that of money, upon the ultimate nature of human existence, the human being's endless journey into the void of time. The second body of ideas which originates the *General Theory* is therefore a description of those circumstances of life which men have built for themselves, their institutions, in especial the institution of money. Book IV proceeds systematically with the binding together of these two strands of thought.

Chapter 11, the first of book IV, sets out what we may call the formal geometry of the four elements or inter-semantic notions involved in the inducement to invest, viz. expectation, profits, interest and present values, all of which are bound together in the statement that the investment flow will tend at all times to be such as to equalize the marginal efficiency of capital with the interest-rate, or (equivalently) to equalize, at the margin of investment, the present value of expected operating profits with the present value of expected construction-costs of the contemplated equipment. In this chapter Keynes insists chiefly on two points: first, that the demand price of equipment (the price it seems just worth while to pay for the marginal unit ordered) logically reckoned, is the present value of that unit's entire series or stream of *expected future* sale-proceeds of output less running-costs, and does not depend merely on the amount of profit expected to be earned in the immediately-future unit time-interval alone; and secondly, that *interest* is something determined in virtual independence of the character of that series or stream of expected trading profits. Keynes makes the size of the business men's attempted investment flow, the size which arises in the aggregate from their individual decisions, to depend on their comparisons of the marginal efficiency of capital with the interest-rate, each, but especially the former, being looked upon as a function of the size of the investment-flow. The marginal efficiency of capital, that is to say, is to be thought of as a schedule, expressible by a curve in a diagram where the abscissae are sizes of the investment flow and the ordinates are percentages per annum at which expected profit instalments are discounted to bring the total of their present values to equality with the first-cost of the machine. It is the dependence of this schedule on expectations concerning distant years which, Keynes insists, makes it sensitive to 'the news', to changes of mood, to ostensibly small-scale events which are treated as straws in the wind and given the power to modify decisively or turn upside down the frail incoherent structure of non-logical inferences and interpretations upon which expectations have to be based. Thus in his conception it is not the shape which the curve or schedule of the marginal efficiency of capital may take in any man's mind at some one moment which matters most, but the large, swift and unheralded changes of form and position which it can undergo, its liability (as we have elsewhere expressed it) to *kaleidic shifts*, shifts necessarily unforeseeable in character and timing by the expectation former himself, but equally undetectable in advance by any detached observer of the scene:

When a man buys an investment or capital-asset, he purchases the right to the series of prospective returns, which he expects to obtain from selling its output, after deducting the running expenses of obtaining that output, during the life of the asset. This series of annuities $Q_1, Q_2, \ldots Q_n$ it is convenient to call the *prospective yield* of the investment. Over against the prospective yield of the investment we have the supply price of the capital asset, the price which would just induce a manufacturer newly to produce an additional unit of such assets. I define the marginal efficiency of capital as that rate of discount which would make the present value of the series of annuities [the series of Q's] given by the returns expected from the capital asset during its life just equal to its supply price.

Keynes's terminology is not wholly felicitous. 'Yield' is used in the literature of finance to mean, in relation to the instalments promised by a borrower, something formally identical with what the marginal efficiency of capital means in relation to the profit instalments, the Q's, expected by a purchaser of equipment. None the less, this definitional passage is perfectly clear. Keynes proceeds a little later to insist upon the *expectation dependence* of the marginal efficiency:

Finally there is the distinction between the increment of value obtainable by using an additional quantity of capital in the *existing* situation, and the series of increments which it is expected to obtain *over the whole life* of the additional capital asset, i.e. the distinction between Q_1 and the complete series $Q_1, Q_2 \ldots Q_r, \ldots$ This involves the whole question of the place of expectation in economic theory. Most discussions of the marginal efficiency of capital seem to pay no attention to any member of the series except Q_1. It is important to understand the dependence of the marginal efficiency of a given stock of capital on changes in expectation, because it is chiefly this dependence which renders the marginal efficiency of capital subject to the somewhat violent fluctuations which are the explanation of the Trade Cycle.*

We are to think of the schedule or curve of the marginal efficiency of capital, not as a stable function whose form can be taken as unchanging throughout an analysis of historical events real or imaginary, but as a tree-branch in a gale, sweeping up and down with the gusts of politics and of the emerging consequences of past action, and by this bodily shift providing the nearest approach which Keynes is willing to allow to a formal link between the inducement to invest and the behaviour of the other variables of the economy or of the model. This scheme of thought, Keynes's invention, is what we have elsewhere called the *kaleidic*† analysis of a development through time in which one situation or event grows out of another. Keynes sums up as follows the content of chapter 11:

The schedule of the marginal efficiency of capital is of fundamental importance because it is mainly through this factor (much more than through the rate of interest) that the expectation of the future influences the present. The mistake of regarding the marginal effici-

---

* *General Theory of Employment, Interest and Money*, pp. 138, 143, 144.
† *A Scheme of Economic Theory* (Cambridge University Press), chapter IV.

ency of capital primarily in terms of the *current* yield of capital equipment, which would be correct only in the static state where there is no changing future to influence the present, has had the result of breaking the theoretical link between today and tomorrow. Even the rate of interest is, virtually, a *current* phenomenon; and if we reduce the marginal efficiency of capital to the same status, we cut ourselves off from taking any direct account of the influence of the future in our analysis of the existing equilibrium. It is by reason of the existence of durable equipment that the economic future is linked to the present. It is, therefore, consistent with, and agreeable to, our broad principle of thought, that the expectation of the future should affect the present through the demand price for durable equipment.

From the formal structure of the inducement to invest, explained in chapter 11 with only a hint of what will be shown to spring from its confrontation with the groping hazards of human enterprise and life in general, Keynes passes in chapter 12 to this latter, totally contrasting theme. This core of Keynes's conception, merely interjected in chapter 12 and suddenly detonated, as it were, in his critics' face in his article in the *Quarterly Journal of Economics*, we have considered in our preceding chapter. The two first chapters of book IV are thus concerned with expectation. Chapter 11 shows formally why expectations have their powerful leverage and basic role in the inducement to invest. Chapter 12 shows what manner of thing it is that thus finds itself at the heart of the economic organism. Having thus given expectation pride of place and by doing so put the emphasis of his theory where he desired it, Keynes comes in chapter 13 to the theory and role of the interest-rate.

If some mechanism existed by which, when the society's general output and aggregate income were those corresponding to full employment of its resources, its desired saving flow and its business men's desired net investment flow were exactly matched to each other, there would be no reason for employment not to be full. For then, that ratio of the goods intended to augment equipment, to those intended to maintain the flow of consumption, which suited the business men, would also suit the income-receivers as such (including the business men in their capacity of receivers rather than payers of income). It is the failure, in real economies, of designed net investment to fill the full-employment saving gap which, in Keynes's theory, drives aggregate income down to the level where the gap is small enough to be filled. Thus an automatic balancing mechanism which worked *regardless of the size of aggregate income* would remove the cause of general unemployment. Now the older theory, the pre-Keynesian theory of value, did suppose that just such a mechanism exists, namely, the rate of interest. If the rate of interest was indeed determined at that level where, regardless of the size of aggregate income, saving and net investment were equal, there would be no need for a theory of unemployment. As always, Keynes had at hand an obliterating retort to those who inclined towards arguments showing that massive general unemployment was impossible: he had but to point to Britain of the 1920s and 1930s. The inference must be that the interest-rate is *not* determined by the equalization of desired saving and designed investment. What, then, determines it?

There could be no theory of massive general unemployment so long as the interest-rate was held to equalize desired saving and desired net investment. Wicksell long since, except that he concerned himself with prices rather than output, had come to this conclusion. Some other influence than those two must dominate the rate of interest and thus sometimes prevent net investment from filling a saving gap large enough for full employment. Keynes's suggestion of the nature, genesis and determining mechanism of interest was revolutionary, and epitomized and intensified the Keynesian paradox of an equilibrium depending, not upon a universal diffusion of complete relevant knowledge, but on its opposite in every respect, that is to say, on uncertainty and a positive contradiction of opinions, leading to a balance which was not simply, as Keynes showed, precarious in the extreme, but which we* can even show to be by its nature automatically self-destructive. In its formal and precisely elaborated version, Keynes's theory hinged upon the interest-rate, because the interest-rate expressed the properties of money, and it was money which, by offering a retreat from the hazards of investment in specialized, concrete equipment, enabled wealth to be divorced from enterprise and so from the giving of employment. It is a peculiar beauty of Keynes's achievement that its central conception is also its most original part.

* G. L. S. Shackle, *Expectations, Investment and Income* (Oxford University Press, 1938), chapter III.

The interest-rate arises from *uncertainty* about the future prices of the bonds given by borrowers in exchange for loans; it depends upon the valuation of *stocks* rather than flows; it balances the conflicting views, about the imminent movement of those bond prices, entertained by *two camps* within the group of holders or potential holders of these bonds. These are the three essential ideas of the Keynesian theory of interest when it is fully exhibited, and in respect of all three of them it sharply contrasts with the idea of settled agreement and stability on which the theory of value rests.

We live by destroying utilities; by eating the food, burning the fuel, and so on; in order to have the prospect of continuing to live, we must re-create today the utilities we destroy today. The price of each such utility will depend on the eagerness to consume it and the sacrifice involved in getting it. This price is the price of a flow, and the quantities referred to in the demand schedule and the supply schedule are numbers of physical units per unit of time. With bonds and with money it is different. Bonds are occasionally produced and occasionally redeemed, but if these transactions are looked upon as flows, these actual flows are small compared with the potential flows which could occur if the great stocks of bonds, which at all times exist, were moved into the market. The prices at which butter and fruit change hands are doubtless influenced by the size of the stocks of these goods in the pipe-line from producer to consumer, and there is here some analogy with the case of bonds. But bonds are not 'in the pipe-line'. Their whole nature is that of an asset *to be held*. The demand for bonds to hold is a differently engendered thing from that of fruit to consume. The supply of bonds to hold is mainly a question, not of what will be produced today or in the coming week, but of what exists at all moments. Similar statements are true of part of the money stock. It is held as an asset. The exchange-rate between money and bonds can change to any extent *without any exchanges of money for bonds*. When existing bonds change hands for existing money, such exchanges are mere incidental consequences and reflections of the revaluations of the existing bonds and existing money for 'asset reasons', not for 'consumption reasons'; for in such cases (the overwhelming majority of the cases of sales and purchases of bonds) there is no 'production' and no 'consumption', but merely change of ownership. Sales and purchases of existing bonds are the *consequence* and not the origin, nor the mechanism, of valuation of bonds, except in so far as such transactions betray or hint at the valuations and perhaps cause various classes of valuers, i.e. holders or potential holders, to revise their opinions of what others are thinking and of what they themselves should think. What, then, is the genesis of the valuation of bonds?

Some have attacked Keynes (mistakenly, we think) with the famous 'bootstraps' argument. For Keynes's *novel* explanation of the valuation of bonds (which he adds to more orthodox lines of thought) is that each individual's present valuation, differing, in general, from that of every other individual, depends on what he thinks will be the market valuation in the near future. All individuals are thus engaged in guessing what the market resultant of the opinions of all of them will be, and the rate of interest which prevails today depends on what the rate is expected to be tomorrow. The rate is said on this account to 'lift itself by its own bootstraps'. This criticism is worthless. Bonds are indeed held in the hope of appreciation in their market value, and will be valued today according to expectations of that appreciation. But these expectations are uncertain. A lender is one who buys a bond, a document which promises future repayments of *specified amounts at specified dates*. It does not promise any repayment on demand. The date when the lender will in fact desire to repossess himself of his money, and the price for which, as the only way of then re-possessing any of it, he will at that time be able to sell his bond, are both of them, at the moment of handing over money to the borrower, *unknown* to him. To lend is to part with a known sum of money in exchange for an unknown sum. Loans will therefore not be forthcoming except on terms which give the lender a presumption that this unknown sum will be not less than the principal which he now parts with; on condition, that is to say, that the total of the borrower's promised repayments shall exceed the lent principal. This condition has two effects. First, it offers a good actuarial chance that the price of the bond, plus any repayments which shall have been made, when the bond shall be sold at an unforeseeable date, will be not less than the lent principal. But secondly the lender, having in view the possibility that he will retain the bond until all the repayments have been made, and thus reap the surplus of these repayments over what he lent, or that a third party, purchasing it from him, will pay a price which allows for this eventual surplus, will be compensated for the psychic discomfort of not *knowing* what the outcome for himself of making the loan will be. The rate of interest of a particular loan transaction is that percentage per time-unit which, when used to discount the borrowers' promised repayments back to the date of his being handed the loan, brings their total discounted value to equality with the lent principal. The fact that lenders can exact interest on money which they lend is thus ascribable to the uncertainty in which lending inescapably involves them. To say that the level of that rate is determined by expectations is merely to apply to the interest-rate something which applies in greater or less degree to all prices. There is no circularity of argument.

The uncertainty which explains interest has nothing to do with any doubts of the borrower's solvency or honesty. It consists in the fact that a lender gives cash in exchange for an *unknown* future sum; unknown, because he can in general know, at the time of lending, neither the date when he will want his money back nor the market price which his bond will fetch at that date; for the borrower has indeed promised repayment, but only at a *stated* date, not *on demand*.

When all holders of bonds, and all holders of spare money, are convinced that bond prices are about to rise, the former group will refuse to sell at the prevailing price and the latter group will seek to buy at it, and the price will rise. Moreover, it will rise in these circumstances without there being at first any transactions, for there can be no transactions until some bond-holders cease to be convinced that a further price rise is imminent. The price cannot stand still, even momentarily, except at a price which, in the given other circumstances, divides the actual and potential bondholders into two camps, the Bulls who still expect a price rise and the Bears who expect a fall; except for those who have neither of these convictions and are therefore content for the moment with the bonds or money, or both, which they happen to hold. Even the establishment of the two camps in appropriate strengths may not serve to stabilize the price unless the existing bonds are in the hands of the Bulls and the existing spare money is in the hands of the Bears. The transactions which are necessary to re-distribute assets in this way may themselves upset the state of expectations and call forth further adjustments of price and re-distribution of assets; and so on. The composition of the two camps out of particular individuals or interests is, of course, volatile in the extreme.

Stock, as opposed to flow, analysis; uncertainty as the basis of interest-rates; and the need for two camps holding opposite momentary expectations; are the elements of Keynes's *speculative* explanation of interest, which so bitterly offended the puritan notion that interest is the reward of thrift. A less provocative term than 'speculative' could no doubt have been chosen; it would not have satisfied Keynes's manifest desire to outrage the believers in automatic full employment, a belief which, in the circumstances of the early 1930s appeared to him inexcusable in view of the facts and disastrous in the policies which flowed from it.

We spoke of 'spare' money, meaning by this that part of the total stock of money which is not mobilized for the making of immediate or near-future payments. To hold money in readiness for making payments is to hold it for the *transactions motive*, and this includes the marshalling of large sums ready to pay for equipment, a purpose which Keynes consented to separate under its own subheading of 'finance'. There is plainly no need for any wealth owner to commit himself precisely, even in his own thoughts, as to what part of his money in the bank is there as an asset or form in which he is for the time being holding some of his wealth, and what part is there in readiness to be soon paid away. It is this natural and necessary overlapping of the two motives which largely defeats any statistical attempt to relate interest-rates with the size of actual cash* balances held by this group or that at any time. It is the central monetary authority which determines how much money shall at any time exist in the society. It is the strength of the desires, for various motives all taken together, to have money at hand which determines the interest-rate that will make it seem worth while to part with this liquid asset. A statistical investigation of the interest-rate, to be effective, valid and meaningful, would have to look into people's thoughts and not merely into their bank statements.

* Bank deposits.

There is lastly the so-called 'precautionary motive' which in the middle 1960s appears to have imposed itself on some Cambridge theorists as the prime motive of all for holding money. They have surely been misled by the language of business men. Business men, when asked why they keep large balances in the bank, may well say that it is as a precaution. If their interlocutors went on to ask why readily saleable gilt-edged securities would not do instead, they might be told that of course these would do, if there were no danger of a fall in their price. And that is not a 'precautionary' motive for holding money, but the speculative motive. The precautionary motive, as Keynes enunciated it, seems to us, except on a very small scale when the purchase and sale of securities would be too expensive, to be illusory. And when small sums of 'reserve' money are held as cash because of the expense of lending and recovering them, they melt into those held for the transactions motive.

The anatomy of the *General Theory*, Keynes's conception under the aspects of both meaning and method, is brilliantly summarized in his chapter 18, 'The general theory of employment re-stated'; whose first words summon our critical attention:

To begin with, it may be useful to make clear which elements in the economic system we take as given, which are the independent variables of our system and which are the dependent variables.

Here by implication is Keynes's choice and faith in the matter of *analytical policy*. Some variables are to be independent and some dependent, not merely in some equations of the system but in the system as a whole. They are to have such status as a permanent and general thing. But a variable which is in all connections and throughout the argument to be treated as independent implies by this status a whole philosophy of explanation, or at least, impels us to search for some such philosophy or outlook. Keynes has, in fact, by the quoted sentence implicitly rejected the closed dynamic model of the type invented, or borrowed from physics, by Ragnar Frisch and developed with fertile zest by Harrod, Domar, Kalecki, Samuelson, Kaldor and Hicks. For in those models each variable has, in effect, its own determining equation, each in turn is exhibited as dependent on some of the others, and we have an insulated, closed and complete set of a very few variables mutually determining (once some 'initial' values are given) the skein of time-paths they shall follow. For Keynes, by contrast, there are economic wind and weather, in the form of politics, invention, fashion and the incalculable movements of expectation, great forces quite outside of and unshaped by the economic ship whose course we seek to understand and control. These are the ultimate and truly 'independent' variables, focused and canalized in their effect as the *marginal efficiency of capital*, the *rate of interest* and the *propensity to consume*:

We take as given the existing skill and quantity of available labour, the existing quality and quantity of available equipment, the existing technique, the degree of competition, the tastes and habits of the consumer, the disutility of different intensities of labour and of the activities of supervision and organization, as well as the social structure including the forces, other than our variables set forth below, which determine the distribution of the national income. This does not mean that we assume these factors to be constant; but merely that, in this place and context, we are not considering or taking into account the effects and consequences of changes in them. Our independent variables are, in the first instance, the propensity to consume, the schedule of the marginal efficiency of capital and the rate of interest, though, as we have already seen, these are capable of further analysis. Our dependent variables are the volume of employment and the national income (or national dividend) measured in wage-units. The factors, which we have taken as given, influence our independent variables, but do not completely determine them. For example, the schedule of the marginal efficiency of capital depends partly on the existing quantity of equipment which is one of the given factors, but partly on the state of long-term expectation which cannot be inferred from the given factors; whilst the rate of interest depends partly on the state of liquidity preference (i.e. on the liquidity function) and partly on the quantity of money measured in wage units. Thus we can sometimes regard our ultimate independent variables as consisting of (1) the three fundamental psychological factors, namely, the psychological propensity to consume, the psychological attitude to liquidity and the psychological expectation of future yield from capital-assets, (2) the wage-unit as determined by the bargains reached between employers and employed, and (3) the quantity of money as determined by the central bank; so that, if we take as given the factors specified above, these variables determine the national income (or dividend) and the quantity of employment. But these again would be capable of being subjected to further analysis, and are not, so to speak, our ultimate atomic independent elements.

For this passage we might claim, as it were, the 'second degree' of precision; the capacity of making apparent by the texture of its sentences just what degree of precision of thought and statement is being attempted. Just in what sense variables are variable, when a governing environment is assumed to be given and specified; who or what varies them; these and such matters are deliberately left as visible but unanswered questions. The reader himself must think and must elect his solution or hold several interpretations in mind. This situation is made clear to the reader, and this obligation imposed upon him, with superlative and engaging skill and tact. The ease and grace of the style itself prepares the reader for a need to seek more harshly exact instruction; and in the end he is invited to provide it for himself, or perhaps instructed not to worry about it: 'The factors, which we have taken as given, influence our independent variables but do not completely determine them.' The values of these variables are, must we assume, the very jetsam of the tides of history in all its depth and complexity, to seek to 'explain' them would be to trespass far beyond the bounds of technical concern which the economist sets himself, and compel him to claim competence where he, and any man, can have none. History herself varies these variables, by an arcane process whose nature we shall do well, for our own purposes, to leave inviolate. The contrast between this attitude, if in discerning it in Keynes's words we do him justice, and that of the builders of 'dynamic' models in the Frisch-Harrod-Hicks tradition, is a very significant one, and has an importance for those who argue for and against a general plan for the economy, in one or other of the many interpretations of this phrase. In the end, Keynes speaks there of the 'ultimate atomic independent elements'. What can 'ultimately independent' mean, except either that they are determined in too complex and elusive a fashion for us to penetrate, or else indeed that they are the upshot of something spontaneous and originative, or 'random', at the very source of history. Keynes does not tell us.

CHAPTER 13

SPENDING, SAVING AND DEMAND

The relation between this book and my *Treatise on Money* is probably clearer to myself than it will be to others; and what in my own mind is a natural evolution in a line of thought which I have been pursuing for several years, may sometimes strike the reader as a confusing change of view. When I began to write my *Treatise on Money* I was still moving along the traditional lines of regarding the influence of money as something so to speak separate from the general theory of supply and demand. When I finished it, I had made some progress towards pushing monetary theory back to becoming a theory of output as a whole. But my lack of emancipation from preconceived ideas showed itself in [my having failed] to deal thoroughly with the effects of *changes* in the level of output. My so-called 'fundamental equations' were an instantaneous picture taken on the assumption of a given output. They attempted to show how, assuming the given output, forces would develop which involved a profit-disequilibrium, and thus required a change in the level of output.*

For one who read the *Treatise* when it first appeared, and then the *General Theory* when that first appeared, and who has now read the *Treatise* again after thirty-five years, it is very hard to say which work deserves the highest marks for radical incisive irradiation of one's mind; for power to loosen, as it were, one's intellectual collar; to delight its reader with an easy, limpid, unpretentious and reassuring exposition; and to excite him with its sense of brilliant novelty and a feeling as of seeing the colours of the sunrise. Novelty of this profound sort is, by a tremendous paradox, everlasting and perpetually unstaled. Nothing can supersede or relegate these books, there is no need to resort to memory for the thrill of the first encounter with them, they can be read again with almost the same feelings as of old.

The difference between the two books is profoundly interesting. The *Treatise* is relaxed, triumphant; the *General Theory* wrestles with a strange, dual and elusive foe, part critic (the

---

* J. M. Keynes, *The General Theory of Employment, Interest and Money*, Preface, pp. vi, vii.

author's self), part conceptual difficulty. The *General Theory* shows signs of strain, as well it might. To start again at the age of nearly fifty, and rewrite one's *magnum opus* in a new, more complex, refined, exact and powerful form was heroic and exhausting. It was, indeed, literally nearly fatal. Was it necessary or worth while? The *Treatise* had efficient machinery, easier, indeed, to grasp than that of the *General Theory*. This was not altogether an advantage, in the circumstances of the time and for the purpose in hand. The mystique, the ascendancy of the later book arose partly from its seeming so difficult, and that difficulty itself arose partly from faults of exposition, even from fallacious reasoning, from which the *Treatise* (if the reader is agile enough to tread in the author's seven-league steps) is free. The appeal to the necessary equality of saving and investment (as defined in the *General Theory* in what we should now call the *ex post* sense) as a proof that the size of general output 'depends' on that of investment, was a fallacious and confusing short-cut of argument. Keynes's Multiplier tried in one of its versions, again fallaciously, to short-circuit Kahn's convergent series by appealing to a trivial, truistical manipulation of the marginal propensity to consume. These things were backward steps, and they seem to have occurred by a false memory on the author's part of how the 'fundamental equations' of the *Treatise* had achieved their results. Those equations illuminated the nature and consequences of disequilibrium. But the *General Theory* confuses equilibrium and identical equality, and quite abandons the formal consideration of *disequilibrium*. The *Treatise*, in the language of the 1960s, is dynamics, the *General Theory* is comparative statics. Nevertheless, of course, the *General Theory* had to be written, if only to make possible its distillation into the article of February 1937 in the *Quarterly Journal of Economics*. And that distillation was already in view when, in December 1935, with his book complete, Keynes wrote in its Preface:

A monetary economy, we shall find, is essentially one in which changing views about the future are capable of influencing the quantity of employment and not merely its direction. But our method of analysing the economic behaviour of the present under the influence of changing ideas about the future is one which depends on the interaction of supply and demand, and is in this way linked up with our fundamental theory of value.

Let us turn to the *Treatise*, books III and IV, and compare it with the *General Theory*, book III.

The question directly sought to be answered in book III of the *Treatise* is: What circumstances produce a change in the general level of the prices of those things which are bought by the people of a country in their capacity as consumers? In a self-contained economy, this price-level is arithmetically the ratio of the quantity of money spent, in the relevant time-interval, by the people of the country in their capacity as consumers, to the quantity of goods which, in that interval, the entrepreneurs insist on disposing of to them for the purpose of consumption. Behind this first and purely formal answer there evidently lies an endless system of further questions and answers, as to what influences bear on the size of the numerator and denominator just defined, what influences or conditions lie behind these proximately determining ones, and so on indefinitely. Keynes's first Fundamental Equation implicitly compares two states of the consumers' price-level. This equation takes an *ex post* view of what we shall call a proper-named unit interval of time, such, that is to say, as the first quarter of the year 1965, and shows both what the price-level would have been in that interval had the entrepreneurs' expectations, prevailing at its beginning, proved correct, and what in fact the price-level was. This realized price-level is thus also exhibited as the sum of two terms, the expected level and the unexpected divergence therefrom. And thirdly, the proximate origin of this unexpected divergence, or of the funds which brought it into being, is specified. Lastly, since we are free to suppose that the expectations which the entrepreneurs entertained at the beginning of this interval, and which led them to pay out to their hired factors, and to count on for themselves, certain remunerations, differ from those which they had entertained at the beginning of earlier intervals, we can point to a further possible source of divergence of the latest realized price-level from earlier ones. For if these remunerations of the factors of production are different from those of earlier intervals, we have here the 'cost-push' mechanism of price-level change to put alongside that of the 'demand-pull' consisting in (welcome or unwelcome) disappointment of expectations. In short, the first Fundamental Equation provides a frame for two comparisons. Explicitly, we are shown the comparison between expected and realized out-turn of the proper-named (i.e. historically identified) interval itself. Implicitly (and also verbally, in the expository text), we are invited to compare what, at its threshold, was expected of *this* interval with what had been expected of earlier proper-named intervals.

The first Fundamental Equation has in it some symbols representing quantities of goods and others representing quantities of money. Keynes's method in this equation has an existentialist flavour, for the unit of physical quantity of goods is special to an implicitly proper-named historical instant, namely the threshold of the interval of which we suppose ourselves to be now taking the earliest possible *ex post* view. Equal units of physical production are units which, in this interval, by the contracts signed or prevailing at its outset, and the price then set by entrepreneurs upon their own services, have had equal money costs. The equation, moreover, states both a record of the immediate past and a presumption about the future. The record tells us what expected price-level of consumers' goods led the entrepreneurs to decide, at the outset of the interval, to make available in it to consumers such-and-such a quantity of consumers' goods, and also what the consumers' actual expenditure, divided by that quantity of goods, has turned out to be. The presumption about the future is that if these two states of the price-level, the one formerly expected and the one now realized, differ from each other, the entrepreneurs will now decide to make available to consumers, in the immediately impending interval, a different quantity of goods from that of the interval just elapsed. There is, however, a gap or unstated supposition in Keynes's formulation. The first Fundamental Equation can display a divergence between the initially expected and the finally realized price-level of the latest interval. Reference is also made in Keynes's expository text to a possible disparity between the price-level expectation which prevailed at the beginning of this just-elapsed interval and the one which prevailed at the beginning of the preceding interval. But nothing is said about the equality or inequality of the realized price-level of that former interval and the one expected at the outset of this latest one. Yet his analysis is incomplete without some reference to this relation.

We have, in short, to ask concerning this equation, which is claimed to show the mechanism of change of the consumers' price-level: change how defined, as difference between what and what? Keynes's apparatus explicitly displays the comparison of the now-realized with the formerly expected price-level. It cannot explicitly display this expectation, held at the beginning of the just-elapsed interval, as dependent on, or as influenced by, the divergence of realizations from expectations in the *preceding* interval. Keynes in his first Fundamental Equation shows how the upshot of decisions taken at the threshold of an interval, by entrepreneurs as such about production and the making available of goods to consumers, and by income-disposers in general about spending or not by spending on consumption, can result in fulfilment or non-fulfilment of the entrepreneurs' expectations, when the record of the interval becomes known at its end. But this equation does not by itself say anything about how this *ex post* result of one interval will influence the decisions concerning the subsequent interval. It is silent also on another matter. Keynes refers in his text, in passing, to the dependence of entrepreneurs' production decisions on the supply prices or supply schedules of factors of production. But the equation cannot display these supply conditions of factors at the threshold of one interval as influenced by consumer prices realized in the preceding interval. All such comparisons of one interval with another are left for the reader to build up from suggestive remarks in Keynes's expository text.

Keynes is discussing change, an event in past or possible history, and the unit time-segment which he examines must therefore be deemed to have its unique and identifiable location in that history. It is for this reason that we speak of a 'proper-named' interval. He speaks as though the measurements, viz. of earnings, spendings and production, of the relevant events of that interval were items of a known and certain record, and thus we must deem him to be taking what we should nowadays call an *ex post* view of this interval. His purpose, nonetheless, is to discover the springs of those events. He finds these, implicitly, in the decisions of the two classes into which the people of the economy are gathered, the entrepreneurs in their capacity as such, and the income-disposers as such, who, of course, include in this different capacity, alongside those who supply factors of production, the same persons who are also entrepreneurs.

We are to conceive, then, of the entrepreneurs deciding at the beginning of the proper-named interval to *thrust upon* consumers as such some specific collection of quantities of goods, a collection which can in some manner be quantified, not merely item by item but as a whole. The hint given in the *Treatise* as to how this quantifying is to be done dimly suggests already the method openly adopted in the *General Theory*, namely, to regard the quantity of employment given in producing these goods as a measure of their quantity. We say that these goods are to be 'thrust upon' consumers. There seems to us to be no escape (even if one were desirable) from interpreting the first Fundamental Equation as exhibiting the confrontation of decisions taken in independence, that is in ignorance of each other. The entrepreneurs must in that case be supposed to decide what quantity of goods to dispose of, during the interval, to consumers as such, without waiting to find out what price this quantity will fetch. The consumers, too, must be supposed to decide what quantity of money to spend in the interval on consumption without waiting to find out what quantity of goods this money will buy. Such a conception of things is no doubt artificial, unless we regard the 'interval' as exceedingly short. But it is scarcely more artificial than the conception of a general equilibrium, where all decisions to buy and sell are to be looked on as the solution of an all-inclusive system of conditional intentions or of demand and supply equations, for such a system must really be treated as timeless. Reality is some blend of the two extremes.

The first Fundamental Equation considers as one whole, and measures as a single quantity, the goods which are thrust upon consumers in the proper-named interval. It does not itself inquire or suggest how this quantity comes to be what it is, but takes it as given. The price of this quantity as a whole, or the price of each of the equal physical units into which it may be supposed to be in some manner divided, thus depends on how much money is spent by consumers as such in the interval. Three classes can be defined, into one or other of which any possible source of these spendings can be placed. There is first the money earned by the suppliers of means of production, the entrepreneurs themselves being included amongst these suppliers, in producing within the interval such a quantity of goods as replaces those sold to consumers in the interval. Since, in a self-contained economy, all goods produced in the interval but not consumed in it must necessarily become a net addition to the economy's pre-existing stock of goods, the second source of spendings on consumption is the earnings from producing such a net addition, that is, the earnings from performing net investment. Thirdly there are withdrawals by consumers from their pre-existing stocks of money, which stocks of money may be initially in the possession of those who spend them, or may be obtained by these spenders in exchange for pre-existing goods which were produced in previous intervals, and may also consist of hitherto unused permission to overdraw at the bank. Such withdrawals, however, can be negative. Less may be spent in the interval on consumption than is earned in it by production. Such negative withdrawals of money from reserve, such *placing to reserve* of money earned in the interval, is positive *saving*. When all three kinds of source of consumer-spending are added together, account being taken of their algebraic sign, we have the result that U, total consumer-spending in the interval, equals E', the earnings in the interval from producing the same quantity of goods as is sold in it to consumers, plus I', the earnings in the interval from producing such quantity of goods as becomes a net addition to the stock of goods, minus what is saved, S, in the interval:

$$U = E' + I' - S.$$

If now the number of physical units, however defined, of goods bought by consumers in the interval is R we have for the price-level P of these goods

$$P = \frac{U}{R} = \frac{E' + I' - S}{R} \quad \text{or} \quad P = \frac{E'}{R} + \frac{I' - S}{R}.$$

Now Keynes's physical unit of production is one and the same no matter whether the goods in question are to be consumed at once or added to the general stock, and so E'/R, the unit production cost of goods sold in the interval to consumers, is the same as E/O, the unit production cost of goods in general. Thus our expression for the price-level of consumers' goods can be rewritten

$$P = \frac{E}{O} + \frac{I' - S}{R} \tag{1}$$

and this is Keynes's first Fundamental Equation. Keynes proceeds:

Let W be the rate of earnings per unit of human effort, W_1 the rate of earnings per unit of output, and let $W = e.W_1$. We can then rewrite equation (1) in the form

$$P = W_1 + \frac{I'-S}{R} \qquad (2)$$

$$= \frac{W}{e} + \frac{I'-S}{R} \qquad (3)$$

The price-level of consumption goods (i.e. the inverse of the purchasing power of money) is made up, therefore, of two terms, the first of which represents the level of efficiency-earnings, i.e. the cost of production, and the second of which is positive, zero or negative, according as the cost of new investment exceeds, equals or falls short of the volume of current savings. It follows that the stability of the purchasing power of money involves the two conditions—that efficiency-earnings should be constant and that the cost of new investment should be equal to the volume of current saving.

This passage enforces the brilliant concise efficiency of Keynes's apparatus. His formula, the first Fundamental Equation, has a peg on which to hang every question that his own later work and that of the host of Keynesians and that of Myrdal have shown to be the essential ones in a theory of money, employment, and general output. Disappointment of initial expectations, if it occurs, is exhibited as a disparity of saving and investment. This is the *nature*, rather than even the proximate source, of the disappointment, which of course can be either a welcome or unwelcome one to the entrepreneurs. So we have to ask what interplay of circumstances proximately governs investment and what governs saving. This is already the *General Theory*, but also, as we have shown in earlier chapters, it is the Wicksell theory, and Keynes acknowledges some acquaintance with Wicksell's work. As to change of efficiency-earnings as another aspect of change of the general consumer price level, this is what nowadays is called cost-push inflation. What is its mechanism and generating circumstances? This question arises as naturally from Keynes's formal dissection of the price-level as the one about inflationary demand. The first Fundamental Equation is, indeed, a supreme example of the 'Cambridge Method'. That method consists in seeking that set of concepts which will enable us to ask the simplest-seeming set of questions. All explanation, after all, is artificial, since all of it depends upon abstraction. In the fabric of the cosmos, all things, perhaps, are bound together. To say that some of these bonds are more essential or in some sense more meaningful than others may be legitimate and helpful, but it is still in some degree subject to interpretation, in some degree arbitrary. To explain some set of phenomena is to display them from a different viewpoint. It was in choosing the viewpoint, like a photographer choosing the 'composition' of his picture, that Marshall, Keynes, Robertson and Harrod ('Cambridge' in the relevant sense) were so successful in making many difficulties irrelevant. They cut the Gordian knot, but first with insight and ingenuity they tied it up themselves, to give their conceptual sword-stroke its maximum effect.

However, the first Fundamental Equation is not by itself enough. It shows us no connection of the state of affairs in the proper-named interval with what has gone before nor with what will come after. If the rate of efficiency-earnings has changed, we wish to know why; and if there is in this proper-named interval a disparity between earnings in the production of goods made available to consumers, and the consumers' expenditure upon them, we want to know what the effect of this will be. Here Keynes gives us a hint, but does not give it that central importance in his scheme which it ought on several grounds to claim. This hint concerns the definition of entrepreneurs' normal remuneration:

We propose to mean identically the same thing by the three expressions: (1) *the community's money-income*; (2) *the earnings of the factors of production*; and (3) *the cost of production*; and we reserve the term *profits* for the difference between the cost of production of the current output and its actual sale-proceeds, so that profits are not part of the community's income as thus defined. The entrepreneurs as being themselves amongst the factors of production, their normal remuneration is included in income. For my present purpose I propose to define the 'normal' remuneration of entrepreneurs as that rate of remuneration which, if they were open to make new bargains with all the factors of production at the currently prevailing rates of earnings, would leave them under no motive either to increase or to decrease their scale of operations.*

* *Treatise*, vol. i, pp. 123–5.

Let us notice the strong but tacit expectational cast of Keynes's thought in this passage and of his whole *Treatise* conception. For *income* is being here defined as *expected* income. It is plainly implied that if entrepreneurs were sure, at the outset of each interval, what the sale-proceeds of each possible quantity of goods thrust upon consumers would be, their individual decisions would result in such a quantity being so thrust as would give them their 'normal' remuneration in Keynes's sense. It is their normal remuneration which they expect. Had Keynes realized and remembered, when he came to write the *General Theory*, this implicit expectational meaning of his concept of income in the *Treatise*, all the confusion in the *General Theory* between the supposed income on which spending decisions of consumers are based, and the realized income which results from those decisions, would have been avoided. Keynes speaks of his definition of entrepreneurs' normal remuneration as only one among many which might be adopted; but any remuneration of entrepreneurs which leads to a change of output will surely lead, at given rates of pay for hired factors working with a given outfit of tools, to a change in efficiency earnings; for in these short-period conditions an increase in output will push the unit cost of production along an upward-sloping supply curve. It follows that if entrepreneurs' normal remuneration were, by definition, such as would tempt them, when they had exactly achieved it by thrusting upon consumers in one proper-named interval a given quantity of goods, to decide upon a larger quantity for the next interval, 'normal remuneration' would be associated with an ever-rising price-level of consumers' goods. This is evidently not that stability of the price-level for which Keynes laid down the conditions (quoted above) on page 136 of vol. 1 of the *Treatise*. Despite Keynes's apparent willingness to consider other definitions, it appears that only that definition will do which makes normal remuneration lead to unchanged quantities of goods being thrust per unit of time upon consumers. One question which may here occur to the reader must be answered. Does an increase in the quantity of goods thrust in the proper-named interval upon consumers necessarily require an increase in total output of goods? Could the extra goods not be provided for by reducing the concurrent addition to stock, so that there need be no movement along the supply curve? The kingpin of Keynes's theory of the general price level in his *Treatise*, as of his theory of general output in the *General Theory*, is the Wicksellian idea that designed investment, the intentional net augmentation, per time-unit, of the total stock of equipment or wealth, is determined on its own by a marginal matching of expected profit with the interest-rate. When this inducement to invest has been satisfied by the appropriate allocation of intended output, any increase of sales to consumers must be matched by an increase in production as a whole, and the movement along the supply curve cannot be avoided. We come now, therefore, to the question how investment and saving, and hence the amount of inflationary demand, come to be of the size they are.

The account which the *Treatise* offers us of the inducement to invest passes, in the course of chapters 10–13, through at least three stages of development. In chapter 10 (iii) the effects, though not the sources, of (for example) a strengthening of liquidity preference are explained. Such a strengthening will lead wealth-owners to sell non-money forms of wealth. If the banking-system buys these 'securities' with money necessarily newly created for the purpose, the desire of non-bank wealth-owners in general for a greater proportion of money to other assets may be satisfied, by this exchange with the banking system of 'securities' for money, without any fall in the price-level of the former. But if the banking system does not compensate in this way the public's increased liquidity preference, the desire of wealth-owners to sell securities cannot result in their being sold to anyone outside the body of non-bank wealth-owners as a whole, and its only effect will be to depress the prices of these securities. (It is even conceivable that such a fall of prices might occur without any changes of ownership whatever. Mere enquiries or probings of the market might convince security-holders that potential buyers had become as much more reluctant to buy as they themselves had become to hold.) The demand price for existing 'securities', however, is also the demand price for new ones, representing equipment which investing entrepreneurs might now order. Why set up a new firm with equipment yet to be constructed, if an existing firm can be bought more cheaply as a going concern? (More cheaply, of course, after allowance for its plant being less efficient than new plant.) Thus a strengthening of liquidity preference can depress the inducement to invest.

One feature of this theory of the inducement to invest (a theory which, 40 pages later, Keynes refers to as 'not intended to be more than a preliminary treatment of this subject') distinguishes it radically from that of the *General Theory*. In this *Treatise* account, the whole burden of changes in the inducement to invest is placed, in effect, on change of the interest-rate. 'Securities' includes both *bonds* (acknowledgements of debt) and *ordinary shares* (titles to the ownership of real buildings and machines, or the going concerns to which these tools belong). The series of prospective instalments of pay, no matter whether these are interest or dividends, which any security of either kind promises, is taken as given, and any change in the valuation of such securities is looked on, in the theory of chapter 10 (iii), as due to a change in the public's present-moment valuation of this *given* prospect. Let us, then, examine this. When the prospective instalments are 'coupon' interest whose due payment at the proper dates is not in doubt, it is of course only the *attitudes* to this prospect, or the comparison of it with other possible use of the price for which it could be immediately sold, which can change. But when the 'prospective' instalments are not the promises of a reputable debtor but the mere conjectures of an entrepreneur or a shareholder, concerning the outcome of the future use of equipment in circumstances now unknown, the most formidable source of change of value of the security is an abrupt shattering or transformation of these profit-expectations. The *Treatise*, in fact, in chapter (10) (iii) entirely neglects the whole phenomenon which in the *General Theory* appears as a *schedule of the marginal efficiency of capital* capable of swift, wide and unheralded bodily shifts of shape and position (changes of form). Chapter 10 (iii) fails to distinguish between bonds and shares, and therefore neglects, or leaves quite unmentioned, the dramatic changes of expectations that can destroy or create in a moment large parts of the value of shares. The profits on which that value depends are future profits; they are, that is to say, in essence mere figments of imagination, they are at base mere matters of opinion, and that opinion can dissolve or emerge incalculably with fresh or reinterpreted 'news' from the technical, political, fashionable or market front: straws in the wind of change. In the *General Theory*, the uncertainty and entre-preneurial nervousness arising from a tacit recognition of these things has taken on a paramount importance, and has indeed become the core of the whole argument about general heavy unemployment. But in chapter 10 (iii) these things make no appearance:

When a man is deciding what proportion of his money-income to save, he is choosing between present consumption and the owner-ship of wealth. In so far as he decides in favour of consumption, he must necessarily purchase goods. But in so far as he decides in favour of saving, there still remains a further decision for him to make. For he can own wealth by holding it either in the form of money or in other forms of loan or real capital [loan capital: bonds, I.O.U.s issued by those who borrow his money from him; real capital: tools, machines, buildings etc. or 'ordinary shares' representing them]. There is a further significant difference between the two types of decision. The decision as to holding bank-deposits [money] or securities relates, not only to the current increment to the wealth of individuals, but also to the whole block of their existing capital. Indeed, since the current increment is but a trifling proportion of the block of existing wealth, it is but a minor element in the matter. Now when an individual is more disposed than before to hold his wealth in the form of savings-deposits [money] and less disposed to hold it in other forms, this means that he favours savings-deposits (for whatever reason) more than before at the existing price-level of other securities. But his distaste for other securities is not absolute and depends on his expectations of the future return to be obtained from savings-deposits and from other securities respectively, which is obviously affected by the price of the latter.*

The marginal efficiency of capital is that percentage per annum which, when used for discounting expected profit-instalments to the present, makes the total of their discounted values equal to the supply price of the equipment in which the capital is to be invested. What is this but a 'return which is affected by the price of securities' when the latter are titles to the ownership of equipment? As an arithmetical formula, the marginal efficiency idea is implicit in the last sentence of our quoted passage. What is not present in it is any hint of the marginal efficiency as a reflector of precarious human hopes and fears, a measure of mens' moment-to-moment appraisal of their situation. This is

* *A Treatise on Money*, chapter III, section (iii), vol. I, pp. 140–2.

that character of the marginal efficiency, *varium et mutabile semper*, that gives it the central role in the *General Theory*. In that sentence there even appears the word 'expectations', also with no hint of uncertainty, plurality or vagueness.

So far as it goes, the account of the inducement to invest given in chapter 10 (iii) is extremely compact and economical. Its counterparts in the *General Theory* are a vital argument from 'The State of Long-term Expectation' (*General Theory*, chapter 12) or alternatively, from 'The Essential Properties of Interest and Money' (*General Theory*, chapter 17), together with a description of the *effects, and the means of control* (not the nature or origins) of liquidity preference and the interest-rate. The mechanism of liquidity preference, the effects, that is, of the desire to hold money (called 'savings deposits' in this connection in the *Treatise*) and of manipulation of its supply, are admirably stated in the passage following our last quotation:

If the banking-system operates in the opposite direction to that of the public and meets the preference of the latter for savings-deposits by buying the securities which the public is *less* anxious to hold and creating against them the additional savings-deposits which the public is *more* anxious to hold, then there is no need for the price-level of investments to fall at all. Thus the change in the relative attractions of savings-deposits and securities respectively has to be met either by a fall in the price of securities or by an increase in the supply of savings-deposits, or partly by the one and partly by the other.*

In the *General Theory* we have the inducement to invest divided into two parts. The rate of interest is shown to be determined at each moment by the confrontation of the liquidity preference felt at that moment by wealth-owners and the quantity of money which the policy of the banking system has caused to exist at that moment. This rate of interest is then in turn confronted with the marginal efficiency of capital, or in more general terms with the entrepreneurs' assessment of the trading profits to be had in the future from equipment which they might order now, and the relation of those conjectural profits to the supply price of the equipment. In the *Treatise's* second

* *Treatise*, vol. I, chapter 10 (iii), p. 142.

stage of development of its theory of investment, this second comparison is given far clearer expression:

It is now evident in what manner changes in the Bank-rate, or—more strictly—changes in the rate of interest, are capable of influencing the purchasing power of money. The attractiveness of investment depends on the prospective income which the entrepreneur anticipates from current investment relatively to the rate of interest which he has to pay in order to be able to finance its production;—or, putting it the other way round, the value of capital goods depends on the rate of interest at which the prospective income from them is capitalised. That is to say the higher (e.g.) the rate of interest, the lower, other things being equal, will be the value of capital goods. Therefore, if the rate of interest rises, the price-level of capital goods will tend to fall, which will lower the rate of profit on the production of capital-goods, which will be deterrent to new investment. Thus a high rate of interest will tend to diminish both the price-level and the volume of output of capital goods. The rate of saving, on the other hand, is stimulated by a high rate of interest. It follows that an increase in the rate of interest tends to make the rate of investment (whether measured by its value or by its cost) to decline relatively to the rate of saving.*

To see the full meaning of this last sentence, we must now return to chapter 10 and examine the second of Keynes's two fundamental equations.

Keynes's second Fundamental Equation takes the price-level P' of new investment-goods as given, that price-level being afterwards explained on the lines we have already quoted:

Let P' be the price-level of new investment-goods, Π the price-level of output as a whole and I ($= P'.C$) the value (as distinguished from I', the cost of production) of the increment of new investment goods.

Then

$$\Pi = \frac{P.R + P'.C}{O}$$

$$= \frac{(E-S)+I}{O}$$

$$= \frac{E}{O} + \frac{I-S}{O} \qquad (4)$$

[where C is the physical measure of the 'increment of new investment goods', that is, the investment done in the proper-named interval].

* *Treatise*, vol. I, chapter 11 (ii), p. 154.

The two fundamental equations are alike, except that in the expression for the price-level of output as a whole the numerator of the second term is the excess of the value, instead of the production cost, of investment over saving. This excess of the *value* of investment over saving is to be looked on (Keynes tells us in section (ii) of chapter 10, 'The Characteristics of Profit') as composed of the excess $I' - S$ of the production-cost of investment over saving, and the excess $I - I'$ of the value of investment over its cost of production (the excess, in respect of those goods which form a net addition in the interval to the country's stock of goods, of sale-proceeds over cost of production). The first of these differences, $I' - S$, is what is spent on consumption goods over and above what they cost to produce, and the other, $I - I'$, is what is spent on investment-goods over and above what *they* cost to produce. The two differences or amounts of profit, $I' - S = Q_1$ and $I - I' = Q_2$, together make up the total profit Q. Keynes is no doubt justified in distinguishing profit from income but the reason he gives in chapter 10 (ii) for doing so is a confusion of thought. He says:

There is one peculiarity of profits (or losses) which we may note in passing, because it is one of the reasons why it is necessary to segregate them from income proper, as a category apart. If entrepreneurs choose to spend a portion of their profits on consumption (and there is, of course, nothing to prevent them from doing this) the effect is to *increase* the profit on the sale of liquid consumption-goods by an amount exactly equal to the amount of profits which have thus been expended. This follows from our definition, because such expenditure constitutes a diminution of saving and, therefore an increase in the difference between I' and S.*

This whole line of thought appears to us quite mistaken. We have, indeed, gone somewhat beyond our brief in insisting that the Fundamental Equations must be looked on as referring to some identified interval in the historical calendar (even if the calendar of a suppositious world) and in speaking as though what happens in any such interval must, for the sake of the logical consistency or intelligibility of the apparatus, be deemed to be the direct outcome and execution of decisions taken at or before the *threshold* of that interval. In postulating this we can claim no warrant from Keynes's explicit text, only from what

* *Treatise*, vol. 1, chapter 10 (ii), p. 139.

seem to be its implications. But one thing is explicitly stated in his exposition: profits are *unexpected*. When the *experience and recorded fact* of such profits leads the individual to *decide upon* a greater expenditure *in the future* (*decision* necessarily looks to the future) we ought to regard him as being at the threshold of a *new* interval. Keynes's Fundamental Equations appear to us to be dynamic, not to be descriptions of an equilibrium. They describe *sequences* of events one stage of which grows out of another, not the result of systematic pooling of conditional intentions in a simultaneous general act. Thus we have to distinguish experiences, decisions and actions as sequential phases, and this must surely be done by considering them to occur in distinct, sequential time-intervals separately described. Let us try to summarize the upshot of these considerations.

The real and crucial distinction between profits and income in the *Treatise* is that the former are unexpected while the latter is expected and counted on. Keynes has no need nor business to talk about entrepreneurs spending their profits on consumption or on investment or on *anything*. They *cannot* spend or dispose of their profits. The meaning which Keynes expressly gives to this word in his text, and the meaning which his apparatus imposes upon it, when that apparatus is interpreted so as to be coherent and self-consistent, forbids any thought of such profits entering their minds at the moment when all their decisions, about producing, buying investment goods, and consuming, are being made, viz. at the threshold of the implicit proper-named interval which the fundamental equations are concerned with. The apparatus of book III, stated, implied or required, is a period-analysis, and spending is something decided on at the threshold of each period. What was not expected, nor counted on, at the beginning of the interval cannot at that moment be assigned to spending or saving. Nor can it be so assigned *within* the interval, for the meaning of the interval is that all its events are the result of decisions taken at or before its beginning. Now the very essence and *raison d'être* of the idea of Keynes's profit in the *Treatise* is unexpectedness. Profit is a windfall. The categories, of course, are all unrealistically clear-cut. To expect a precise figure of income, when, as with the entrepreneurs' income, this is of its nature an unknown and not the subject of a contract, is not reasonable or natural. But it is what Keynes's simplified, abstract apparatus (resembling in these respects all *theory*) requires us to suppose. Windfall profit is *nothing* until experienced, until recorded, until, that is to say, it is already something in the *past*. Its existence as a fact of the record may influence decisions as to what shall be done in the future. But these future acts cannot then be carried back to modify the past.

There is no hint in the explicit text of book III that we are to regard the Fundamental Equations as applying to a time-interval of finite length. That book does indeed suggest in many places that entrepreneurs, for example, will decide, or seek, to do certain things (necessarily in the future) because of the experiences they have had (necessarily in the past). But the period-analysis interpretation which we have imposed upon the Fundamental Equations and upon the arguments based on them is an endeavour on our part to elucidate them, not something warranted by what Keynes himself puts into words in that book. However in book IV he speaks on p. 270 of 'excess loans [being] balanced by the accrual of profits at the end of each production period, and [being] therefore again available for the next production period'. In describing a process of sequential changes or events, Keynes himself is thus driven to a period-analysis form of thought.

We are not yet at the end of the evolution, to be found in the *Treatise*, of Keynes's ideas on the inducement to invest. A page or two after our last quotation we are carried even nearer to the *General Theory*:

The most usual and important occasion of change [of prices] will be the action of the entrepreneurs, under the influence of the actual enjoyment of positive or negative profits, in increasing or diminishing the volume of employment which they offer at the existing rates of remuneration of the Factors of Production, and so bringing about a raising or lowering of these rates. Moreover, there is a further reason why it is appropriate to regard the above as the normal mechanism of change. For when the Central Currency Authority of a country wishes to change the level of money-incomes in the country and thereby the quantity of circulating money which they require, the only alteration which it has a power to order relates to the terms of lending. This alteration affects the attractiveness of producing capital goods, which disturbs the rate of investment relatively to that of saving, which upsets the rate of profits for producers of consumption-goods, thus causing entrepreneurs to modify the average level of their offers to the factors of production, and so finally achieving the ultimate objective of changing the level of money-incomes. In so far, however, as production takes time, it is obviously the anticipated profit or loss on new business, rather than the actual profit or loss on business just concluded, which influences them in deciding the scale on which to produce and the offers which it is worth while to make to the factors of production. Strictly, therefore, we should say that it is the *anticipated* profit or loss which is the mainspring of change.

Many things about these sentences are noteworthy. Here almost for the first time in the *Treatise* we get a reference to the 'volume of employment', but this is still looked on merely as a link in the mechanism of a rising or falling price-level. But later the business men are 'deciding the scale on which to produce' and the words which come before and after this remark convey a suggestion that the scale is important in its own right and not merely as a means or effect of price-level changes or even of cost-changes. And at the end the leap is made at last from *realized* to *anticipated* profit. In chapter 12 this fresh idea becomes almost the equivalent of that in chapter 11 of the *General Theory*:

What happens to the price-level of new investments, i.e. of the goods which are added to the stock of capital? It depends on the utilities which these investments will yield up at some future date and on the rate of interest at which these future utilities are discounted for the purpose of fixing their present capital value. Thus, whether producers of investment goods make a profit or a loss depends on whether the expectations of the market about future prices and the prevailing rate of interest are changing favourably or adversely to such producers.

There is even a hint here of the *volatility* of capital-goods prices.

'It follows that I could do it better and much shorter if I were to start over again' (*Treatise*, preface, p. vi). Did he succeed? In some important respects the *General Theory* is not merely a deepening or clarifying of the *Treatise* but a turning aside from it. The *Treatise* is thoroughly Wicksellian. Keynes is asking and answering in book III precisely the question that Wicksell asked and answered in *Geldzins und Güterpreise*, namely, what circumstances entail a general rise of prices (or what opposite circumstances entail a general fall) and consequently what circumstances are necessary, and perhaps sufficient, to ensure the absence of any such tendency? His answer is the Wicksellian one: Any difference between the value of the net investment which entrepreneurs all taken together are doing, and the saving which the people of the country all taken together are doing, will lead, at once or after some chain of reactions, to a change of the price-level of consumers' goods. Keynes articulated Wicksell's theory by distinguishing two classes of entrepreneurs, or, when he was speaking more carefully, two capacities in which entrepreneurs operate, namely, as suppliers of goods to consumers and as performers of net investment. For any given quantity, per unit of time, of goods which they are thrusting on consumers, there is some amount of sale-proceeds which will just induce them to continue the same offer of employment, at the same rates of pay, as heretofore to their hired factors of production in order to continue supplying to consumers that same quantity per unit of time. This amount of sale-proceeds is the *cost of production* of that quantity of consumers' goods. If, after the event, sale-proceeds from this supply turn out to have exceeded that amount, the difference or profit, Q_1, will not only mean that the price-level of consumers' goods has already been carried above their cost of production, but also that the entrepreneurs will now plan to supply consumers with a larger quantity per time-unit and for this purpose will offer higher rates of pay to hired factors in order to employ more of them, and thus the new total cost of supplying consumers, viz. the income of more factors, more highly paid, producing more goods, will be higher. More highly paid factors imply that W_1, the rate of earnings per unit of output, will have risen and thus the first term of the first Fundamental Equation will have been disturbed. Restfulness of the consumers' price-level, therefore, requires as one necessary condition that Q_1 be zero, and this is equivalent, as we have seen, to the equality of the *cost of production* of new investment (similarly defined to that of consumer-supply) with saving. But if entrepreneurs, all taken together, are paying each other more for, or valuing more highly, goods constituting new investment than these goods are costing to produce, they will have a profit, Q_2, in their capacity as performers of net investment (no matter whether this profit goes to the *buyer* or the *maker* of the equipment). This will lead them to plan an increase in their net investment (whether measured by cost or value) and thus there will arise an increase in the income of the community and a further possible source of divergence between saving and the cost of investment.

In the foregoing passage we have taken care not to use notions that Keynes himself does not use in book III of the *Treatise*. In particular, we have abandoned our use of expressions appropriate to a period-analysis interpretation of the Fundamental Equations, and instead of speaking of what entrepreneurs or income-disposers intend or decide to do, we have referred to 'the net investment which entrepreneurs are doing' and to 'the saving which the people of the country are doing', intending to render thus Keynes's 'current net investment' and 'current saving'. But these latter expressions, so simple-sounding and straightforward, are in this context delusive. To claim an explanatory power for the Fundamental Equations is to claim that they show choice or action growing out of circumstance. Choice is about the future, however immediate. What people 'are doing' is what they *have chosen* to do, and to understand that choice we must look at the circumstances, or their mind-picture of the circumstances, which prevailed when that choice was made, not the circumstances which prevail when their resulting actions are being performed. Keynes indeed gives countenance to our period-analysis gloss upon his words. On p. 153, for example, he refers to 'the decisions of the members of the community as to how much of their money incomes they shall spend on consumption'. Period-analysis, the attempt to exhibit events as the consequence of the inter-play of previous decisions, and subsequent decisions as the outcome of these events, is of course what emerged from Myrdal's and Lindahl's 'immanent criticism' and reformulation of Wicksell. But Keynes in the *General Theory* turned in the other direction. The *General Theory* is expressed in terms of a comparison of equilibria. Each such equilibrium is the fragile coalescence of momentarily held expectations, a change in which, nervously waiting upon any change or rumoured change of news, can abruptly destroy it. But the cascade of events which must be supposed to follow such destruction and lead to a new equilibrium cannot be described or analysed by the *General Theory's* formal method. The contrast between the two books can be expressed in a sentence: the *Treatise* is a formal and explicit study of *disequilibrium*, a type of situation of which, in its formal analysis, the *General Theory* knows and can know nothing. At each curtain rise the *General Theory* shows us, not the dramatic moment of inevitable action but a tableau of posed figures. It is only after the curtain has descended again that we hear the clatter of violent scene-shifting. Must it be said, then, that the *General Theory*, so far from 'doing it better and much shorter'' was a backward, and an unnecessary, step? Can it not, after all, be claimed that the *Treatise's* theoretical machinery was briefly expressed and perfectly efficient, and that the recommendations based upon it, though nominally aimed at controlling prices rather than output, were in fact the same as those of the *General Theory* so far as monetary measures are concerned? 'When money incomes fall away, lower the interest-rate; when they swell too much, raise it' is what both books say. Nonetheless, the *General Theory* has a quite different theoretical message, and the fact that its formal method is that of comparative statics, while that of the *Treatise* was a close approach to what we nowadays mean by dynamic economics, gives it a positive advantage for the conveying of that message. For that message is that events in men's minds, the *unaccountable* sudden seizure of their thoughts by hopes and fears, not the mechanism and arithmetic of money flows, are what give to our modern economy its violent impulses and hesitations. The *Treatise* in regard to the interest-rate went far towards this view, showing interest as dependent on, and even necessitated by, the divergently uncertain expectations held by Bulls and Bears. But the *Treatise* had still a lot of mechanism, and though that mechanism is highly convincing in itself, it may obscure those springs or inhibitors of action, the psychics of investment, which in the end, in his final summing up in the *Quarterly Journal of Economics*, Keynes came to look on as his great discovery.

The argument of the *Treatise* is presented in brilliant incisive and convincing summary in section (iv) of chapter 12. As a basis of policy for those in charge of a country's banking system, the theory there given is complete and impeccable. Only one thing from Keynes's ultimate thought is missing from this theory, only one thing is there which he would later have wanted to change. The degree to which the whole *General Theory* is here anticipated is worth briefly considering:

In conditions of equilibrium both the price-level of the goods coming forward for consumption and the price-level of the goods added to the stock of capital are determined by the money-rate of efficiency earnings of the factors of production.

For each size of output that he might contemplate, an entrepreneur will have in mind some minimum reward for himself which if realized would make it seem just worth while to have produced and offered for sale that output. Some one size of output will be the biggest that he thinks he could sell for proceeds just sufficient to give him the minimum reward of that size. He will not produce a larger output than this, but competition will broadly deny him any advantage from producing less. Thus that aggregate output, in each of the two categories of goods (and so, of course, in both taken together) will be produced whose sale-proceeds are *expected* to precisely match the cost, including the entrepreneurs' minimum satisfactory reward, of production. But in the event, when the interval to which expectations and decisions referred has gone by, the sale-proceeds actually realized can prove to have exceeded or fallen short of what was expected: a profit can emerge. If price-expectations were grounded in the record of the then-recent past, such a profit represents a *movement* of the price-level:

Movements in our two types of price-level are connected at one remove, and are, generally speaking, in the *same* direction. For if producers of investment-goods are making a profit, there will be a tendency for them to endeavour to increase their output, i.e. to increase investment, which will therefore tend, unless savings happen to be increasing in the same proportion, to raise the prices of consumption-goods. If producers as a whole are making a profit, individual producers will seek to enlarge their output so as to make more profit.

If we take the two above-quoted passages together, and put upon the former of them the gloss which we have suggested, the whole result comes very close to the idea that the absence of any tendency for aggregate *output* to be changed depends on an exact filling of the saving-gap by the flow of net investment. When we turn the *General Theory's* identities, referring to the realized past, into meaningful *ex ante* equilibria, we have precisely the foregoing proposition. If now we turn to the passage, already quoted on p. 179 above, which occurs between these two, we find an explanation of investment values identical with that of the *General Theory*:

The price-level of new investments [equipment which might be constructed] depends on the anticipated price-level of the utilities which these investments will yield up [the services which the equipment will render] at some future date and on the rate of interest at which these future utilities are discounted for the purpose of fixing their present capital value.

Investment *profit*, an excess of the valuation placed on equipment over its production cost, must then arise as an ephemeral consequence of sudden changes of expectation:

Whether producers of investment-goods make a profit or loss depends on whether the expectations of the market about future prices are changing favourably or adversely to such producers, [and whether] the prevailing rate of interest [is so changing].

The theory which emerges from all these passages taken together is nothing else than the central construct of the *General Theory*, namely, an account of the genesis of change of general *output* in terms of the inducement to invest.

What, then, is missing? It is the recognition, the insistence, that the future trading profits which are the whole and sole foundation of any ascription of value to a piece of proposed equipment, are in essence a figment, something conjectural and, of course, in an important sense and in a considerable measure believed in, but not something subject in the present to any objective test or confirmation, save very indirectly by analogy and precedent. But it is in the present, the moment of deciding whether or not to order this equipment, that the valuation has to be made. A recognition and insistence on the depth and the role of *uncertainty* are what the *Treatise* lacks and the *General Theory* has.

What is present in the *Treatise* that Keynes might have wished to express differently? It is the sentence in the middle of p. 182 which refers to the adequacy or otherwise of the public's saving, and makes this matter bear, not on the *cost of production of investment goods* where it belongs, but on the cost of borrowing money, to which it is (virtually) irrelevant. If intended investment exceeds intended saving, the price of factors of production may rise. Thereby the marginal efficiency of capital will be reduced. But as to the cost of *financing* the investment, the *rate* of interest which will have to be paid on the needed loans or will have to be sacrificed by using any reserve cash depends on the bearishness or bullishness, not on the thriftiness or prodigality, of wealth-owners and on the lending policy of the banking system. The amount to be borrowed or otherwise provided does, of course, depend on the cost of production of the equipment which is to be ordered. The theory of the interest-rate, however, is for chapter 15, on Liquidity Preference.

CHAPTER 14

THE MULTIPLIER

Chapter 1 of Professor Hegeland's *The Multiplier Theory* is concerned with the question of anticipators of Kahn. Interesting as his cases are, only one or two contain the essence of Kahn's idea, that is, that the generating of an extra money-income-stream by the production of goods such as cannot themselves be consumed, and the spending of this extra stream of money-income wholly or in part, will call into being an extra output of consumption goods, which must be of such an ultimate size as to satisfy not only those newly employed in producing non-consumable output but *also its own producers*. Both groups of those newly employed, namely the factors producing non-consumables and the factors producing consumables, will spend on consumption some proportion of their new incomes. Equilibrium, the absence of inducement to further change, will consist in the equality between the *saved* portion of the total new income of both groups taken together, and the value of the new non-consumable output. Thus the total extra income of both groups taken together will be some multiple of the value of the new non-consumable output, and that multiple is the Kahn Multiplier. This is a radically different proposal from that of starting with an increase in the output of some consumable good. For who has the income with which they are able and willing to buy such extra consumable output? Only its own producers. And if the propensity of these producers to consume is less than unity, they will leave part of their own output unbought and unconsumed. The Kahn Multiplier multiplies *extra income not matched by extra consumable output*, and it is of no consequence to the people of one country, seeking a means to increase their own employment, whether that original extra income is generated by an extra output of tools, or of goods for export uncompensated by extra imports, or whether it is a free gift of the government or of private philanthropy. Kahn chose road-building as his example, doubtless because it is unnecessary to explain that roads cannot be sold to consumers.

There appear to be four effects or mechanisms which Professor Hegeland is too readily inclined to assimilate to the Multiplier. One of these is the Accelerator or mechanism of induced investment, between which and the Multiplier the only similarity is that each provides a stimulus to increased output. But whereas the Multiplier shows what incremental flow of general output will be needed in order to match, with an extra flow of saving, a given incremental flow of intended net investment, the Accelerator shows what incremental stock of equipment will be called for to make possible a given incremental flow of general output. If we divide the economy into a consumers' goods sector and an investment goods sector, the two sectors are made, by our turning from the Accelerator to the Multiplier, to exchange the role of source and of recipient of the impulse.

Secondly, there is what we may call the Leontief mechanism, the mere expression of the fact that industries supply each other with materials, components, power and services. Any extra demand for the objects whose finishing stages are performed in any one sector (any one firm or industry) will be thence partly distributed to the suppliers of that sector. An increase in the sales of any sector of the system will call for corresponding increases, each evidently, in absolute and value terms, smaller than the first, in many other sectors. If this process ultimately leads to the re-employment of 1,000 men, no doubt only a few of these will be found in the sector for whose goods extra demand first appeared. In this sense there has been a multiplication of the first 'packet' of re-employment. And if, in any sector, additional durable equipment is called for to satisfy the new demand, an Accelerator mechanism will be at work, by which a stock of, say, ten years' worth of machine-services will have to be bought in one transaction and at one moment, in order that the corresponding flow of such services may be at once available. But all this, again, is something quite different from the Kahn Multiplier.

Thirdly, Professor Hegeland draws on Pigou for what Hegeland calls the 'double Say's Law effect'. Suppose that increased efficiency of the workers and others who produce a certain good leads to an increase of their output. The smallest consequent decrease in price, if the price elasticity of demand of the rest of the community (supposedly its preponderant buyers) for this good is infinite, will lead to the whole of the extra output being absorbed. But whence will come the necessary income to buy it? The rest of the community must be supposed to increase their own outputs of the goods they produce, so that they may have the wherewithal to buy the extra output of the first good. Thus there will be increased employment, or at any rate increased work, amongst them. But when (Pigou argues) they bring their increased output to market, it will in its turn elicit extra exertions on the part of the first group of producers, whose price elasticities of demand for the products of the rest of the community are also assumed infinite. Thus both groups of producers, according to Pigou's theory, will increase their exertions and their outputs until a new balance is attained on the basis of the first group's increased productivity. There are many strange features of this argument. A price-elasticity of demand is usually thought of as a measure of the reaction of people with *given* incomes to a price-change of some good on which they spend a very small part of those incomes. It is certainly not inconceivable that the opportunity to buy some commodity more cheaply than heretofore might encourage extra exertion in earning income, but this reaction is not a logical consequence of the supposition of an infinite price-elasticity of demand. That concept belongs to partial, not aggregative analysis. Nor does Pigou seem to follow out his own idea fully. For the original increase of output of the first group's product is due to increased *efficiency*. Thereafter there is a second, due to increased *exertion*. Why does not the rest of the community respond to this second increase of output with a second increase of its own, and so on? At any rate, this is not the Kahn Multiplier.

Fourthly, there is the notion that the numerical value of the Multiplier can be estimated from that of the income velocity of circulation of money: 'I am surprised that [Mr Robertson] should think that those who make sport with the velocity of the circulation of money have much in common with the theory of the multiplier.'* Of all lines of thought which have been supposed to bear on the Multiplier, the most misguided is that of tracing identified 'packets of money' (as it were, particular bundles of banknotes) round the economic system

---

* J. M. Keynes, 'The General Theory of Employment', *Quarterly Journal of Economics*, February 1937.

as though only those incomings and payments-away could be related to each other, which are embodied in one and the same tangible tokens or their equivalent. Such a reduction of economics to hydraulics is not merely unilluminating but positively misleading. Particular firms might, of course, be prevented from increasing their output in response to an increase of orders through being unable to pay for the necessary extra labour, materials and power, that is to say, through having no spare money of their own and being unable to borrow money or to obtain materials, etc. on trade credit. Such a lack of *finance* might no doubt be relieved if it were the universal business practice to make small payments at short intervals instead of large ones at long intervals. The bank balance which each person or firm would then require, in order to mediate a given flow of incomings and outgoings, would on an average over time be smaller, and this fact could be alternatively expressed by saying that the velocity of circulation of the money stock would be faster. It is also true that if the society's aggregate income is increased while its stock of money remains constant, and if the uses other than the mediation of production, income and expenditure, to which money is put, remained unchanged in character and requirements, the velocity of circulation would have increased. But all this is very far from implying a rigid constraint on the numerical value of the Multiplier, imposed by some maximum attainable velocity of circulation of the money stock as a whole, or of that part of it used in mediating the real activities of production and of income payment and disposal. Still less does it mean that the Multiplier is a phenomenon intimately bound up with the mechanics of money circulation. On the contrary, it is an expression and upshot of people's *propensity to consume* some proportion of what they produce. Money has a strong influence on the course of economic events, but its movements neither constitute nor dominate the Kahn Multiplier. The size of expenditure on consumption, which people intend to make, may well be more closely influenced by their *expected* income than by the past income which has already arrived in their pocket or bank account. *Orders* for supplies can be given, by persons or firms, without their having to show the colour of their money on the spot when they give these orders. A firm whose order-book is lengthening will itself give more orders per week, or larger ones, in anticipation of being able to pay 'when the time comes' even if it could not do so at once. Even labour is obtained on a few days' or weeks' credit, and the newly re-employed can get their groceries on a few days' or weeks' credit also. And the Multiplier is a matter of orders and production decisions, not of the thumbing over of cash.

Closely linked with the misconception that the Multiplier principle concerns the mechanical transit of packets of cash from one hand to another, is the confusion between the extra *saving* which the extra general output and income provides, and the *finance* required for the public works or private schemes of investment which are the multiplicand of the Multiplier mechanism. To save is to abstain from consuming during some time-interval some part of the value of what one produces during that interval. To save is to produce without consuming, and is thus to *release*, from the stream of general output, goods which thereupon add themselves (whether according to the plans of business men or the government, or against those plans) to the pre-existing stock of general producers' goods. Realized saving and realized investment, *ex post* quantities, are equal by definition, and this is the meaning of the equation which Professor J. E. Meade, as he now is, contributed to Kahn's thinking on the Multiplier. (For an economy with foreign trade relations, 'investment' or the 'multiplicand' includes the export surplus.) The essence of the Multiplier principle is, indeed, that society has a built-in business mechanism working to increase general output up to that size out of which income-receivers all taken together are *willing* to leave unconsumed a flow of production equal to that which investment decision-makers, i.e. business men and the government, wish to direct into the augmentation of their productive equipment. During, and in aid of, the process of attaining a new balance between the absolute size of the desired or intended saving flow and that of the desired or intended net investment flow, *assets* of different kinds will be exchanged among the members of the society. Firms intending to increase output will sell shares or I.O.U's to the general public or the banks, then the money which they have thus gathered will begin to be paid out as an extra stream of wages and other incomes, in exchange for which the firms will build up a stock of goods in process, which when ready they will start to sell to each other and the public. Out of their extra stream of income earned in producing these goods, the public will buy part of the goods for consumption and, with the remainder of the income, replenish the cash balances which they depleted in buying the firms' shares or I.O.U's; and so on. The Meade equation is an ex post *identity* which does nothing to solve the problem of how *to marshall money in the right place at the right time* for the execution of plans, intentions, decisions; and which has, moreover, nothing to say on the question whether, in any given circumstances, a scheme of public works or other large additional flow of net investment will or will not be 'inflationary'.

The Kahn Multiplier, considered by itself and apart from the Accelerator or any reaction such as Hegeland's early writers refer to as 'psychological', is an equilibrating mechanism. It is an account of the chain of reactions which carries up aggregate income, reflecting the value of general output, to a level where the society's desired saving is equal to its desired investment. It leads from one equilibrium to another. But those early writers, by contrast, were mostly concerned with a cumulative self-reinforcing process of slump or boom in the business cycle. In neoclassical economics the dominant notion, the key to understanding, is that of price, and when writers who had been brought up in this tradition turned to study the business cycle, they saw in it a phenomenon where prices were both mechanism and chief manifestation. In the boom, prices rise, or in the terminology which has survived the outmoded Quantity Theory of money, there is inflation. Thus one preoccupation of those who, before or after Kahn had written in 1931, discussed the potentialities and dangers of schemes of public works as a means of relieving unemployment, was whether such schemes might cause inflation. One of Kahn's best practical contributions was to point out that when there are unemployed productive factors of all kinds, the supply curve of each kind of factor, and therefore that of each product, is likely to be a straight line parallel to the quantity axis, and so an increase of general output can occur without price increases.

Let us turn now to see in more detail what Professor Hegeland has found among pre-Kahnian writers. He says that Jevons's climatic theory of the business cycle 'paved a way of thinking which inspired Bagehot to the first clear statement of the Multiplier principle'. Bagehot says

There is a partnership in industries. No single large industry can be depressed without injury to other industries. Each industry when prosperous buys and consumes the produce probably of most (certainly of very many) other industries, and if industry A fails and is in difficulty, industries B, C and D, which used to sell to it, will not be able to sell that which they had produced in reliance on A's demand. Then as industry B buys of C, D, etc., the adversity of B tells on C, D, etc., and as these buy of E, F, etc., the effect is propagated through the whole alphabet. And in a sense it rebounds. Z feels the want caused by the diminished custom of A, B and C, and so it does not earn so much; in consequence it cannot lay out as much on the produce of A, B and C. The fundamental cause is that under a system in which every one is dependent on the labour of everyone else, the loss of one spreads and multiplies through all, and spreads and multiplies the faster the higher the previous perfection of the system of divided labour.

Interdependence of economic sectors takes two forms. There is Leontief interdependence, the technological need of one kind of activity for the products of others. And there is final-demand interdependence, the fact that goods are bought for final use, in consumption or in net investment, out of incomes earned in producing other goods. It is the second of these which embraces, though not confined to, Kahn's Multiplier, but it is the former which Bagehot seems in our quoted passage to have in mind. Or at best we may say that he is describing generally the consequences of specialization. Kahn's Multiplier is concerned with the Great Categories, not individual and finely distinguished activities. If Bagehot's industry A, whose order-book is the first to decline, is that of road-building contractors, naturally the orders they give for granite or cement will also be reduced, and the orders that quarrymen give for explosives will in turn be reduced, and so on. But when Kahn and Keynes speak of a reduction of the investment flow, we may best understand them to mean that some whole block of technologically linked activities, bounded where the quantitative relations become unimportant, has reduced its output of some products not directly bought by consumers, so that the reduced income of the people who operate this block leaves part of the society's directly consumable output unprovided, at its existing level, with demand. The consequent reduction of a series of activities leading to consumable output, and the further consequences, for demand, of a reduction of incomes earned in these latter activities, and so on, is the Kahn Multiplier effect (working, of course, in the downward direction in contrast to Kahn's own example). Bagehot is not proved by this passage to have been more than vaguely aware of a Multiplier effect, and can, we think, have had no influence in suggesting it to Kahn.

If we consider a Bagehot-Leontief process and suppose it to work upwards, it is plainly true that the ultimate new level of employment of all kinds, and the corresponding new level of general output, will be attained only by successive stages as the activity or sector which receives the first increase of orders gives corresponding extra orders to its own suppliers, and these to their suppliers, and so on. In this sense the increment of production in the first sector appears to be multiplied. But there is a difference, and it is the practically essential one, between this multiplying process and Kahn's. For here the whole finance of the increment of general output is provided by those who give the extra orders to the first-affected activity. Thus if one hundred extra loaves a week are demanded from the baker, the money paid to him for them goes only partly into his own and his workpeople's pockets, while the rest passes to the miller to pay him and his workpeople for grinding each week the extra flour that goes into a hundred loaves. And not all the extra money which the miller receives stays in the mill, but some goes each week to the farmer for the extra grain that provides the flour for a hundred loaves. In a Kahn process, however (or in the Kahnian aspects of Bagehot's process) the initiator of the whole effect need only finance a part of it. He must pay for the extra stream of net investment, that is, of creation of equipment which will augment the existing stock, but he need not pay for the extra streams of consumable output that will be elicited by the spending of those who make the equipment. It is in the aspect of finance that a genuine leverage or amplifying effect is obtained, and it is this aspect which encouraged Keynes and Henderson originally to urge public works upon the British Government in 1929.

Among Hegeland's theorists it was Julius Wulff, a member of the Danish parliament, who earliest described in exact terms a leakage mechanism identical in form with Kahn's. Wulff makes income leak into imports rather than saving. Citing an article by Fr. Johannsen (whom we must distinguish from another Johannsen who will concern us below) in the Danish journal *Ingeniøren* of 1925, Hegeland tells us that

Already in 1896 Julius Wulff computed the secondary effects of public works and of other measures giving rise to changes in total employment by using the multiplier formula. He thus declared that if wages increased by a given sum, say A, due to an increase in employment, 60 per cent would be spent on Danish goods and services whereas the remaining part would be spent on imports, which from the viewpoint of the home market constituted a corresponding amount of leakages. The subsequent increase in receipts at home, 60 per cent of A, would then, in turn, be spent on home production in the same proportion, and so on, thereby giving rise to the following series:

$$A + \tfrac{3}{5}A + (\tfrac{3}{5})^2 A + (\tfrac{3}{5})^3 A + \ldots = \tfrac{5}{2}A$$

Wulff did not receive any acknowledgement of his ideas until three decades later.

Here is the whole Kahn mechanism precisely anticipated, except that a propensity to buy foreign consumable goods is substituted for a propensity to save. The extra sum of wages, A, is evidently paid to men, formerly unemployed, who have just been taken on for a scheme of public works, the product of which will doubtless be something non-consumable. These newly re-employed men have, in Keynesian terms, a propensity to consume of unity, but their consumption-expenditure, though it absorbs the whole of their income, is spent only as to 60 per cent in the home country while the rest goes abroad. The same is true of those who are newly taken on to make extra consumable goods in response to the extra spending. Thus we have as a convergent series of terms the additional streams of output of consumable goods and of the corresponding income, converging in this case to a limit of $\tfrac{5}{2}$ times the original extra wages. The Multiplier, in its formal essentials, was perfectly envisaged by Wulff. We cannot suppose that Lord Kahn had ever heard of him, nor of the journal where his work was described, in Danish, in 1925. Why is there so often, in the world of ideas, a lone premonitory flash of illumination, then a long silence of years before the outbreak of the lightning in earnest? Why Gossen, so brilliant in his obscurity, so long before the great blossoming of the 1870s? Why Wulff and the other Johannsen, a whole generation before Kahn and Keynes? Why Cournot a century before Yntema, Harrod, Mrs Robinson and Chamberlin? Why were indifference-curves utterly disregarded from Edgeworth to Pareto, and from Pareto and Barone to Hicks?

We come now to the second, and better known, of the two men who were real Kahnian precursors, unknown though they were to Kahn. N. A. L. J. Johannsen, a German, must doubtless be regarded as perfectly contemporary with Julius Wulff, neither of them having presumably ever heard of the other, since Joahnnsen's first manuscript was already in the hands of a critic in 1898.

In his analysis of how depressions develop (Professor Hegeland tells us) N.A.L.J. Johannsen realized the cumulative effects of a given decrease in expenditure. The explanation of the cause of the depression simply implies that planned saving exceeds planned investment expenditure, but this is not sufficient to account for the total decline in output. By means of a so-called fundamental example he demonstrates how the initial cause is gradually enlarged because of 'Das Multiplizirende Prinzip'. Johannsen starts with a very simple economy of only five 'trading bodies', A, B, C, D and E situated on an isolated isle. Each of them produces [goods worth] 30 marks per week, of which he retains $\frac{1}{3}$ for his family and sells the remainder to the other four men, from whom he simultaneously buys an equal [value of goods]. Total [marketed] output thus amounts to 100 marks and equals the quantity demanded, being all consumed. Suppose now that A refrains from consuming his income acquired from sales—living, together with his family, only on the 10 marks' worth of his non-marketed production—and uses his receipts for building a barn instead. Of total purchases, 80 marks are thus spent on consumption-goods and 20 marks on investment goods, market equilibrium still being maintained. But suppose that A, when the barn is finished, continues his production of consumption goods for sale and his saving, not undertaking any new investment project. His saving then appears as 'impair' saving [i.e. saving not matched by desired investment] whereas saving that is transformed into (desired) investment is called 'capitalistic saving'. What happens? Johannsen answers as follows. Total production still amounts to 100 marks but total sales to only 80 marks—because of 'impair' saving—out of which 20 marks constitutes A's income, the remaining 60 being equally distributed between B, C, D and E. Hence, their purchases exceed their sales by A's income. Johannsen now supposes that B, C, D and E reduce their purchases during the next period to the same amount as their receipts of the preceding period i.e. to 60 marks. Thus the purchases from each seller, including *A*, are reduced to 12 marks, which implies that *A*'s income also is affected by the decrease in total demand. And this is exactly what Johannsen means by 'Das Multiplizirende Prinzip'.

Johannsen even more than Wulff has captured the essential notion which Kahn eventually crystallized. The Multiplier process begins with the sudden emergence of an excess of intended investment over intended saving or the reverse. The process itself, in case of an excess of investment, is the succession of increments of consumable output elicited from business men by the persistent growth of consumer-spending, a growth for which they themselves are of course, by their successive acts of augmenting output, partly responsible. Johannsen, in Professor Hegeland's account of him, has all these elements. Like all the rest of Hegeland's candidates for the honour of first discoverer, Johannsen describes a downward and not an upward process. This fact itself is enlightening: it shows that before Kahn and Keynes there was no employment theory, only trade cycle theory where general unemployment was a transient phase and not a state of repose. In Johannsen's 'fundamental example' we see, first, that designed investment abruptly declines while intended saving stays the same. And then we see that the consumable output, now partly unwanted and unsaleable, is cut down by its producers, who by that act cut down still further the demand for the remaining output, and so on in a geometrical progression. A discrepancy between saving and investment; more than that: between *ex ante* saving and *ex ante* investment; and the recoil of diminishing employment upon the demand for the goods still being produced. All is there.

The theory of monopolistic competition lay for forty years unnoticed in Marshall's *Principles*, disregarded even by Marshall himself, until the great outburst of rediscovery in the late nineteen twenties. Just so, the Multiplier principle went largely unregarded by professional economists from the time when the 'amateur'* N. A. L. J. Johannsen first propounded it (and

* Contempt for the 'autodidakt' is universal among continental academics. The founders of the Royal Society and the makers of the English industrial revolution, to say nothing of Michael Faraday, would have been beyond the pale. Keynes himself was an 'amateur' amongst probability theorists. And what of Albert Einstein among the mathematicians?

he, after all, showed his ideas at the outset to a professional, Adolf Wagner) until that same era of renewal, and was then re-discovered, in some approximation or hint, by half-a-dozen writers. If the German Johannsen was, perhaps, the most complete anticipator, the Danish contribution was brilliant both early and late. Writing in 1925 and again in 1927, the Danish Johannsen, Director of the Copenhagen Telephone Company, recorded Julius Wulff's idea of 1896 and illustrated it with calculations of his own. The final Danish effort virtually coincided with Kahn's. Professor Hegeland tells us that

Fr Johannsen's writings were studied particularly by his fellow countryman Jens Warming, professor of statistics. Warming objects to Johannsen's view according to which the total amount of employment of the whole world seems to be treated as a given figure. He suggests the idea, often recurring in his later articles, of creating employment by producing goods and services which the re-employed are going to purchase themselves. This is said to mean a real solution of the problem of unemployment and not merely throwing away the problem on some other country. Savings are estimated at 12 to 15 per cent of individual income and Warming correctly perceives their weakening effect on the total increase in production. This is still more evident in a later article published in October 1931, where Warming by means of a hypothetical example demonstrates how new streams of saving will finally amount to the same figure as the original spending, but how, during the process, (desired) investment and (desired) saving do not co-incide. No reference appears in this article to Kahn's analysis, which was published in June 1931, and it may be that Warming had no knowledge of Kahn's contribution when writing his article.

The Danish multiplier theorists were very naturally preoccupied with the situation of a very small country, highly specialized to agriculture and fishing and entirely non-industrialized, without even any coal. In such a country any increment of income was bound to be largely spent on products from abroad. Any import surplus which thus resulted would have, in effect, to be borrowed by Denmark from the rest of the world. Professor Hegeland does not tell us by what detailed measures Warming would have eliminated the newly re-employed people's propensity to import: whether by building factories for making import-substitutes or by cottage industries; but this is not our theoretical concern. What would be the meaning and practical implications of a public programme of 'harmonious' production, where extra streams of various goods would be produced in just those relative quantities in which they could precisely and completely satisfy the extra demand arising from the new incomes earned in producing them, and exactly absorb those incomes? Professor Hegeland points out that there would in such a case be no secondary effects whatever; there would appear to be no Multiplier. But another way of expressing this is simply to say that the new equilibrium, which is attained by the Multiplier process, would be built into the public employment programme, and the *whole* of the new employment, instead of just that part which was engaged on output not available for home consumption, would be publicly financed. Let us, then, glance back over the early work which Professor Hegeland has cited.

These examples compel us to look again at the notion of a Multiplier and ask again what is its essence. Underlying all such phenomena is the interdependence of all sectors and components of the economic society, an interdependence in both the economic and hence in the mathematical sense, arising from specialization of role and product, from 'division of labour'. This interdependence brings it about that an event happening in, or an action taken by, any one sector or individual decision-maker is bound to affect very many, or all, others. However, interdependence is not integrated unity, it does not mean that a single centre of intelligence and decision is in charge of all. On the contrary, there are a multitude of sources of initiative, of decision-makers, each needing to gather, sift and interpret information about the actions of the others in order to decide its own. Thus decisions in the society do not each prescribe the part to be played by every sector, element and individual, making known to all participants and all who are to be affected, precisely their part or designed experience in the affair. A decision, an action, taken by one person or sector, on the reckoning that it will bring advantage to that initiator, can (we may say, must) have repercussions *unforeseen* by that initiator and *unfinanced* by him. 'Multiplier' ratios in unlimited numbers can be calculated as comparisons of mutually related events or movements in distinct sectors or elements of the society. They are interesting and relevant in the Kahnian or Keynesian sense when they describe the *leverage* available to one initiating sector or decision-maker in eliciting reactions on the part of other sectors, for which those others themselves can be counted on to provide the motive power and necessary resources, the 'finance'. Kahn's example showed these features at their clearest. Roads do almost nothing to satisfy the consumption needs of those engaged in building them, while they are so engaged. A road must be completed in some sense and degree before it can be used. Even when complete, it may give a little direct pleasure to travellers, but it cannot directly feed, warm, clothe or house its builders. All but the saved part of their earnings thus goes to stimulate production on the part of others, and these further responses can be left to the self-interest of others to be directed, financed and executed by them, with no further action on the part of the governmental sponsors of the road-building. The meaning of the Kahn Multiplier is in a sense somewhat arbitrary and *ad hoc*. We can choose cases where there is more, and cases where there is less, prevision and control, by the initiating sector, of the later repercussions and responses. The Multiplier can be a measure of the relation to each other of parts of one encompassing design, seen as such by the initiators of action. Or it can be so seen by those seeking to persuade some authority to take action, but not so seen, at first, by this authority itself. The Multiplier principle may be said in this aspect to belong to a fluid stage in the spreading acceptance of economic knowledge. But its practical definition can always rest on the matter of finance. When in Bagehot's picture we see industries successively re-employing each other, we can ask two different questions. If, after a *given* change in the bill of goods for final use, the new bill of goods has an annual value $£A$ greater than the old, how much will be the annual value of the extra employment given to factors of all kinds, that is, how much will be the extra income generated by the productive system as a whole with its new bill of goods for final use, compared with its old? We know that the answer is $£A$ a year. But we can further ask: If such and such an initial change is somehow induced in the bill of goods for final use, what further changes in the bill of goods will be implicit in this initial change, given the tastes and propensities, and perhaps also the expectations, of income-disposers? In particular, if the initial change consists in increasing the outputs of some investment goods, or other 'multiplicand' goods, what will be the ultimate new, equilibrium, bill of goods for final use?

Kahn's precise formalization of the Multiplier idea found Keynes's mind attuned and ready. Keynes and Sir Hubert Henderson had urged already, in their pamphlet of 1929 called *Can Lloyd George Do It?* that the employment-giving effect of public works would not be confined to the hitherto unemployed men who were directly taken on to execute such works or to supply materials and tools for them. These men, having now more income, would demand more consumption goods. Whence would such goods be supplied? The Keynes-Henderson pamphlet saw in this demand for extra consumption goods the source of the extra employment-giving power of public works. But they failed to work out either the mechanism or the arithmetic of the matter. Keynes was grappling with an unfocused problem, and in the *Treatise on Money* we find first appearing in his thought the need for some conception of how the size and use of the flow of available consumption goods is affected when the volume of employment is first increased:

An increase in working capital resulting from an increased volume of production and employment (and not from a lengthening of the productive process) also necessitates investment; but in this case investment does not require any reduction in the level of consumption below what it would have been if the increase in production had not taken place. That is to say, an increase in working capital due to increased employment does not involve an equal abstention from, or a reduction of, current consumption by the community as a whole, as does an increase in fixed capital, but mainly a redistribution of consumption from the rest of the community to the newly employed. When such a transference is effected, there is, in spite of there being no decreased consumption of available income, an increment to the wealth of the community in the shape of an increment of non-available income which serves to increase the volume of net investment—this increment being brought about by increased production and not by diminished consumption. Nevertheless, this too requires diminished consumption *on the part of particular individuals*, namely, those who would otherwise have consumed what is actually being consumed by the newly employed factors of production.*

Some explanation of Keynes's *Treatise* terminology is called for. *Working capital* means goods in process at any stage other than

* J. M. Keynes, *A Treatise on Money*, vol. II, book VI, chapter 28, pp. 124, 125.

that of readiness for sale to consumers or, in the case of durable tools and equipment (*fixed capital* in the *Treatise* language), readiness for use by producers. Its quantity is of course measured by value. *Available income* means that part of general output which is in the form of goods ready for consumption in contrast to output in the form of durable equipment or of additions to goods in process, these latter two categories composing *non-available income*. In this passage Keynes recognizes that men newly taken back into employment with a view to their providing an extra flow of net investment, will have extra income and will spend it on consumption goods. Whence are these to come? The answer of the *General Theory* is that they are likely to come at first from the depletion of stocks of goods ready for consumption (*liquid capital* in the language of the *Treatise*) and very soon from the output of *further* re-employed men taken on to supply the new extra consumption demand, these further men having ultimately to be so many that their voluntary saving-stream, out of their now increased incomes, equals the extra consumption of those engaged in producing the new stream of non-available output. Keynes in our quoted passage was aware of the question whose answer is the Multiplier, but he did not, in the *Treatise*, perceive this answer.

Who, then, first put in print a clear conception of the Multiplier mechanism, as that term is understood by Keynes in the *General Theory* and has an essential place in modern macroeconomics? A score of names from time to time have been canvassed as having made somewhat related suggestions. Nearly all can be dismissed. Some amount to little more than the banality that economic agents demand things from each other, and that services sold by one man provide the income with which he buys the goods of others. Some are total misconceptions, confounding the true Multiplier's propagation of beliefs and stimulation of decisions with the almost irrelevant hydraulics of money. Some mix up the Multiplier with the Accelerator. Dr A. Llewellyn Wright in an article of wide-ranging erudition has discovered one writer whom Professor Hegeland does not mention, who like N. A. L. J. Johannsen, but thirty years later, hit upon the essential notion of increments or decrements of expenditure passed on in a convergent series. In his book *Australia, 1930*, published in 1930, Professor

L. F. Giblin shows precisely by this scheme how a decrement of income due to a reduction of exports, operating through a propensity to consume home goods of two-thirds, would lead eventually to a reduction of income three times as great as the initial reduction of sales of exports. Since the export surplus is as valid and relevant a component of the 'multiplicand' as net investment or as public works expenditure, we might be tempted to say that Professor Giblin had the whole Multiplier mechanism in his mind. However, it would not be quite true to say that there is no essential difference between a Multiplier working downwards and one working upwards. For one of the chief purposes of Lord Kahn's article of 1931 was to demonstrate the absurdity of the idea that investment not induced in the private sector by comparisons of profit and the rate of interest, but superposed, in the form of public works, on private-sector investment, would necessarily cause a general rise of prices, even in conditions of general heavy unemployment. It may be claimed that the upward Multiplier, working in a 'fixprice'* situation, was in 1931 an idea more alien to accepted thought than a downward Multiplier where no inflationary tendency could be in question. Dr Llewellyn Wright's final judgement is in that sense:

Professor Pigou's series was not a multiplier because his damping factor did not consist of a leak, but in doubtful price changes. Mund's analysis, on the other hand, was built on the basis of a leak proportion, but not on the basis of a geometric series. Giblin's analysis conforms to these characteristics and is, therefore, entitled to be regarded as a multiplier analysis. Giblin's model, however, failed to bring out the significance of the concept. It is Professor Kahn's analysis alone which clearly sets out the implications of the fact that consumption and investment might expand *together*. Here is the originality which makes his article the pioneering work in this field.†

* I borrow Sir John Hicks's admirable and self-explanatory coinage. See *Capital and Growth* (Oxford: Clarendon Press, 1965).

† A. Llewellyn Wright, 'The Genesis of the Multiplier Theory', *Oxford Economic Papers*, New Series, vol. 8, no. 2, 1956.

CHAPTER 15

LIQUIDITY PREFERENCE

By a bond we mean a marketable promise by a borrower to pay stated sums at stated future dates to whomever shall at such a date hold the bond. When he hands money to the borrower, the lender cannot know at what price the bond will be saleable at a future date, and he cannot know at what date he may wish to sell it. Thus to lend is to give a known in exchange for an unknown sum of money. To afford the buyer of a bond (whether a bond newly created by a borrower, or an old one) some presumption of getting back at least as much as he pays, and to compensate him for the irksome uncertainty of not knowing how much he will get back, the market will price bonds at less than the sum of the remaining payments due from the borrower. The percentage per annum (or other unit interval) which if used for discounting all the borrower's remaining promised payments to a given date, makes the sum of the discounted payments equal to the then price of the bond, is the interest-rate on that bond at that time. Interest exists, and is positive, because of the lender's inescapable uncertainty. Its rate is determined on the bond market. For if at one date a bond promising stated sums at stated deferments from that date can be bought more cheaply than the price, at some other date, of the promise of the same sums at the same respective deferments from this other date, the rate of interest is lower at this other date. By what set of influences, and by what mode of their interaction, then, are prices governed in the bond market?

All those bonds which at some moment offer roughly similar schedules of deferred payments (so that equal payments at any one randomly chosen deferment are promised by each of these bonds) form a class of assets or means of holding wealth. Many other classes are at all times available to the wealth-owner, and these include bonds offering markedly different schedules of deferred payments; shares in companies; land, buildings and their contents; and money. A free market will at all times value each such class of asset at such a price that all the existing stock of this class can find willing holders. If any items are in the hands of unwilling holders, the matter can be adjusted either by exchange of ownership or by change of relative market valuations; for a wealth-owner must accept some one or other kind of asset. Transactions are not essential to a market dealing in stocks of assets to hold rather than in flows of products to use up: enquiries rather than actual exchanges can serve to establish prices; or the announcement of the prices of a few transactions can enable the mass of holders to decide whether to sell, buy or retain. An active participant in the market will not be willing to retain an asset when he is convinced that its price in terms of other assets is about to fall. This principle applies to the prices of bonds in terms of money, and thus it has been justly said that today's interest-rate is influenced by expectations of tomorrow's; and this proposition has been supposed, with no justice, to mean that the rate of interest 'hauls itself up by its own bootstraps'. The desire to have one's wealth in the form of money is, however, influenced by other considerations besides that of expected changes in the money prices of non-money assets; and thus the motives of the asset market, in so far as they affect the price of bonds, can be conveniently summarized under the heading of desire to hold money; or, as Keynes called it, *liquidity preference*. Keynes did not express the matter quite as we have expressed it in the foregoing; but what we have here said about the mechanism or interplay of considerations which governs interest-rates flows directly from what he did say. My own endeavour has been to refute the 'bootstraps' argument by a new statement of the liquidity preference theory in one sentence: the origin of positive interest is the lender's inescapable uncertainty concerning what he will in fact get back from a given sum lent now.

The accountancy of business and of everyday life requires a *unit* of account. If every account could be so managed that its inflows and outflows equalled each other at every moment, every account could at all times have a zero balance, and money, in any other sense than that of a purely abstract unit, need not exist. Such an arrangment being impossible, stocks of generalized purchasing power do at all times exist and are necessary to the working of our system of exchange. People or businesses who are about to make payments need to command sufficient money for the purpose. This motive for keeping a stock of bank notes, bank balances or unused bank overdraft permission, Keynes called the transactions motive, or, when the purpose is to pay for expensive blocks of equipment, the finance motive. There is thus a basic reason for the existence of a money in the sense of a stock of generalized purchasing power, comprising the three types of money mentioned above. When such a money exists, people, firms and governments will be continually wanting to borrow it from each other. But lending, we saw, involves uncertainty and thus calls for a positive rate of interest, the expectation of changes in which provides a further reason for sometimes desiring to hold money, not for making payments but as an asset. This is the 'speculative motive' for 'preferring liquidity'. Keynes distinguished further a precautionary motive. But the bonds of a solid borrower, when a nearly perfect market for such bonds exists, are as well able as money to provide a fund for sudden contingencies, except only when there is grave doubt about how their price may behave. But *that* doubt is merely the speculative motive. When we have properly conceived and expressed the transactions motive and the speculative motive for holding a stock of money, no separate precautionary motive remains.

One great enigma to this day afflicts the theory of interest. Bonds are all the time being created in exchange for loans of money, others are all the time being cancelled in part or whole in exchange for repayments of money. In general the stock of bonds is thus continually being added to or depleted. The excess in money value of the bonds which were issued on some day over those which were cancelled on that day is necessarily equal to the excess of the money which was paid for new bonds on that day over the money which was repaid for old bonds on that day. These two measurements of one aspect of one past day's transactions, being both of them measurements of the same thing, are necessarily equal. So far as the repayments are concerned, they were stipulated, perhaps, in the terms of the original loans. But what induced lenders to make fresh loans, exceeding the repayments of that day by the amount which we observe to have occurred? What induced borrowers to issue new bonds in excess of cancellations to just the amount which we observe to have occurred? The necessary equality of the two sides of any transaction *which actually occurs* is assured by logic. But what induces that transaction to occur? The market induces it by suggesting a *price* to which both lender and borrower can agree. The total net addition, per day, hour, or minute, to the stock of outstanding bonds becomes what it does become because a larger net addition would not, in those complete market circumstances which include the beliefs and the resources of every potential dealer in it, find lenders willing to lend at terms which would make borrowers want to borrow that larger amount; and because a smaller net addition would not, in those entire market circumstances, find that lenders were content to lend only that smaller net addition at terms as attractive as those which borrowers would offer for it. The rate of interest, or the skein of various rates for various types of loan, are required by the nature and purpose of the market to balance the quantities of net new bonds and net new money which, in some proper-named interval, the two sides are willing to exchange. Because each of the two quantities refers to a time-interval of stated length, each is a *flow*, and so we may say that the interest-rate is required to select, from the range of potential sizes of *flow of net lending*, and from the range of potential sizes of *flow of net bond-issuing*, a pair which are equal. But the market in which new bonds are bought and sold is the market in which old bonds are bought and sold. The very same interest-rate variables which have the task of matching the willingness of lenders, and the willingness of borrowers, to create a net addition to the stock of bonds, have also the task of matching the willingness of holders or potential holders of existing bonds with the quantity of existing bonds requiring to be held. The enigma and dilemma of interest-rate theory is whether the interest-rate, or the system of simultaneously prevailing rates, can do both of these things together; or, if it does appear to do them in fact, how we are to conceive its mode of achieving this result.

Keynes's resolution of this dilemma is part of the core of his theory of employment. If we can conceive of the interest-rate being determined only on a market for net new lendings and borrowings, and if, alternatively, we can conceive of its being determined only on a market for old bonds, the two rates, thus determined in otherwise similar circumstances, might differ from each other. This implicit conflict, however, is solved by *force majeure.* Within any brief interval that we care to select, the quantity of old bonds that can be released on to the market for sale, or the quantity of money, held hitherto as an asset, that can be released for the purchase of bonds, by a change of the interest-rate, is overwhelmingly greater than the quantity of net new borrowing and lending that might be induced by the same change. The market for old and new bonds combined is dominated by the vast stock of old bonds and by the great mass of money which at all times exists in the hands of those individuals or firms who for the moment fear a price-fall of securities. Against these great pre-existing masses, always poised for release on to the market by any sufficient movement of the interest-rate, little influence can be exerted by the quantities of new bond issues, or of savings newly accumulated, within a brief past interval, in the hands of those waiting to return them, via purchase (directly or indirectly) of new bond issues, to the business community. It is thus that the interest-rate, or the system of rates, can be too high to allow full employment. For if an economic system were conceivable, where the interest-rate was determined only by the supply of new bonds for the finance of net investment and the demand for such bonds as the sole destination of new saving, the outcome might balance the saving-flow out of a full-employment aggregate income with the net investment flow planned in those conditions by business men, and thus full employment would be secured. 'Liquidity preference' is an explanation of the level of interest-rates which relieves them of their duty or their competence to equalize the full-employment intended saving-flow with the full-employment intended net investment flow, and leaves them free to be 'too high' for this equalization, so that there is general heavy unemployment as there was in the 1930s; or to be 'too low' for this equalization, so that there is a persisting rise of the general price-level, as there has been from 1945 to 1965.

General heavy unemployment occurs when a society desires to save a larger proportion of its income than that which arises from the production of goods intended by business men, or by the government, as net augmentations or improvements of the society's stock of equipment. If there exists a mechanism which prevents any such excess, there can be no general heavy unemployment. But the theory of value, which until the 1930s was the whole central body of economic theory, explains interest as the price which brings to equality the desire of a society to save and its temptation to invest. Thus Keynes imperatively needed to find an explanation for interest which could displace and disprove the established one, and he had already done so when he wrote the *Treatise*. We have already quoted a passage in which the stock-versus-flow conflict is resolved in favour of stocks:

The decision as to holding bank-deposits or securities relates, not only to the current increment to the wealth of individuals, but also to the whole block of their existing capital. Indeed, since the current increment is but a trifling proportion of the block of existing wealth, it is but a minor element in the matter.*

Keynes's theory of employment also explains what happens when the two modes of determination of interest (if these distinct modes are conceived to be both in operation) are in conflict with each other. Suppose that the 'stock' mechanism, being dominant, has carried the rate of interest above the level which would have resulted from the 'flow' mechanism operating alone, and that at this high level the society's desired saving flow exceeds its desired net investment flow. Since, *ex post*, these flows must by logical necessity be equal, we have to explain how it comes about that one or other or both of the realized flows differs from its corresponding intended flow. The first result of disparity may be that some goods, intended for immediate sale to consumers, will be left with their producers and constitute unintended investment. Later it seems likely, or inevitable, that production as a whole will be reduced. Out of the smaller income which measures this lower production, the society will desire to save less than it had formerly hoped to out of its former relatively large income. Too high an interest-rate will have caused unemployment and a reduced general output. If the 'flow' mechanism is prevented (by the dominant 'stock' mechanism) from performing its task at a high level of general output and aggregate incomes it will compel the reduction of that output and income to a level where it can perform its task. Keynes's theory of employment *requires* the supposition that the 'stock' mechanism is, or at least can be, dominant.

* *A Treatise on Money*, chapter III, section (iii).

In interest-theory as elsewhere, the *Treatise on Money* was a livelier and more zestful, a far more relaxed and genial book than the *General Theory*. The 1920s were not economically a good time for Britain, but they were a time of confidence in a peaceful future, they were not the grim and menacing 1930s. Keynes in writing the *General Theory* faced a personal intellectual crisis. The *Treatise* had had its decisive novelty, but nonetheless its carefully elaborated connections with orthodox Quantity Theory. Its concern (ostensibly, and at its inception) was with an orthodox problem, the governance of the value of money. But in the *General Theory* Keynes had something to say that was going, if accepted, to subvert the body of established doctrine and reverse its political injunctions. Could he produce and perfect a genuine solution of the great enigma of general unemployment? Would the key which he believed he had found really turn in the lock? This was the source of that *angst* which shows at many places through the brilliant and incisive phrases of the *General Theory*.

Looked on as a formal system rather than a Treatise on Human Nature and the Human Condition, Keynes's theory of employment has at its heart the rate of interest, and the rate of interest in its turn has as its central nerve the speculative motive for holding money. The theory of the speculative motive is presented in the *Treatise on Money*. It appears there with a lively naturalness, as part of the description of the business world which Keynes was passing on from the *cognoscenti* like himself, the frequenters of the City, to the academic world of economists; it has the air of a mere familiar piece of knowledge, obvious enough to the experts, who had only to reflect upon their everyday experience to be aware of it. Yet, except for the ultimate foundation, the appeal to the inhibiting effects of uncertainty on investment decisions and the unmanageable consequences of the struggle to ignore this uncertainty, upon which in the end the whole theory of employment was seen to rest, it is the 'speculative' theory of interest that claims our admiration for its originality and novelty more than any other single idea in either book. The *Treatise* is, in large part, an analysis of the economy's total need for a stock of money into various sources of demand, and of the mutual struggle of these various component demands each to satisfy itself at the expense of the others. The questions it seeks to answer are concerned with the relative adequacy of the stock of money which the banking system supplies, to the various purposes, taken singly and together, which this stock must serve in this or that set of circumstances. The rate of interest, or the system of rates, comes in as the policy instrument of the banking system for regulating the size of the stock. The monetary authorities are credited with a powerful measure of control over the size of the total stock and are supposed to exercise it largely by changes of 'Bank Rate' and the system of other bank lending rates which by convention move with the central bank's official rate.

In what does the stock of money consist? What is to be included in money? In this regard the *Treatise* raises a question of high theoretical and practical importance, decisively answers it, but then lets it fall completely, and in its statistical discussions ignores it:

We have characterized *cash-deposits* as furnishing the ready command over money which is required for the convenient transaction of current payments. But the analysis is complicated, in a modern community, by the fact that a cash-deposit is not the only means of providing this facility. It is provided, equally well, by the *overdraft*. A customer of a bank may draw a cheque against his deposit, thus diminishing his *credit* with the bank: but he may, equally well, draw a cheque against his overdraft, thus increasing his *debit* with the bank. It is just as effective to pay by increasing the debit balance of the debtor and decreasing the debit balance of the creditor as it is by decreasing the credit balance of the former and increasing the credit balance of the latter.*

In other words, unused overdraft permission is money, and ought for all logical and practical purposes to be included in measurements of the stock of money. It is perfectly possible that a section of the community might run its affairs entirely by such transfers from firm to firm of these borrowing facilities, and those business deposits B, the money used in their business by members of the Stock Exchange, whose extremely high apparent velocity needs some special explanation, may perhaps largely consist of such facilities.

The *Treatise* offers us a four-fold scheme of the non-bank

---

* *Treatise*, book I, chapter 3 (iii).

community's demands for stocks of money (all kinds of which are here included in 'deposits'):

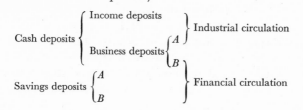

The *General Theory* would place all of these, except the savings deposits, under the head of the Transactions Motive. The savings deposits alone are held, not in readiness to make payments, but as a form in which to store wealth, an asset. The Speculative Motive applies only to the savings deposits.

The income deposits and the business deposits *A* together compose that part of the money stock which is used in production and consumption. Looked on as a stream continuously flowing round a closed system of channels, these two classes of deposits are a unity which Keynes calls the industrial circulation. Some part of this stream flows out from each employer in two directions, on one hand towards the hired factors of production and on the other towards firms who supply this firm with materials, power or services. From these other firms again it flows partly to employees and partly to yet other firms, and so on. Eventually the whole *value added* of the community in any year has been paid out to its factors of production. From these it flows back again partly by their consumption spending and partly by their eventual purchases of bonds and shares out of their saving. The business deposits *A* are thus a reservoir fed by the revenue or the capital-seeking of firms and drained by their out-payments for means of production, while the income deposits are a reservoir fed by the earnings of the factors of production and drained by their consumption or, via the savings deposits, by their purchase of bonds or shares. These two reservoirs compose the industrial circulation, the first of the two great divisions into which the total stock of money falls. The other is the financial circulation, made up to two remarkably and doubly contrasted portions.

Business deposits *B* are the money used on the Stock Exchange. If indeed all stock and share transactions were paid for by cheque drawn on a credit balance, the velocity of these deposits would seem extremely high, for the total annual value of such transactions is many times the flow of the industrial circulation, while it is inconceivable that Stock Exchange firms could have at their disposal a quantity of positive bank balances comparable to the industrial circulation. If they had, there would be no need for them to remain in business, they could retire upon the interest of their money. If, then (contrary to reason but in conformity with statistical practice), we include as money only those sums which banks *owe* to their customers and not those which they are *ready to provide them with*, we must regard business deposits B as a very small part of the financial circulation but a part having a tremendous velocity, while the rest of the financial circulation, by far the greater part of it, is regarded by Keynes in the *Treatise* as having a zero velocity. For this other part is the savings deposits, the holding of which has to be made worth while by a suitably low level of the interest-rate.

In Keynes's intersecting classification which we have schematized above, the industrial circulation and the business deposits B together compose the cash deposits. Between these cash deposits and the savings deposits

the broad distinction is clear, and can be expressed as follows: the amount of the savings deposits depends upon the comparative attractions, in the mind of the depositor, of this and of alternative securities; whilst the amount of the cash-deposits depends upon the volume and the regularity of what he receives and pays by means of cheques and the length of the interval between receipts and expenditure.*

This passage has many interesting points, not least of which is its clear suggestion that the attraction of savings deposits is a matter of individual judgment, taste and circumstances, which presumably, therefore, will bear upon the 'price' of savings deposits. Another such point is more puzzling. It is plainly suggested that the non-bank community, by the decisions of its constituent individuals, can control or powerfully influence the amounts of both the savings deposits and the cash deposits, and consequently their sum, the quantity of money. The *General Theory*, by contrast, is more prone to treat the quantity of money as something given, an upshot of central monetary authority

* *Treatise*, book I, chapter 3 (ii), p. 38.

decisions to which the non-bank community must respond as best it may. Keynes of the *Treatise* seems, in fact, to have looked on the banking system as more passive, more subservient and more *able* to be subservient to the commercial needs of the country, while Keynes of the *Theory* thought of the system as strongly directed from the centre. It is hard to tell whether this appearance has any solid foundation. We may ask ourselves how, supposing the non-bank community came at some time to like savings deposits less in comparison with bonds or shares, it was able to reduce the quantity of savings deposits as distinct from altering their price, the interest-differential which was sacrificed by holding them instead of bonds. For those who buy bonds do not *destroy* deposits, they merely transfer them to the sellers of the bonds; unless those sellers are banks. To suppose that the non-bank holders of savings deposits can, as a body, reduce the amount of those deposits is to suppose that the banks readily sell bonds to that community as soon as it shows a stronger taste for them and begins to drive up their price. Keynes of the *Theory* ascribes no such complaisance to the banking system:

It is impossible for the actual amount of hoarding to change as a result of decisions on the part of the public, so long as we mean by 'hoarding' the actual holding of cash. For the amount of hoarding must be equal to the quantity of money (or—on some definitions— to the quantity of money *minus* what is required to satisfy the transactions-motive); and the quantity of money is not determined by the public. All that the propensity of the public towards hoarding can achieve is to determine the rate of interest at which the aggregate desire to hoard becomes equal to the available cash. The habit of overlooking the relation of the rate of interest to hoarding may be a part of the explanation why interest has been usually regarded as the reward of not-spending, whereas in fact it is the reward of nothoarding.*

Interest is explained by liquidity preference in the *Treatise* as it is in the *Theory*, but the contrast of methods or of outlook between the two books is scarcely less evident here than in the discussion of profits and prices. The *formal* tools of the *General Theory* are stable functions and the concept of equilibrium:

Liquidity preference is a potentiality or functional tendency, which fixes the quantity of money which the public will hold when the rate

* *The General Theory of Employment, Interest and Money*, chapter 13, p. 174.

of interest is given; so that if r is the rate of interest, M the quantity of money and L the function of liquidity preference, we have $M = L\ (r)$. This is where, and how, the quantity of money enters the economic scheme.

Yet only the mutability of such functions, their proneness to change their form at each breath of 'news' or suggested re-interpretation of circumstances, can convey the essence of liquidity preference, which makes interest the outgrowth of un-certainty. In the *Treatise* we seem to see the tides of opinion sweeping round the City, their own later state and movement affected by the consequences of their earlier state. The *Treatise* is dynamic, almost in the modern sense and manner. Having defined savings deposits A as 'a stable sub-stratum held for personal reasons and likely to change in amount only slowly', Keynes describes the psychology underlying Savings deposits B:

A 'bear' is one who prefers at the moment to avoid securities and lend cash, and correspondingly a 'bull' is one who prefers to hold securities and borrow cash—the former anticipating that securities will fall in cash value and the latter that they will rise. Now when bullish sentiment is on the increase, there will be a tendency for savings deposits to fall. The amount of this fall will depend upon how completely the rise in security prices relatively to the short-term rates of interest offsets the bullishness of sentiment. But (apart from compensating variations in the requirements of the Industrial Circulation) the volume of savings deposits can only be maintained or increased in face of an increase of bullish sentiment, if the banking system directly brings about the rise in security prices by itself buying securities or if it takes advantage of the fact that *differences* of opinion exist between different sections of the public so that, if one section is tempted by easy credit to borrow for the purpose of buying securities speculatively, security-prices can be raised to a level at which another section of the public will prefer savings deposits. Thus the actual level of security prices is, as we have seen in chapter 10, the resultant of the degree of bullishness of opinion and of the be-haviour of the banking system.

'The level of security prices' is, of course, another expression for the level of the interest-rate, since any such rate is the annual percentage at which a borrower's outstanding promised pay-ments must be discounted to make their present value equal to their market price. If we are willing to put sufficient weight on Keynes's references to the responsiveness or activity of the banking system, so that we do not feel troubled by the question how the quantity of money can be varied by the actions of the non-bank public, the foregoing passage is a better account of liquidity preference, because more impregnated with the feel of markets and their constant tip-toe alertness to every breath of suggestion, than is to be found in the *General Theory*.

In the *Treatise* we are told of the wild intricate play of market forces, the forces of the game of self-interested catch-as-catch-can endeavour, the urgent, watchful, anxious and temerarious speculative struggle. In the *Theory* this account has been tamed and civilized. There is a curious bifocal quality about chapter 13 of the *Theory*, where the elusiveness, the moment-to-moment mutability and the unformulable complexity of the interest-rate 'weather' is allowed to appear, and is then brushed aside, and a tidy model is presented which shows the community's desired stock of money as a smooth function of the interest-rate. The comparison of those two books is that of romantic versus classic; the novel with its varied twists and shifts versus the Greek tragedy with its fateful and unified march of development. Keynes in the *Theory*, as many years earlier in the *Treatise on Probability*, wishes to make order and certainty out of what he had himself shown to be uncertain and lacking in the necessary basis of complete explanation. In economic theory, conduct is a rational coping with circumstances; in real life it is a leaf blown in the wind. For some reason (why, is a question that concerns us in this book) Keynes, when he came to rewrite the *Treatise*, felt driven to mathematize it, to bring it into line, in *form*, with the 'classical' (the neo-classical) analysis of whose content he so much despaired.

Liquidity is general purchasing power of known nominal amount available at any time. In a properly-working economy, money best answers this description, because in such an economy, the exchange of any non-money object for another object must be made via money, and thus the definition is twice violated, for the exchange *into* money will both take time and involve uncertainty as to the nominal quantity of general purchasing power, that is, the quantity of money, that will be available. In a modern economy, moreover, the statement is not circular, for there is a money-unit which has none but a book-keeping existence and serves (even in the form of token coins) none but a book-keeping purpose, and thus can be recognized independently of the question whether it *best* embodies a known amount of ever-available purchasing power. In chapters 13 and 15, Keynes distinguishes three reasons why a stock of money may be desired. 'Convenience in the transaction of current business', or 'bridging the interval between the receipt of income (or sale-proceeds) and its disbursement' are unsatisfactory accounts of one such reason, for we are led to ask, as Hicks in his 'Suggestion for Simplifying the Theory of Money' (*Economica*, New Series, no. 5, vol. II) had already done, why money received and not immediately wanted should not be lent at interest. The precautionary motive is the desire for a stock of money 'To provide for contingencies requiring sudden expenditure and for unforeseen opportunities of advantageous purchases, and also to hold an asset of which the value is fixed in terms of money to meet a subsequent liability fixed in terms of money'. Contingencies, opportunities and liabilities could all be provided for by non-liquid assets, if only the price obtainable for each such asset at an unforeseeable moment and without notice was knowable for certain in advance and was not less than the price so obtainable after some delay. But the non-fulfilment of these conditions is what generates the speculative motive, and we must maintain that the precautionary motive has no separate existence from it. We shall return later to the transaction motive as treated by Hicks in the article which we have cited. Meanwhile we turn to Keynes's account of the speculative motive in chapters 13 and 15 of the *General Theory*.

Keynes starts by pointing out that no speculative motive could operate if the interest-rates which were going to prevail for every kind and maturity of loan at every future date were known for certain. He is not content, however, merely to refer to the fact that such present knowledge of future interest-rates would amount to present knowledge of future bond prices, which, therefore, could not be the object of speculation. He presents in detail the idea, not relevant to his theme, that a knowledge of future interest-rates would imply a set of definite relations amongst the rates prevailing at present for loans of different maturities. This digression gives a needless air of complication to a simple inference from the unarguable fact of *uncertainty* about future rates. Knowledge of the future, in the sense of the possession of facts which cannot be wrong, is a self-contradictory combination of words. Such knowledge, if conceivable in relation to interest-rates, and if possessed by everybody, would of course eliminate any *differences* of opinion about future rates and bond prices, and thus the whole monetary machinery would be utterly changed in character. This character as Keynes sees it is admirably summarized on p. 171 of the *General Theory*:

If the liquidity preferences due to the transactions-motive and the precautionary-motive are assumed to absorb a quantity of cash which is not very sensitive to changes in the rate of interest as such and apart from its reactions on the level of income, so that the total quantity of money, less this quantity, is available for satisfying liquidity preferences due to the speculative motive, the rate of interest and the price of bonds have to be fixed at the level at which the desire on the part of certain individuals to hold cash (because at that level they feel 'bearish' of the future of bonds) is exactly equal to the amount of cash available for the speculative motive. Thus each increase in the quantity of money must raise the price of bonds sufficiently to exceed the expectations of some 'bull' and so influence him to sell his bonds for cash and join the 'bear' brigade.

In this and a number of other passages Keynes speaks as though the quantity of money desired on account of the speculative motive was predominantly governed simply by the level of the interest-rate; in other words, as though this quantity were a stable function of a single other variable. Yet the speculative motive is an expression of *uncertainty*; it depends on expectations so mutable and precarious that *opposite* ones are normally held by two camps of even strength and equal expertness. It seems obvious that the relation between the level of the interest-rate and the 'Bear' demand for cash must be extremely changeable, and that, in fact, the relevant functional dependence involves not just the one 'independent' variable but a host of influences, so that if we insist on drawing a curve relating the interest-rate to the demanded quantity of speculative money, this curve must be looked upon as a thread floating in a gusty wind, continually liable to change its form not only because of 'the news', but even because of a change in the total quantity of money itself. Keynes's own position on this matter seems changeable:

As a rule, we can suppose that the schedule of liquidity preference relating the quantity of money to the rate of interest is given by a smooth curve which shows the rate of interest falling as the quantity of money is increased. In the first place, as the rate of interest falls, more money will be absorbed by the transactions motive. In the second place, every fall in the rate of interest may increase the quantity of cash which certain individuals will wish to hold because their views as to the future of the rate of interest differ from the market views. It is interesting that the stability of the system and its sensitiveness to changes in the quantity of money should be so dependent on the existence of a *variety* of opinion about what is uncertain.*

A stable function involving only the two variables, quantity and interest-rate, is at first envisaged in chapter 15:

Experience indicates that the aggregate demand for money to satisfy the speculative motive usually shows a continuous response to gradual changes in the rate of interest, i.e. there is a continuous curve relating changes in the demand for money to satisfy the speculative motive and changes in the rate of interest as given by changes in the prices of bonds and debts of various maturities. Indeed, if this were not so, open market operations would be impracticable. In normal circumstances, [however], the banking system is in fact always able to purchase (or sell) bonds in exchange for cash by bidding the price of bonds up (or down) in the market by a modest amount.†

But in the next paragraph the other aspect appears:

In dealing with the speculative motive it is, however, important to distinguish between the changes in the rate of interest which are due to changes in the supply of money available to satisfy the speculative motive, without there having been any change in the liquidity-function, and those which are primarily due to changes in expectation affecting the liquidity function itself. Open-market operations may, indeed, influence the rate of interest through both channels; since they may not only change the volume of money, but may also give rise to changed expectations concerning the future policy of the Central Bank or of the Government.‡

From a detached and general viewpoint, we have in such a case as this the choice of two approaches. We can have in mind a functional relation which formally associates two variables only, but which is highly unstable and mutable in its form, through

* *General Theory*, chapter 13, pp. 171, 172.
† *Ibid.* chapter 15, p. 197.
‡ *Ibid.* chapter 15, pp. 197, 198.

the action of extra variables upon the numerical values of its parameters. Or we can include these other variables in a more penetrating functional association, which may then be deemed stable. Why did Keynes apparently regard the former method as natural and inevitable? He was, in the first place, a Cambridge economist steeped in Marshallian 'two-by-two-ism'. But secondly, he was here interested in the effects of changes in the quantity of money. Such changes were, in the conception he deemed relevant, the fountain-head, and if the influence of these changes could be seen to flow through many complex and shifting channels, still they converged in the end upon the interest-rate and worked, in Keynes's *Theory* view, almost solely through it. Moreover Keynes wishes to contrast a sinking of the interest-rate, occupying time and due to a gradual increase of the quantity of money in existence, and representable by a movement *along* a liquidity curve of unchanged form, with an abrupt alteration of the rate due to an abrupt alteration of the form ('shape and position') of the curve:

Changes in the liquidity function itself, due to a change in the news which causes revision of expectations, will often be discontinuous, and will, therefore, give rise to a corresponding discontinuity of change in the rate of interest.*

And then there comes a passage which one would suppose was never read, and certainly was never understood, by those critics who continued to think of the interest-rate as determined by a duty of equilibrating two *flows* and as governed by transactions:

Only, indeed, in so far as the change in the news is differently interpreted by different individuals or affects individual interests differently will there be room for any increased activity of dealing in the bond market. If the change in the news affects the judgement and the requirements of every one in precisely the same way, the rate of interest (as indicated by the prices of bonds and debts) will be adjusted forthwith to the new situation without any market transactions being necessary.†

It is now, quite at the end of the formal interest-rate discussion, that we come upon a piece of the ultimate foundations of Keynes's theory of the nature of business. It is his answer to the question: If all enterprise is sustained only by expectation, and

---

* P. 198.   † *General Theory*, chapter 15, p. 198.

expectation is mere conjecture or invention about something (to wit, the future) which in the nature of things cannot be observed and hence cannot be the object of any real knowledge, what is it that can lend any appearance of even short-term stability and consistency to the conduct of business? His answer is that men desire, and therefore assume, the reality and meaningfulness of some 'normality'. They accord some authority to what *is*. They assume that things will in some degree go on as they are, or as they have broadly been in the past, in at least a few fundamental respects. There is a tacit, instinctive *convention* to believe in the rightness and reassertive power of things as they have known them, broadly, to be. The interest-rate is Keynes's first and most impressive example of this. It is a main source of the *actual* stability that shows itself in the bond-market. The further the interest-rate falls below some narrow band of 'normal' levels, to which (so it is assumed) it is bound eventually to return, the larger the capital losses to which buyers of bonds at these high prices expose themselves. The smaller, also, is the yield by which the 'coupon' income from these bonds rewards them for taking these risks. So interest-rates are constrained within some lower limits the operation of which reinforces the belief in the existence of a 'normal' range of interest-rates. For when bond prices are high but have not *risen* for some little time, their promise of further capital gains begins to fade, the risks of holding them at their high prices become more insistent, and a movement to sell may begin. But this will start the price downwards, and the whole fabric of hopes on which the price climbed to these high levels will collapse. The 'normal' will have reasserted itself, dragging back the interest-rate to the safety of the conventional zone. At 'abnormally' high rates there is an evident capital gain to be made by buying and waiting for the return to normality. 'Normal', however, need by no means mean 'what corresponds to full employment'. There is no mechanism whatever which leads men to adjust their ideas of a 'normal' zone of interest-rates to that level which would induce, in the other prevailing circumstances, a flow of net investment sufficient to fill the full-employment saving-gap between production and consumption.

In chapter 15, Keynes writes the society's total desired stock M of money as the sum of two parts, M_1 which is desired for transactions and precautionary reasons, and is regarded by him as a function of aggregate income Y, and M_2 which is desired for 'speculative' reasons (i.e. distrust of the impending movements of money prices of assets other than money), and is regarded as a function of the interest-rate r:

$$M = M_1 + M_2 = L_1(Y) + L_2(r).$$

The 'liquidity preference' theory of the interest-rate asserts, of course, that r will seek that level where, when there has been time for the designed net investment flow to adjust itself to the interest-rate and for general output (= aggregate income) to adjust itself to the new net investment flow, L_1 will leave enough out of the *actual* total stock of money to satisfy L_2 at this interest-rate. Keynes is chiefly interested in L_2:

Finally there is the question of the relation between M_2 and r. We have seen in chapter 13 that *uncertainty* as to the future course of the rate of interest is the sole intelligible explanation of the type of liquidity preference L_2 which leads to the holding of cash M_2. It follows that a given M_2 will not have a definite quantitative relation to a given rate of interest of r:—what matters is not the *absolute* level of r but the degree of its divergence from what is considered a fairly *safe* level of r, having regard to those calculations of probability which are being relied on. Nevertheless, there are two reasons for expecting that, in any given state of expectation, a fall in r will be associated with an increase in M_2. In the first place, if the general view as to what is a safe level of r is unchanged, every fall in r reduces the market rate relatively to the 'safe' rate and therefore increases the risk of illiquidity [i.e. the risk involved in being illiquid]; and in the second place, every fall in r reduces the current earnings from illiquidity, which are available as a sort of insurance premium to offset the risk of loss on capital account.

There is here illustrated another facet of Keynes's art of thought. A change of expectations, since its possible causes and its possible natures are infinitely diverse and beyond all survey, can have any effect we care to conceive. Thus the *analysable* region of economic events consists in those chains of cause and effect, or those internal structures of situation, which exist in the presence of a *given* 'state of expectation'. The notion of a *state of expectation* which can be supposed unchanging for a certain span of time or of events, but which is essentially fragile and radically

changeable from unnumbered sources which no one can foresee, is his special version of *ceteris paribus*. It lends to Keynesian
economics an exceptional power to combine reasoning and
realism. It was adopted and used with great effect in the years
after the second world war by Professor Joan Robinson, who
has always been the most in-seeing and skilful interpreter and
user of the pure Keynesian method. Keynes's tool of thought
in the passage we have quoted is that of a function, associating
values of M_2 and r, which is stable and unchanging in form for
so long as we care to suppose the general state of expectation
to be unchanged. If the *actually existing* quantity of money can
change without changing the state of expectation, then the
mutually associated movements of r, Y, M_1 and M_2 can be
thought of as movements *along* the curves $M_1 = L_1(Y)$ and
$M_2 = L_2(r)$. Keynes draws from his theory of the *conventional*
nature of the interest-rate a conclusion for practical policy:

Thus a monetary policy which strikes public opinion as being experi-
mental in character or easily liable to change may fail in its objective
of greatly reducing the long-term rate of interest, because M_2 may
tend to increase almost without limit in response to a reduction of r
below a certain figure.

Ten years after the publication of the *General Theory*, the
'Dalton incident' gave to these words a dramatic illustration.
During the latter half of 1946 the stock of money in the United
Kingdom was increased by some 10 per cent in addition to the
seasonal increase. The yield of consols was reduced from 3 to $2\frac{1}{2}$
per cent. Within the first few months of 1947, after a Treasury
miscalculation in the price of a new issue, and after the fuel
crisis, the yield sprang up to a higher level than where it had
begun, while the stock of money continued to rise.

We come now to one of the most remarkable papers contributed to the journals of theory in our period. 'A Suggestion for
Simplifying the Theory of Money' illustrates Sir John Hicks's
special gifts at their highest level. Some seed of thought flung
down by another writer is made to germinate and blossom into
a complex pattern of surprising possibilities and implications.
And, let us add, what more can a man do? What was suggested
in simple and realistic style in chapter 10 of the *Treatise on
Money* is now taken by Hicks and expressed as a refined theory

whose very precision is the source of unlooked-for revelations and new twists of ideas:

> Mr Keynes's *Treatise*, so far as I have been able to discover, contains at least three theories of money. One of them is the Savings and Investment theory, which seems to me only a quantity theory much glorified. One of them is a Wicksellian natural rate theory. But the third is altogether much more interesting. It emerges when Mr Keynes begins to talk about the price-level of investment goods, when he shows that this price-level depends upon the relative preference of the investor—to hold bank deposits or securities. Here at last we have a choice at the margin! And Mr Keynes goes on to put substance into [the idea of the marginal utility of money] by his doctrine that the relative preference depends upon the 'bearishness' or 'bullishness' of the public, upon their relative desire for liquidity or profit.*

One question instantly arises. Hicks's 'Suggestion' is to marginalize the theory of money. But is that Keynes's suggestion? If a man feels *sure* that the prices of bonds and shares are going to fall fast and far, there will be no margin at which he will be happy with his portfolio, short of selling the whole of it for money. Even a small fall, if it takes only a week or two, will outpace the accrual of interest or dividends and result in a net disadvantage. If Bears are really bearish, they will want to be right 'out of the market' and hold only money; and if Bulls are really bullish they will want (as Keynes himself in several places says) to borrow money from the banks in order to buy securities with more than their whole fortunes. The Bullish-Bearish seesaw may, for any one speculator, be one which shows little inclination to balance half way up; it may be that he splits his fortune into two parts: a reserve whose form remains fixed over long periods, and a *masse de manœuvre* the *whole* of which is switched into and out of money according to 'the news' as seen through his own personal interpreting spectroscope. There will, of course, on all occasions be speculators who cannot make up their minds, and who resolve to 'hedge' by holding some money and some securities. But Hicks's idea of considering the implications of a marginal utility of money finds its best and proper application to the transactions motive; and, if so, we must claim for it more originality than Hicks does for himself.

* (Sir) J. R. Hicks, *Economica*, New Series, no. 5, February 1935.

One way of expressing the change of attitude in monetary theory that the *Treatise* had suggested and that Hicks was now, in one direction, so felicitously refining would be to say (Hicks does not say it) that the older theory was about holding money *because of income* whereas the new one is about choosing to have money *instead of income*. The new theory is about the motives for holding money in preference to holding certain capital values. But capital values themselves intimately depend on some notion of income (Hicks himself refers to Erik Lindahl's brilliant article 'The Concept of Income' in *Economic Essays in Honour of Gustav Cassel*, 1933, pp. 399–407), and it is not clear why Hicks at the outset takes pains to push aside any relevance of 'income' to his problem. Income, as Lindahl in especial has shown, is a forward-looking concept, and capital values are entirely forward looking. Indeed it is true, of course, that the whole subject-matter of economics is forward-looking, for economics is about choice and choice is about the future. What Hicks is really concerned to dispense with is any connection with the Quantity Theory. He also very puzzlingly refers to Wicksell's *natural rate of interest* as an idea from which we must dissociate the essence of monetary theory. This is, presumably, because the natural rate belongs to the 'savings and investment' theory of money, which Hicks had rejected in the passage we quoted above. Wicksell's ideas may have been somewhat mutually entangled, but they were, at the very least, the proximate source of Keynes's and Myrdal's great surge forward in the theory of general output. Hicks, however, has the basic question, which is sought to be answered by 'liquidity preference' (he does not call it that) in view:

What has to be explained is the decision to hold assets in the form of barren money, rather than of interest- or profit-yielding securities. So long as rates of interest are positive, the decision to hold money rather than lend it, or use it to pay off old debts, is apparently an unprofitable one. This, as I see it, is really the central issue in the pure theory of money. Either we have to give an explanation of the fact that people do hold money when rates of interest are positive, or we have to evade the difficulty somehow. It is the great traditional evasions which have led to Velocities of Circulation, Natural Rates of Interest, *et id genus omne*.

The deep impression that Hicks's article made on at least one reader is evidenced in the margin of my copy, which shows that

I read it first on 4 March 1935; for a second time on 2 October and yet again on 3 October; and for a fourth time on 4 February 1937; on Christmas Day 1965 I have read it a fifth time. On those earlier occasions I wrote six marginal notes and two longer interleaved passages. We have noticed above that Keynes treats the transactions motive as self-evident in nature and needing no analysis. It is this gap which Hicks fills with such *éclat*. Yet in filling it he accords the Bulls and Bears of the *Treatise* no more than an initial reference, and the briefest acknowledgement that capital appreciation or depreciation is a component of the gain to be looked for by a wealth-owner who contemplates exchanging money for other assets. These matters, nonetheless, are relevant, in Hicks's argument, to the *transactions* motive and not merely to a separate speculative motive. For what Hicks does is in fact to amalgamate the two motives into a single theme:

The net advantage to be derived from investing a given quantity of money consists of the interest or profit earned less the cost of investment. It is only if this net advantage is expected to be positive (i.e. if the expected rate of interest plus or minus capital appreciation or depreciation is greater than the cost of investment) that it will pay to undertake the investment. Now, since the expected interest increases both with the quantity of money to be invested and with the length of time for which it is expected that the investment will remain untouched, while the costs of investment are independent of the length of time, and (as a whole) will almost certainly increase at a diminishing rate as the quantity of money to be invested increases, it becomes clear that with any given level of costs of investment, it will not pay to invest money for less than a certain period, and in less than certain quantities. It will be preferable to hold assets for short periods, and in relatively small quantities, in monetary form.

The short periods and small quantities are those involved in the income–expenditure circuit, and thus what Hicks has explained and given a structure of reason to is the transactions motive. But in thus explaining it he has invoked the speculative motive, in the anonymous and rather dismissive phrase 'plus or minus capital appreciation or depreciation'. One of the present writer's marginal notes to Hicks's article, written on 3 October 1935, says

One cannot help feeling that the second term of this net advantage, namely the 'capital appreciation or depreciation' which is expected to have happened between the date when money is available for investment and the date when it is expected to be required in liquid form, is the dominating influence in the relative valuation of money and other assets. It seems likely to be quantitatively so much more important than changes in the nominal [i.e. coupon] rate of interest.

Perhaps this is still a fair comment, and suggests, if so, that Hicks in the ingenious and surprising elaborations to which he proceeds was missing the chance to emphasize, what emerges clearly from his argument, the *unity* of all motives for holding money instead of income-yielding assets, namely, the *expense and danger* of doing otherwise in certain commonly recurrent circumstances.

Despite his early reference to Keynes and the bullishness and bearishness of the public, despite his seizing on the Keynesian question as the starting-point of interest-rate theory: what makes people willing to hold some of their wealth in ostensibly barren money rather than in interest- or profit-yielding securities: Hicks's belief in the capability of theory is quite different from Keynes's. Keynes displays to us a number of paths along which things can develop, the choice of the particular path being made from case to case by an unforeseeable context of 'outside' events. But Hicks wishes to catch things at an earlier stage, and to derive (by observation, not logic) a knowledge of what particular expectations will be generated by what visible circumstances. There is even a flavour of suggestion that we can in principle know all the relevant circumstances so as to have a considerable foresight of the monetary course of events:

Now the fact that our 'equilibrium' [of the public's holdings of different types of asset] is here determined by subjective factors like anticipations, instead of objective factors like prices, means that this purely theoretical study of money can never hope to reach results so tangible and precise as those of value theory. The whole problem of applying monetary theory is one of deducing changes in anticipations from the changes in objective data which call them forth. Obviously, this is not an easy task, and, above all, it is not one which can be performed in a mechanical fashion. It needs judgement and a knowledge of business psychology more than sustained logical reasoning. When once the connection between objective facts and anticipations has been made, theory comes again into its rights.

'This is not an easy task.' Keynes would, I think, have declared it utterly impossible. Those who exhibit even the smallest gift for an occasional success at it make large fortunes on the Stock Exchange. They are able to do so precisely because this task is, broadly and for most people, and always with any precision or certainty, impossible *in the nature of things*.

Throughout the four numbers of the *Economic Journal* for 1937 there proceeded a great debate on interest-rate theory. In March and June Professor Bertil Ohlin presented, under the too-modest title of Some Notes on the Stockholm Theory of Savings and Investment, a clear and complete statement of the macro-economic theory (as it would nowadays be called) which had been attained by the intellectual heirs of Wicksell, and compared it with that of the *General Theory*. In the June number Keynes made his first reply, called Alternative Theories of the Rate of Interest. In September, a symposium by Professor Ohlin, Sir Dennis Robertson and Sir Ralph Hawtrey (as they became) offered Three Rejoinders, and in December Keynes made, in The 'Ex-ante' Theory of the Rate of Interest, a promise tragically destined to be frustrated by illness and war:

I restrict myself in what follows to the discussion between Professor Ohlin and myself, because this, I think, may prove to be a fruitful one. He has compelled me to attend to an important link in the causal chain which I had previously overlooked, and has enabled me to make an important improvement in my analysis; and as regards the difference which still remains between us, I do not yet abandon the prospect of convincing him. Whilst, however, the latter must probably await a future article which I intend to write dealing with the relation of the 'ex-ante' and 'ex-post' analysis in its entirety to the analysis in my *General Theory*, I have, meanwhile, some comments on his latest contribution.

Had Keynes been spared by events to write the 'fourth edition', here foreshadowed, of the great conception begun in the *Treatise*, reworked in the *General Theory* and potently distilled in his article in the *Quarterly Journal*, an incomparable synthesis would surely have resulted, and would have dissolved a mass of confusion, partly Keynes's own and partly that of critics who fastened on faults of exposition and exposed their own blindness to the essence of something radically new. Unhappily, in the December article Keynes had still not appreciated the real power and necessity of the *ex ante* approach. What he refers to, justly enough, as an 'important improvement' was the recognition that liquidity might be desired by *anticipation* of large-scale investment. He was not yet fully seized of a vital notion: that decision and choice refer to actions *not yet become actual*, and thus are elements in an *essentially ex ante* theory. Myrdal had not invented a new analysis, he had pointed out the true nature of the existing one.

Somewhat aside from this remarkable debate there appeared in the March issue of the *Journal* a paper which must be said to have eclipsed and superseded both the attack upon Keynes and his defence. In 'Liquidity-premium and the Theory of Value' Hugh Townshend, a civil servant, argues direct from the nature of expectation to show that money prices are basically indeterminate and retain their stability only by convention. Townshend's paper contains also an astonishing judgement, based upon pure theory, which events in the twenty years since the Second World War have borne out:

The inference that there is no reason to believe in the probable indefinite recurrence of a *regular* cycle of price-fluctuations...seems to follow from Mr Keynes's conclusions.*

Townshend's brilliant paper, although thirteen pages long, appeared only under Notes and Memoranda. It leapt too far ahead for the mass of Keynes's critics, still tapping the wheels of his theory to see whether it would clank decently round like the sort of thing they were used to, and Townshend attracted no attention. His article was a fit companion piece for Keynes's own in the *Quarterly Journal*, both of these pieces, published in successive months, having evidently been independently written, and both bringing into the heart of monetary and 'macro-economic' theory the same notion, society's resort to *convention* as a substitute for the *reason* (the logic) which could not work for lack of data. We shall first trace Ohlin's attempt at glossing Keynes in Myrdalian language and Keynes's reassertion of his elliptical mode of thought, then show briefly how Townshend had already cut through to a conclusion more heretical than theirs. Ohlin describes as follows the origins and thought-scheme of the Stockholm School:

Wicksell's *Geldzins und Güterpreise* contained the embryo of a 'theory of output as a whole', although this fact was not clearly perceived

* Hugh Townshend, *Economic Journal*, vol. XLVII, p. 166.

until the late 'twenties, when Professor Lindahl presented his elaboration of Wicksell. Lindahl showed that Wicksell's cumulative process depended on special assumptions concerning the entrepreneurs' expectations, thereby utilising the analysis of 'anticipations' which had been presented in Professor Myrdal's work, *Pricing and the Change Factor*, 1927. Myrdal discusses the influence of the uncertain future on price formation. Of the pre-depression treatises only Marshall seems to have had it in mind; at least he used a terminology which protects him from much of the criticism which can be directed at other writers. In fact, Keynes's analysis in chapter 5 [of the *General Theory*] can be regarded as the following up of numerous suggestions in Marshall's *Principles*. Myrdal tries to build these expectations into a picture of the forces existing at a moment of time. He does not attempt to construct a dynamic price theory which considers the *rate* of change. This analysis was continued by him in 'Der Gleichgewichtsbegriff als Hilfmittel in der Geldtheoretischen Analyse', published by Hayek in 1933. He there works out in detail the vitally important distinction between 'looking forward' and 'looking backward'. The third decisive factor in the development of the Stockholm theory was Lindahl's book on *The Means of Monetary Policy* (published in 1930 but circulated in proof a year earlier), which used Myrdal's expectation analysis to follow the Wicksellian line of approach by means of periods of time, perhaps somewhat under the influence of Mr D. H. Robertson in this latter respect.

This passage sets out for us with the authority of an insider the intricate sequence of publications and their influence on each other. It is fascinating in the questions that it prompts and the suggestions that it offers. Why did price dominate the minds even of monetary and business cycle theorists to the exclusion of output, and why did this dominance obscure for thirty years the relevance of Wicksell's work for a theory of general output and employment? If Myrdal analysed *the moment* in respect of its charge of expectations and decisions waiting to react with each other, in what respect and degree did the other Stockholm theorists go beyond this? What claims have they to have considered any '*rate* of change'? How many steps can the sequence analysis take, and are not all steps, in so much as they are pure theory, one and the same step?*

* Perhaps they are not. See the present writer's *Expectations, Investment and Income* (Oxford University Press, 1938), Appendix, pp. 117–19.

A little later, Ohlin refers to the four economists, Hammar-skjöld, Johannson, Myrdal and himself, who were asked by the Swedish Government's Unemployment Committee to write monographs on four different aspects of unemployment:

The high degree of unanimity between them and the fact that they were all influenced by the Wicksell-Myrdal-Lindahl writings and by Cassel with regard to the anti-classical approach to price and distribution theory, make it justifiable to talk about a Stockholm school of thought. (The only non-resident in Stockholm is Lindahl, who worked in Stockholm for many years.)

These monographs and the discussion of them led to the Committee's Final Report by Hammarskjöld on *Remedies for Unemployment*, of which Ohlin says that 'While there is only a scanty discussion of the determination of the rates of interest, there is an extensive analysis of "frictional" unemployment and possible remedies, matters which are almost entirely ignored by Keynes'. How a committee advised by Myrdal and Ohlin can have so lamentably misconceived its real problem, to which the interest-rate is at least theoretically central, as to think 'frictional unemployment' more important than effective demand, in the conditions of the early 1930s, is hard to understand. Nor is it easier to believe that Ohlin considers 'frictional unemployment' a worthwhile substitute for a thrust into the heart of things.

Ohlin's discussion of interest-rates occupies six pages at the beginning of his second part, in the *Journal* for June 1937. His first concern is to dissolve Wicksell's conception of a 'normal' rate of interest. Wicksell, we saw, has three criteria for this normalcy: the rate of interest at which money can be borrowed is normal if it is equal to the 'natural' rate of interest; it is normal if it equalizes the supply of and demand for saving; it is normal if it holds constant the general level of prices. Did Wicksell think of these as equivalent alternative formulations, the fulfilment of any one guaranteeing the fulfilment of the others? We think so, but Myrdal has indicated some necessary glosses upon them, and we have others to propose. Myrdal has shown that 'the natural rate of interest' cannot be made sense of as a technical productivity, but must be understood as an expected profitability; and we have shown, in chapter 10 above, that such profitability has to mean the same as Keynes's marginal efficiency of capital. However, there will at all times be an incentive for business men to place such orders for equipment as will, for each of them, bring his own marginal efficiency of capital (a percentage per unit time which reflects his own judgments and expectations in all his uncertainty concerning them) into equality with the interest-rate at which he can finance such orders. Thus there can be no persisting discrepancy between the 'rate of expected profitability' and the market rate of interest. The market rate drags down the marginal efficiency or 'natural rate' to equality with itself. But this equality in itself does nothing to bring to equality the business men's aggregate of intended net investment and the income-disposers' aggregate of intended saving. Of Wicksell's two first criteria, intelligibly interpreted, it is only the second which can remain for long unfulfilled. When it is unfulfilled there will be a source of excess demand, or of insufficiency of demand, which if it is an excess in circumstances of full employment, will push general prices up; if it is an excess when there are unemployed factors of all kinds, will lead to a bigger general output; and if it is an insufficiency, may lead to a fall of both output and prices. Ohlin rightly (as we think) rejects the notion of a 'natural rate' with any independent stability of its own; but he says nothing which destroys the meaning of Wicksell's second criterion. All he does is to point out that intended saving and intended net investment can be equal whether or not each of them, and aggregate income, is the same for the coming unit-interval as it was for the previous one, and that an all-round increase of this kind can result in, or be associated with expectations of, an increase of the general price level. All this is plainly true, and it means that Wicksell's second condition of monetary equilibrium is a necessary but not a sufficient condition for the absence, in circumstances of full employment, of any source of price-raising demand. Ohlin's liberation of ideas goes beyond Wicksell's and beyond Myrdal's, and it goes further than we can agree with:

Ceteris paribus, increased investment without a corresponding increase in planned savings raises the sum total of purchases, and, thus, production or prices or both. But it should be noted that the *ceteris paribus* assumption includes 'constant income expectations'. If they rise, and consumption with them, an expansion will result even if planned saving should happen to be equal to planned investment.

No, it includes *given* income expectations for the impending short interval to which also the investment and savings decisions are taken to apply. Expectations or desires concerning subsequent intervals may and will influence decisions concerning the nearest future interval. But the Myrdalian construction, Myrdal's interpretation of Wicksell, calls for a consideration of the compatibility, or otherwise, of plans for the nearest interval. This interval is, for the purpose of this construction, an 'atom of time' in which *new* decisions cannot be taken, and in which the only possible events are the attempted execution of the decisions, that is, the commitments, prevailing at its threshold. There is no need, or meaning, therefore, for any assertion that income expectations are 'constant'.

Other things being equal, a change in the interest rate will cause a different kind of economic development. Which [i.e. what] rate of interest one wants to call 'normal' depends on what kind of economic development one considers 'normal'. If the interest level should be lower and the volume of investment greater than what corresponds to this development, then a process of relative expansion—of output or prices or both—is the outcome. Thereby the total quantity of savings is increased. Wicksell's idea was that the normal rate—which he thought of as closely related to a natural rate corresponding to the marginal productivity of capital or of round-about methods of production in some Böhm-Bawerkian sense—changed very slowly if at all through the increase in savings caused by the process of expansion.

These passages evidently refer to a whole time-extended process. The expressions 'development', 'process', 'change very slowly', can mean nothing else. Thus the whole argument, in relation to Wicksell-Myrdal, is beside the point. History germinates in moments, it does not spring up in complete segments ready made, and the analysis and explanation of it must proceed by the study of momentary situations. The alternative is to be wholly determinist and thereby render meaningless any explanation in terms of choice amongst alternatives. When Ohlin says 'Thereby the total quantity of savings is increased', and speaks of 'the increase in savings caused by the process of expansion' he shows himself to be taking a quite different viewpoint from that of Wicksell or Myrdal. To understand a process we must surely articulate it into its momentary elements, even if these elements all have so much in common that we can properly describe a typical element of the process.

What Ohlin is insisting on is that equality between intended
saving and intended net investment is not a sufficient condition
to prevent an increase of output and a rise of prices. But what
we must insist on is that whenever intended saving and intended
investment are equal, the rise of output and prices will occur,
not as an unexpected and disconcerting divergence between
what was earlier expected and what is now recorded about a
just-elapsed period, but as something intended and expected by
those concerned. The rise of prices will come into view when
the business men seek, at the threshold of some interval, to
engage factors of production to work for them in that interval.
For what drives up prices in conditions of Wicksellian monetary
equilibrium is not the sudden emergence of a demand for more
goods than have been produced, but the emergence of a demand for more factors than are available, or more than are
available at the hitherto prevailing factor prices. In the
language of the *Treatise on Money*, Ohlin is failing to distinguish
between Income Inflation and Profit Inflation. For in Myrdalian language, income inflation will be known to both employers and employed at the time when contracts of future
employment are signed; that is (in terms of the stylized 'sequence analysis' model) at the threshold of the interval. Profit
inflation will not be known until the end of the interval. Ohlin
goes too far in his liberating efforts, and in seeking to deny
significance to the *ex ante* saving-investment equality he is
rejecting a valuable means of insight, one which in essence is
accepted by Wicksell, Myrdal and Keynes.

From the later pages of Ohlin's discussion of the interest-rate
(*Economic Journal*, vol. XLVII, pp. 224–7) it is evident that he had
then no grasp of Keynes's meaning. The repeated reference to
savings, the adherence to a flow analysis, the belief that it makes
no difference whether the market in *existing* bonds is included
or excluded from the class of transactions by which the interest-
rate is manifested, the very fact that 'transactions' are looked on
as part of the essence of the matter, instead of *valuations* which
may or may not call for transactions; all these things betray a
habit of mind quite alien to the liquidity preference approach:

What governs the demand and supply of credit? Two ways of reasoning are possible. One is *net* and deals only with *new* credit, and the
other is *gross* and includes the outstanding *old* credits. The willing-

ness of certain individuals during a given period [a *flow* analysis involving a *period*, in contrast to a stock analysis concerning the situation at a moment] to *increase* their holdings of various claims and other kinds of assets *minus* the willingness of others to *reduce* their corresponding holdings gives the supply curves for the different kinds of new credit during the period. Naturally, the quantities each individual is willing to supply depend on the interest-rates. The total supply of *new* claims *minus* the reduction in the outstanding volume of *old* ones gives the demand—also a function of the rates of interest—for the different kinds of credit during the period.

A similar kind of reasoning can of course be applied *gross* i.e. including the old claims which were outstanding when the period began. It is quite obvious that this reasoning in gross terms leads to the same result as the net analysis above.

It is quite obvious, at any rate, that Ohlin's view of the matter has nothing to do with Keynesian liquidity preference, where the interest-rate is dominated by valuations, at each and any moment, not 'per period', of the stocks of old bonds.

Later, Ohlin refers to 'the market which is given a special position by Keynes, the demand and supply for cash and claims "quickly" convertible into cash'. Liquidity preference can be stated in terms of money or of bonds. The market where bonds are exchanged for money will evidently be influenced by other markets, such as those for the ordinary shares of companies, or those for real property and even those for consumable goods. The concentric rings of influence can be conceived as widely as we like. It is still true that a rate of interest is the answer to a sum whose data are the terms and the current price of some type of bonds. Nothing essential is involved in the choice of regarding such a market as a market where money is bought with bonds or where bonds are bought with money. This matter is the first that Keynes deals with in his reply to Ohlin.

'Alternative Theories of the Rate of Interest' immediately follows Ohlin's part II in the *Journal* for June 1937:

The liquidity-preference theory of the rate of interest which I have set forth in my *General Theory of Employment, Interest and Money* makes the rate of interest to depend on the present supply of *money* and the demand schedule for a present claim on money in terms of a deferred claim on money. This can be put briefly by saying that the rate of interest depends on the demand and supply of money; though this may be misleading, because it obscures the answer to the question,

Demand for money in terms of what? The alternative theory held, I gather, by Professor Ohlin and his group of Swedish economists, by Mr Robertson and Mr Hicks, makes it to depend on the demand and supply of *credit*, or (meaning the same thing) of *loans*, at different rates of interest. The theories are, I believe, radically opposed to one another.

The word 'credit' suggests perplexities quite irrelevant to the matter in hand, and 'loans' directs attention to the act rather than the consequences of lending, and for these reasons they are bad. But they are not the locus of the error that Keynes is seeking to pin down. 'Loans' could be understood as 'bonds', and would then mean simply the 'deferred claims on money' which Keynes himself refers to. Keynes in his next main paragraph successfully exposes Ohlin's source of confusion, but at once falls into a trap which has already engulfed Ohlin, namely the appeal to the *ex post identical* equality of saving and investment to prove that the interest-rate does not ensure their *ex ante contingent* equality. This error is precisely equivalent to the assertion that price cannot bring to equality the quantity demanded and the quantity supplied, because what is bought is identically the same quantity as what is sold. After quoting Ohlin, Hicks and Robertson, Keynes takes up Ohlin's statement as the clearest for comment:

The net supply of credit [as defined by Ohlin] is exactly the same thing as the quantity of saving. The net demand for credit at different rates of interest is exactly the same thing as the quantity of net investment at different rates of interest. Thus we are completely back again at the classical doctrine which Professor Ohlin has just repudiated—namely, that the rate of interest is fixed at the level where the supply of credit, in the shape of saving, is equal to the demand for credit, in the shape of investment.

It is now that things go wrong. Keynes should have pointed to the massive stock effects of the 'old' bonds, whose revaluation, to almost any extent, can occur in a moment, and, if sufficiently unanimous amongst holders of bonds and holders of money, need engender no transactions, still less depend on them. But instead we have the grossly fallacious appeal to the *ex post* identity, which Keynes supposes Ohlin to endorse:

Exactly the same argument applies as that which Professor Ohlin has used at the very commencement of his article, where he writes:

'Obviously the rate of interest cannot—with the terminology used above—be determined by the condition that it equalises savings and investment. For savings and investment are equal *ex definitione*, whatever interest level exists on the market.' For—with the terminology used above—the net supply and demand of credit are equal *ex definitione* whatever interest level exists on the market.*

We can perhaps scarcely blame Keynes for not appreciating the imperative need for an *ex ante* view, if he supposed that the very spokesman of the Stockholm School itself had here dispensed with it. The need *is* imperative, since otherwise the whole supply and demand analysis, in any and every application, and thus the whole of value theory from start to finish, goes by the board.

Keynes next propounds an important fresh aspect of the 'transactions' need for a stock of money, namely, the advance arrangements which a business man must make when he has decided to order a large piece of new equipment and knows that he will have to make large payments for it. The man who has decided to buy a ship or an oil refinery is in the same technical position as one who has decided to buy a pair of shoes: he has to be ready to pay for it when the time comes. It is only the scale and elaboration of his arrangements, and the length of time he must allow for them, which are different. To make an investment decision, to give an order for a piece of equipment, is therefore to incur a need for a stock of money. Keynes recognizes in this need something distinct from the ordinary transactions motive, and elects to give it a separate name, 'finance'. We think that the constriction of investment, and thus of general output, employment and aggregate income, which may arise from an insufficiency of finance in this sense, rather than any difference in the nature of the two sources of demand for money, is what justifies the distinction:

An investment *decision* may sometimes involve a temporary demand for money before it is carried out, quite distinct from the demand for active balances which will arise as a result of the investment activity whilst it is going on. There has to be a technique to bridge the gap between the time when the decision to invest is taken and the time when the correlative investment and saving actually occur. This service may

* J. M. Keynes, 'Alternative Theories of the Rate of Interest', *Economic Journal*, vol. XLVII, p. 245.

be provided either by the new issue market or by the banks. Even if the entrepreneur avails himself of the financial provision which he has arranged beforehand *pari passu* with his actual expenditure on the investment, either by calling up instalments in respect of his new market-issue exactly when he wants them or by arranging overdraft facilities with his bank, it will still be true that the market's commitments will be in excess of actual saving to date and there is a limit to the extent of the commitments which the market will agree to enter into in advance. But if he accumulates a cash balance beforehand, then an accumulation of unexecuted or incompletely executed investment-decisions may occasion for the time being an extra special demand for cash. Let us call this advance provision of cash the 'finance' required by the current decisions to invest. Investment finance in this sense is, of course, only a special case of the finance required by any productive process; but since it is subject to special fluctuations of its own, I should (I now think) have done well to have emphasized it when I analyzed the various sources of the demand for money.*

We may notice that if Keynes had included unused overdraft facilities within the definition of money, there would have been no need to distinguish between banks and new market-issues as the two sources of 'finance'; except that unused overdraft facilities, until a recent (November 1965) proposal in Australia, have cost nothing in interest.

In this article on 'Alternative Theories', Keynes is mainly concerned to deny that the propensity of people to save out of their income has any but an indirect and quite unimportant influence on the interest-rate, and to deny that the latter has any part to play in bringing to equality the flow of saving and that of investment. The article is unhappily marred and crippled by the repeated appeal to a mysterious equality between these two variables, an equality which, it appears from Keynes's words, is both guaranteed by logical necessity and the meaning which he assigns to these terms, and yet requires to be ensured. Of this we can say only that it represents an ellipsis of thought. Keynes attained a right conclusion by a leap of argument which, for the step-by-step logician, involves a chasm in the path and a pit of fallacy. It may be wearisome to read the increasingly confused statements that follow one another. But

* J. M. Keynes, 'Alternative Theories of the Rate of Interest', *Economic Journal*, vol. XLVII, pp. 246–7.

this confusion, able to entrap a mind of such untrammelled power, arises from something in the very nature of the economic subject-matter, that is to say, from the nature of a study involving human conscious conduct and its results. The *sources* of that conduct are thoughts, judgments, conjectures, even figments only tenuously supported by evidence; things which are themselves invisible; only the results of their confrontation and interaction can be seen. But this confrontation resolves all their conflicts and incompatibilities into a logically inescapable *ex post* harmony, whose character does not itself tell us what those conflicts and tensions were. It appears to us very important to illustrate the intellectual toils which arise from this aspect of the philosopher's prime puzzle: What is time? or (is it the same question) What is consciousness? The ultimate explanation is that Keynes telescopes the *moment of decision* and the moment of *confrontation of the acts implied* by decision; the two ends of the Myrdalian interval; the *ex ante* and the *ex post*. His constant reiteration that investment and saving cannot be unequal, but are brought to equality by changes of income, means that he defines income, not as the value-added which the business men imagine and look to when they sign contracts of factor-employment relating to the coming interval, but as the value-added which they *would* assign to their production plans were they able, in some Wellsian time-machine, to move forward to the end of that interval and see what quantities, at what prices, will actually be sold, and then move back again to its beginning to note that when correct valuations are placed upon their production plans, saving and investment are equal. The burden of adjustment of *ex ante* disparity to *ex post* equality is placed by Keynes wholly on prices, not at all (in most of his writing) on the retention by business men of unsold stocks which constitute formerly unintended investment. It is the equilibrium method invoked without specification of an equilibrium mechanism:

The theory of the rate of interest which prevailed before (let us say) 1914 regarded it as the factor which ensured equality between saving and investment. It was never suggested that saving and investment could be unequal. This idea arose (for the first time, so far as I am aware) with certain post-war theories. In maintaining the equality of saving and investment, I am, therefore, returning to old-fashioned orthodoxy. The novelty in my treatment of saving and investment consists, not in my maintaining their necessary aggregate equality, but in the proposition that it is, not the rate of interest, but the level of incomes which (in conjunction with certain other factors) ensures this equality. I should, however, like to take this opportunity to correct a misunderstanding which runs through Mr Hawtrey's criticisms of my work. Mr Hawtrey is convinced that I have so defined Saving and Investment that they are not merely *equal*, but *identical*.*

It is sad that Keynes was led to spend so much time and effort on an argument of which he had no need. His sole concern and legitimate endeavour was to show that we cannot assign to the interest-rate the role of bringing saving and investment to equality in face of a full employment income. For this purpose, all he needed to do was to admit that (*ex ante*) saving and investment *are not brought to equality by anything whatever*, save the purest accident. For they do not confront each other simultaneously in one and the same market.

Having, by whatever means, dismissed the interest-rate from its role of guarantor of full employment, and having by the same act deprived it of the mechanism which had been thought to determine it, he was obliged to seek for it a new explanation. What he found is expressed near the end of the article with an incisive simplicity that could not be surpassed:

The resulting theory, whether right or wrong, is exceedingly simple —namely, that the rate of interest on a loan of given quality and maturity has to be established at the level which, in the opinion of those who have the opportunity of choice—i.e. of wealth-holders— equalizes the attractions of holding idle cash and holding the loan [i.e. the bond]. The function of the rate of interest is to modify the money-prices of other capital assets in such a way as to equalize the attraction of holding them and of holding cash.†

The dialogue between Ohlin and Keynes was in some sense a dialogue between the letter and the spirit of the law. In the brief re-statement of his views which Ohlin contributed to the symposium of the September *Journal*, we find a formally impeccable account of the liquidity preference view, endorsed and adopted now, as it would seem, by Ohlin. But there is little evidence that Ohlin perceived the consequence of this view,

* J. M. Keynes, 'Alternative Theories', *Economic Journal*, vol. XLVII, p. 249.
† *Ibid.* p. 250.

namely, that *stocks*, of bonds and money, will dominate the market where old and new bonds are exchanged for pre-existing and, perhaps, newly bank-created money. Ohlin does, however, here expose with incisive force the irrelevance of *ex post* considerations to the meaning, attainment and determination of an equilibrium. He comes very near, also, to the essential fact which disqualifies even *ex ante* investment and saving, considered as a pair of interacting forces, from being deemed to determine the interest-rate, namely, that they are never confronted with each other in any market:

As already indicated, *any* rate of interest is possible, irrespective of how much saving or new investment is planned. For the resulting economic development provides unintentional saving and investment (positive or negative). Not so with credit. Given a certain willingness to grant and to take credit—on the part of individuals, firms and banks—*only one interest level is possible in a free* market. The truth is that the price of 3 per cent bonds—and thus the long term rate of interest—is fixed on the bond market by the demand and supply curves in the same way as the price of eggs or strawberries on a village market. There *is* a credit market—or rather several markets —but there is no such market for savings and no price for savings, with the definitions used by Mr Keynes and myself.

In its reliance on an equilibrium method, the *General Theory* suffers from a basic handicap. For its formal method obliges it to discuss only equilibria, and these equilibria are of a kind whose occurrence is *purely accidental*, and can in no way claim to be the natural and inevitable result of a self-operating adjustment process. Equilibrium, in any context, is either an accidental or a systematic outcome of affairs. If systematic, it results from an exchange or pooling of conditional intentions, that is, of information. But at no moment is there any exchange of information between potential savers and potential investors about their conditional, or even their committed, intentions. There is no mechanism for such a pooling. The rate of interest, because dominated by a market in pre-existing acknowledgements of debt, does not provide such a mechanism. This is the essence of the matter, which Keynes saw but failed to provide with an efficient conceptual vessel, and which Ohlin, in the brief symposium note, distilled very well into the highly suitable Stockholm bottle, but still without a full acknowledgement of what this essence is. The interchange in the 1937 *Journal* between Keynes and Ohlin was like a formal old-fashioned dance, each partner taking up in succession the position just vacated by the other, but never quite managing to walk arm-in-arm in one and the same direction.

Keynes's last shot was 'The "Ex-Ante" Theory of the Rate of Interest', in the *Journal* for December 1937. It begins with the tragically frustrated promise to reconsider the whole bearing of *ex ante* analysis on his ideas. Its main effort is to hammer home the point that liquidity preference, and liquidity itself, are *stock* conceptions and not *flows*. Only in so far as saving is a use of income which calls for fewer transactions per time-unit than consumption expenditure does, can saving, at the time when it is being performed, be said to affect the liquidity situation by reducing the quantity needed of transaction balances. The *flow* of saving from one set of wealth-owners to another, as when income is received from employers and lent to borrowers, does nothing in itself to affect directly the *aggregate* desire for liquid stocks of wealth or to provide them to *the community as a whole*. Yet Keynes in this article still shows himself insensitive to the real meaning and necessity of an *ex ante* analysis. He deems investment to be seen *ex ante* only when it is a project to be executed months or years ahead, and seems unwilling to recognize that every act, however trivial and instantly realizable, is being seen *ex ante facto* at the moment when it is chosen from a set of rival available acts. Thus Keynes spends his effort in this article, not to search for and make contact with the idea of *ex ante* quantities or schedules as having *general* relevance for *all* economic analysis, but to elaborate the concept of 'finance', or anticipative marshalling of spending power in view of investment plans. This latter idea is of prime importance, but it is not so basic and vitally needful as a frame of thought able to accommodate the notion of choice. Keynes ends his article with a further reflection on unused overdraft facilities:

In Great Britain the banks pay great attention to the amount of their outstanding loans and deposits, but not to the amount of their customers' unused overdraft facilities. The aggregate amount of the latter is not known, probably not even to the banks themselves, nor their division between the purely precautionary facilities which are not likely to be used in the near future and those which are associated with the impending planned activity. Now, this is an ideal system for mitigating the effects on the banking system of an increased demand for *ex ante* finance. For it means that there is no effective pressure on the resources of the banking system until the finance is actually used, i.e. until the phase of planned activity has passed over into the phase of actual activity. Thus the transition from a lower to a higher scale of activity may be accomplished with less pressure on the demand for liquidity and [on] the rate of interest.

Sir Ralph Hawtrey, though for many years a civil servant, is in the essential sense a 'Cambridge' economist. Not only was he, like Marshall and Maynard Keynes, a Wrangler in the Mathematical Tripos, but he brings to economics the same feeling as they did for psychological and institutional reality, and the same instinctive wish to avoid too cut-and-dried a formalism in the shape of his economic theory. He distrusts the Stockholm School's artificial division of time into periods separated by instants at which, and only at which, every kind of economic agent takes his decisions. In the third of the contributions making up the September symposium, Sir Ralph compares a number of Keynes's, Ohlin's and his own definitions. He deals uncompromisingly with Keynes's ambiguities concerning the equality of saving and investment:

If demand were defined to mean purchases and supply to mean sales, any proposition about economic forces tending to make demand and supply equal, or about their equality being a condition of equilibrium, or indeed a condition of anything whatever, would be nonsense. If [saving and investment] are defined as 'different aspects of the same thing' how can it possibly be 'the level of income which ensures equality between saving and investment' (*Economic Journal*, vol. XLVII, p. 250)?*

We must not, of course, allow the falsity of Keynes's argument to blur the truth of his insight. It *is* the level of incomes which *moves in search* of an equilibrium between (designed, *ex ante*) saving and (designed, *ex ante*) investment. When there is a disparity, a disequilibrium, between the two *ex ante* quantities, there will almost inevitably follow one period later, that is, so soon as this disparity is revealed *ex post*, a set of decisions by business men to change designed general output, and thus aggregate income, with the purpose (doubtless at first self-frustrating) of bringing

* *Economic Journal*, vol. XLVII, p. 437.

the designed saving and investment of the *next* period to equality; or rather, of bringing, for each one of the business men, realized sales into equality with what he had expected. But *this* action of income is a dynamic, time-extended process, a series of entrepreneurial reactions, not a magical transformation, within one and the same moment, of a disequilibrium into an equilibrium. In this and other matters Sir Ralph's patient, exact and unimpassioned formulations steadily build up in his reader a solid trust in Sir Ralph's logic, and a disposition to look a second and a third time at any proposition which seems at first sight to endanger this faith. It is hard in this contribution (or elsewhere) to fault Hawtrey's words, but he nonetheless leaves the strong impression of neglecting the vast mass of the *existing* stocks of wealth, and their dominance of the market, and of regarding liquidity preference as merely affecting people's disposition of their new, 'current', saving or intended saving:

And indeed the action of withholding savings from active investment and accumulating them in idle balances is simply the outward manifestation of liquidity preference.

Not 'the' manifestation; *a* manifestation, naturally and necessarily accompanying the quantitatively more important one of selling, or not buying, non-monetary assets already in existence.

A point of terminology to which Sir Ralph devotes a few lines deserves much more attention:

In criticising Mr Keynes's work I have made the distinction between active and passive or designed and undesigned investment. Mr Keynes suggests that Professor Ohlin's definitions might suit me better than my own. But is there any difference? 'Unexpected new investment', Professor Ohlin writes, 'can mean simply that stocks at the end of the period are different from what the entrepreneur expected' (*Economic Journal*, vol. XLVII, p. 65). If there is any difference between undesigned and unexpected, I prefer undesigned. A trader may foresee quite clearly that he is going to be burdened with a redundant stock, and may be unable to avert it. It may be possible to go back to some time in the past at which he as a free agent took action which has had this outcome, and to say that at that time he did not expect it. But at that time he may not have formed any expectation about the consequences so far ahead at all.

'He formed no expectation' and so, as the present writer would say,* the outcome when it emerged was *un*expected rather than *counter*-expected. The distinction between judgments which turn out to be wrong, and a total absence of any judgment, is, we think, important; for a bolt from the blue can be more disconcerting, and destructive of plans and hopes, than a question long asked but now answered in a way which causes surprise.

The sheer elusiveness and uncapturable quality of 'expectations' is admirably suggested by Sir Ralph:

However important the part played by expectations may be, it is not to be inferred that they can or should be given precise quantitative measurement. Any forecast of a future economic quantity is likely to be not merely vague and approximate, but actually incomplete. The expectation often relates only to an upper or a lower limit, or it is contingent upon factors of which no forecast is made at all. Even the directors, managers and experts who concur in the plans of one and the same concern may have widely divergent views as to what the actual results are likely to be. Mental processes that may be discrepant in so many ways cannot simply be added together like the items in a ledger.†

Despite the subjectivist revolution, which accorded to tastes an equal status with technics in the scholarly account of the economic process, economic theory has retained one basic premiss and preconception. It regards human conduct as a rational response to given and known circumstances. It sometimes admits a question as to how far those circumstances can reasonably be supposed to be known to the responders. But it refuses, save in a few outlying departments, to face the consequences of a lack of such knowledge. If a ship strikes the rocks through faulty navigation, the principles of navigation themselves and the facts of geography are by no means thereby called in question. If two ships collide, that is a failure to exchange conditional intentions and find an equilibrium solution which, if its respective prescriptions for the various participants are all acted on by them, will guide them all successfully. Equilibrium theory does not accept that valuations can have an *ex nihilo* spontaneity and an autonomous influence on affairs. Valuations, according

* See 'The Logic of Surprise', *Economica*, May 1953, reprinted in *Uncertainty in Economics and Other Reflections* (Cambridge University Press, 1955).
† *Economic Journal*, vol. xlvii, pp. 439, 440.

to economic theory, are *derived* from tastes and resources. Pareto regarded them as merely secondary and instrumental, expressing, at most, the implications of the clash of tastes and obstacles. But valuations, in the context of production and investment, depend on *expectations*. If then expectations have a life of their own, if they are born in some degree of imagination and originative thought, in that same degree valuations lose their dependent status and become unaccountable. Expectations, not derived in stable and discernible fashion from other facts, become prime sources of events, and any determinate future must dissolve. Such is the argument that the present writer has elsewhere advanced. Some breath of such thoughts must have come to him from the two contributions to the *Journal* of 1937 by Mr Hugh Townshend, Keynes's most audacious and extreme interpreter:

[Sir Ralph] Hawtrey has, I think, failed to get to grips with Mr Keynes. I believe, indeed, that he has altogether missed his central idea, which I conceive to be the *direct* causal influence of expectations on *all* prices. There is surely a good deal in Mr Keynes's book which represents, not quite the most general form of his thesis, but rather earlier stages of his thought before he had arrived at a self-consistent new theory of value, subsuming the new theory of interest at which he had originally been aiming. The mechanical analogy breaks down; as it surely must, if prices are influenced, through liquidity premium, by *mere* expectations. There is no position of equilibrium. The foundation of the theory has disappeared. The future is not merely unknown to the economic man; it is also undetermined. The prospect of future returns (whether from enterprise or from the realisation of accumulated assets) is not expressible as a mathematical expectation. This, at least, is what I conceive Mr Keynes to mean.*

'Through liquidity premium.' The thesis which Mr Townshend distils from Keynes's work is simple and extremely destructive. The value put *now* upon any lasting asset by an individual or a market depends, in measure varying with the particular character and assumed economic life-span of that asset, upon suppositions as to what value it will be assigned at this and that *future* date. Such suppositions can in the nature of things have no solid basis of observed or deductive fact. They are expectations, that is (I would myself say) figments of

* *Economic Journal*, vol. XLVII, pp. 321–6.

imaginative thought drawing upon facts of the present as mere sources of suggestion, and entertained in consciousness of their uncertainty. Values of assets of 'lasting' type can thus be created and destroyed in a moment, without any accompaniment of time-using acts of production, consumption or exchange. Not merely Say's Law but Walras's Law, applied to any interval of finite length however short, must be abandoned, for between its beginning and end a man's total wealth can increase, not by productive effort and saving, but 'out of nothing'; and can likewise dissolve. Thus the inducement to invest, which depends upon values assigned to projected equipment, eludes accountancy and orthodox ascription to listed quantitative influences, and becomes an autonomous source of events.

We have quoted Mr Townshend's review of Sir Ralph Hawtrey's *Capital and Employment*. We shall end this chapter by returning to the outset of the great interest debate, to an article that lay outside the formal course of that debate and touched a more general and more basic theme. 'Liquidity-premium and the Theory of Value' is a criticism of Hicks's review-article on the *General Theory*, which had appeared in the *Journal* for June 1936:

Dr Hicks proceeds to identify Mr Keynes's doctrine of liquidity preference with the view that the rate of interest is still a price determined by conditions of supply and demand at the margin (of 'production')—namely, the price of *new* money-loans sold in exchange for free money. But it would not seem that Mr Keynes's doctrine can be re-stated in any such form. On the contrary, it surely implies that the rate of interest is an independent variable in the scheme of economic causation. The rate of interest—better envisaged as a simple function of the money-price of a negotiable money-debt not payable at sight—is not causally determined by the conditions of supply and demand for new loans at the margin. Rather are the demand and supply schedules for new loans determined by the value set by the market on existing loans (of similar types). That is to say, psychologically-determined changes in the latter influence largely, though they do not wholly determine, the former. Since in most cases the volume of existing loans of any one type is large compared to the volume of new loans of that type (if any) being created in any short period, the influence of expectations about the value of existing loans is usually the preponderating causal factor in determining the common price. Moreover, the price of the existing loans can of course change (to any extent, in theory) without any new similar flotations occurring; and, if opinion is unanimous, it can change (without limit) without any actual exchange or movement of money.

One man at least had understood that Keynes's long following of the logic where it led had destroyed the conception of economics as *hydraulics*. One more stroke, and the view of it even as accountancy, in the sense which validates Walras's Law, must go by the board:

Dr Hicks begins with the following premiss: 'Over any short period, the difference between the values of the things an individual acquires (including money) and the value of the things he gives up (including money) must, apart from gifts, equal the change in his net debt.' But what is meant here by a 'short period'? Clearly not any finite period. For any period long enough for the individual to be able to carry out any transactions at all is long enough for expectations, and hence the market price of his assets of any kind, to change during the period. But the possibility of any such change while his debts remain fixed invalidates the arithmetic of the premiss.

Mr Townshend concludes, as Keynes had done a week or two earlier in the *Quarterly Journal* (long after Townshend's article was written), that the basis of such order and stability in the economic world as we enjoy is *convention*:

Perhaps economic (price)-stability really depends on the prevalence of custom in regard to price-offers among the majority who all 'think' alike, combined with the prevalence of a divergency of views among the minority who think for (literally, for) themselves.

The interest-rate in a money economy. This was the enigma that led Keynes to the nihilism of his final position, made explicit by him in the *Quarterly Journal of Economics*, and by his interpreter Mr Hugh Townshend in the *Economic Journal*, virtually at the same moment. The interest-rate depends on expectations of its own future. It is expectational, subjective, psychic, indeterminate. And so is the rest of the economic system. The stability of the system, while it lasts, rests upon a convention: the tacit general agreement to *suppose* it stable. This stability, once doubted, is destroyed, and cascading disorder must intervene before the landslide grounds in a new fortuitous position. Such is the last phase of Keynesian economics. But Keynes had shown governments how to prolong the suspension of doubt.

CHAPTER 16

FORMAL DYNAMICS:
CYCLES AND GROWTH

When a principle was sought by economists which should have universal application and explanatory power, playing the part in economics which gravity does in celestial mechanics, such a principle was found in *self-interest*, which led men to apply reason to their circumstances in order to extract therefrom the greatest attainable satisfaction of their desires. It was then observed that each man's circumstances, in part, consist of other men's desires, so that there appeared to be a conflict. But it was further seen that the *market* is a mechanism whose purpose is to resolve such conflict, by finding, in effect, a comprehensive scheme in which each man would find prescribed that action for himself which he would choose, out of all actions open to him, given that each other man undertook to perform the action which the scheme prescribed for *him*. This conception of a *general equilibrium* depended on four conditions amongst others: (i) equal and complete freedom of individuals to make bargains with each other; (ii) perfect knowledge on the part of each man of the satisfaction he would get from each and every conceivable situation; (iii) the announcement to each person of an exactly specified action prescribed for him by the scheme; (iv) the absence of any field or time of action except that concerned in the general and simultaneously determined set of actions constituting the equilibrium scheme. Conditions (ii) and (iv) in this list are even more remote from everyday experience than the others, and it is number (iv) in particular which excludes from 'equilibrium', understood as in the foregoing, many familiar aspects of economic life. For the circumstances existing now which shape the decision we now take can be seen as the outcome of actions of ourselves and others stretching back through the past. We discern a structure, variously interpretable as 'cause and effect', as a stereotype of association, or in other formulas, in which actions, events and situations of different dates seem to be linked in a manner which in some sense repeats itself in the course of time. It may be plausible, that is to say, to express today's events as functions of past events, or today's situation as a function of past situations; to state a rule by which, if those past events or actions are known, we can calculate today's and tomorrow's. Such stereotypes, functions or rules need not be looked on as permanent. But if they link the events of a few months or years and remain valid, in a given approximate form, for a few months or years, they may serve as the means of explanation and prediction, that is, as the basis of theorizing. Such considerations evidently give us a different sort of theory from the general 'static' or timeless equilibrium which we outlined above. Conforming to the usage which seems to have crystallized, we may reserve for systems which conceive the states or events of different dates as bound together in mathematical functions, the collective name of dynamics. Let us, however, distinguish them from other non-static systems by calling them as a type 'formal' or 'calculable' dynamics. Until the end of our period, all such models had been concerned with cycles of prosperity and depression in a society whose trend of growth of output or resources was not considered relevant. But in the *Economic Journal* for March 1939 there appeared Sir Roy Harrod's 'An Essay in Dynamic Theory'. Here suddenly there was pointed out a new problem, resulting from the invention of the Multiplier and its confrontation with the much older idea of the Accelerator. Or it was asked: Whence can come the extra capacity of equipment to make possible the growth of general output? and: Whence can come the demand sufficient to absorb the general output at each size to which it will have grown? Harrod shows that the questions answer each other. Growth of output provides the incentive for net invest-ment and net investment provides the physical means of growth of output. Net investment also, by its direct and its multiplier effects on demand, can, if its own flow is of just the right size, assure the absorption of the general output at each stage of the latter's growth. Net investment has *two* effects which, by right choice of its level, can be made to *sustain each other*. Harrod's answer gave us a new branch of economic theory, in which the balance of the different aspects of *growth* took the place of the balance of the different aspects of a stationary existence.

A decision to invest, to order equipment, has two consequences. While the equipment is being produced, employment and general output are higher than they would otherwise have been. When the equipment is ready for use, productive capacity is higher than it would otherwise have been. Is there, in given circumstances, some pace of percentage growth of orders such that the extra capacity resulting from earlier orders just makes possible the extra output needed to satisfy the direct and multiplier demand arising from later orders? Were the flow of investment orders to grow during an appropriate time-interval by the percentage, thus defined, of its size at the threshold of that interval, the expectations which led business men to give the earlier orders would, in the aggregate, appear at the end of the interval to have been exactly justified by the absorption of the extra output they had envisaged. Such intervals can moreover be conceived to be *échelonned*: the later orders of one interval are the earlier orders of another, and, if growth continues at the appropriate percentage per time-unit, will themselves be justified by the demand arising from still later orders, and so on. Growth of investment orders, capacity and output, all at the same appropriate percentage, will provide its own *warrant*.

In this scheme of thought the word *interval* occurs, on one hand, because we are concerned with flows and accelerations of flow, quantities of dimension xt^{-1} and $xt^{-1} t^{-1}$ (where x is a number of physical- or value-units and t a number of time-units); and, on the other hand, because we are concerned with the lapses of time required to construct equipment after orders for it are given. The measurement interval can be arbitrarily chosen, and has no necessary relation with the time which elapses between the ordering of an equipment item or equipment system and its readiness for use. These latter intervals can conceptually be échelonned, arranged to overlap, in such a way as to give any desired approximation to a smooth acceleration of flow everywhere differentiable with respect to time. We can thus claim if we like that the whole conception of self-justifying growth, thus described, refers to a 'single moment'. It is this claim which Harrod likes to make when he states his conception of regular growth, that is, growth of output, capacity, demand and investment all at that percentage per time-unit which provides its own warrant. Harrod goes direct to such a 'momentary' interpretation, and in suggesting above the approach to it via the conception of *échelonned intervals*, or a structure of lagged events, we have gone outside his own presentation. We have thus sought to demonstrate at the outset, however, that Harrod's conception of the regularly progressive economy is an example of formal or calculable dynamics in the sense we described above. His own view of it, derived by analogy from physical mechanics, merely appeals to that notion of time-intervals of vanishing length which is characteristic of the Newtonian calculus. Let us first briefly derive Harrod's 'fundamental equation' by an argument which slightly glosses his own and then examine his own development of the matter stage by stage.

Let us suppose that equipment, no matter how physically and technologically diverse, can be measured as a single 'quantity of capital', and that the production done with its aid in a unit of time, no matter how diverse its forms, can also be treated as a single quantity called general output or aggregate income. And let us suppose that for each unit of general output the business men *desire* to have in use a quantity of capital C. If now ΔY is the increment, occurring in a unit of time, of Y the general output, the extra capital-in-use desired will be $\Delta Y C$. If, at the threshold of the unit-interval in which Y increases by ΔY, the whole existing capital stock is already in use, the extra capital desired for growth of output must be provided out of the production done in the interval itself. Suppose that the saving which income-disposers all taken together desire to do out of their aggregate income is a proportion s, so that in a unit-interval whose production is Y, society is content to provide extra capital sY. Then the growth of general output that corresponds to desired saving, the extra demand created by the one being precisely matched by the extra capacity allowed to be created by the other, will be that which gives $\Delta Y C = sY$ or $(\Delta Y / Y) C = s$. The character of this 'growth equilibrium' is more subtle than the simplicity of its expression suggests. Each side of the equation plays, as it were, an active and necessary part in the continuous renewal of the situation which encourages growth at a given percentage per time-unit. At each moment, or in each interval of vanishing length, the growth of output supplies investment demand for the products of that moment, or interval, sufficient to fill the gap left by the saving of that moment, or interval; and in each interval or at each moment the saving of that time supplies the exact quantity of extra capital desired for the growth which occurs in, or at, that time. Thus the expectations of the business men, whose combined decisions give rise to growth of their combined output by a given percentage, are continually fulfilled by the experience of finding their output exactly matched by demand, while their need for extra capital is exactly matched by the portion of their output which income earners desire to leave unconsumed.

The *Economic Journal* for March 1939 carried the first of a series of articles now extending through twenty-five years,* in which Sir Roy Harrod has stated, defended and refined his dynamic theory. That theory pushes to an extreme the method of Marshall and Maynard Keynes, where difficulties, complexities and intricacies are imprisoned in a few verbal capsules which then can be mutually related in a simple construction. The incisive power and compelling simplicity of all these writers' work is achieved by a skilful, brief indication of the area of ideas covered by such terms as propensity to consume, wage-unit, capital–output ratio, rate of growth; together with some suggestions of how the contents of each such capsule can be in some degree conceived as homogeneous and measurable. The question of whether and how the contents which must be assigned to these capsules, if the theories are to give insight into reality, can be deemed susceptible to the kinds of manipulation implied by the handling of the capsules themselves, lends itself to endless and on the whole futile discussion. The theories make their way by an appeal which is partly that of beauty and partly that of efficiency. They explain so much, so easily. Only those who will dispense with their efficacy are really entitled to complain of their summary disposal of complexities. In the long course of his thought, Harrod has been led to make some nominal interpretive concessions, but has defended throughout the formal simplicity of his first construction.

The axiomatic basis of the theory which I propose to develop consists of three propositions—namely, (1) that the level of a community's income is the most important determinant of its supply of saving;

---

* At the present writing, Sir Roy Harrod's latest contribution to the subject is 'Themes in Dynamic Theory', *Economic Journal*, vol. LXXIII, September 1963.

(2) that the rate of increase of its income is an important determinant of its demand for saving, and (3) that demand is equal to supply. It thus consists in a marriage of the 'acceleration principle' and the 'multiplier' theory, and is a development and extension of certain arguments advanced in my *Essay on the Trade Cycle.**

In the third of these propositions the word 'is' seems puzzling and out of place. Equality of demand and supply is surely a special circumstance which, in general, may or may not prevail. It is a condition capable of being unfulfilled. A *market* is a mechanism specially adapted to bring demand and supply to equality, and it may be permissible to postulate a market so perfect that demand and supply in it are equal at all times. But Harrod is far from being concerned with such a market. There are here two issues. Such a model as Harrod's is, in the first place, aggregative, and depends at best, for the balancing of demand and supply, on a great number of distinct markets, one for each class of product, these markets being only very indirectly and unreliably linked with each other, and being very far from the equivalent of a single unified market where a homogeneous investment good might be fancifully supposed to be dealt in; and in the second, but by no means less important, place, such a model essentially involves non-simultaneous decisions, which, therefore, cannot have been the subject of an operation of pooling and solving a system of simultaneously stated conditional promises or intentions, such as may be said to constitute the ideal equilibrium and provide the only means to perfect rationality of choice.† In short, in the Harrodian dynamic model, despite Harrod's claim that 'the fundamental concept in dynamic economics...is the rate of increase that obtains *at a given point of time*',‡ we are essentially concerned with lagged relations. If things appear otherwise, it is because Harrod appeals to the physical analogy of a particle accelerating under the influence of *contemporary* forces. That analogy can be misleading. Perhaps Harrod's proposition (3) might state

---

* Sir Roy Harrod, 'An Essay in Dynamic Theory', *Economic Journal*, vol. XLIX, pp. 14–33.

† This theme is developed in the present writer's *A Scheme of Economic Theory*, chapter 2 (Cambridge University Press, 1965), and in *Cahiers de l'Institut de Science Economique Appliqueé*, Suppl. No. 134. Février 1963: L'équilibre: étude de sa signification et de ses limites.

‡ Second essay in dynamic theory, *Economic Journal*, vol. LXX.

that equality of demand and supply for saving is a condition for the renewal of growth from moment to moment, or from unit-interval to unit-interval, at a constant percentage.

Throughout the evolution of his dynamic theory, Harrod's reasoning has centred on his Fundamental Equation, which has appeared under three interpretations. The theory consists essentially in the statement of a condition, the proof that in a real economy this condition can be only precariously fulfilled, and the tracing-out of the broad consequences of its non-fulfilment. Thus the principal purpose which the Fundamental Equation must serve is to express a condition. Harrod however sought to introduce and substantiate his argument by exhibiting the equation in the first place as a book-keeping identity between two ways of describing one and the same past event, namely, a certain accretion to the formerly existing stock of capital. In this policy we think he was mistaken. The validity of the condition is a matter of logic, and not of appeal to a historical record where the condition may or may not have been fulfilled, and its non-fulfilment may well have been associated with the consequences which Harrod's theory predicts. The identity is irrelevant. In 'An Essay in Dynamic Theory' Harrod explains thus the *conditional* equation:

I now proceed directly to the Fundamental Equation, constituting the marriage of the acceleration principle and the multiplier theory. Let G stand for the geometric rate of growth of income or output in the system, the increment being expressed as a fraction of its existing level. Let G_w stand for the warranted rate of growth, [namely] that rate of growth which, if it occurs, will leave all parties satisfied that they have produced neither more nor less than the right amount, [that is] will put them into a frame of mind which will cause them to give such orders as will maintain the same rate of growth. Let s stand for the fraction of income which individuals and corporate bodies choose to save. Let C stand for the value of the capital goods required for the production of a unit increment of output. The unit of value used to measure this magnitude is the value of the unit increment of output. The [numerical] value of C depends on the state of technology and the nature of the goods constituting the increment of output. We may now write the Fundamental Equation in its simplest form $G_w = s/C.$*

* *Economic Journal*, vol. XLIX, pp. 15–17.

Provided the 'income and output' of the system and the 'capital' it uses are each accepted as measurable in ways which render it legitimate to speak of a ratio between them, a ratio having, for technological reasons, some short-period constancy, Harrod's logic in relating to each other the three capsules or black boxes of his scheme is simple and invincible. So much so, that the reader is already on his side in confronting the difficulty of proposing a principle for such measurement. A definition of economics which, however disturbing to economists, would contain a great deal of truth would be 'The study of collections of essentially diverse objects as though these collections were always quantifiable by one constant unit'. Economics is inherently and essentially imprecise. The only question is how heroic we are prepared to be, or what choice we make between simplification of the type of the Crusoe economy, where most major problems of reality are assumed away and arguments about the remainder can be logically impeccable, and simplifications of the Keynesian and Harrodian type where the need for rough-and-ready quantification is accepted. Any principle for quantifying collections of essentially (i.e. relevantly) diverse things must amount to valuation. In the passage we have quoted, Harrod explicitly resorts to this term. He says a little later 'The [numerical] value of C [the capital–output ratio] may be somewhat dependent on the rate of interest'. Harrod is here referring (I think) to the changes in technology that will be rendered profitable by changes in the interest-rate. But there is another and quite different effect of an interest-rate change, much more awkward since it operates arithmetically and therefore instantaneously, in contrast with technological changes which are inevitably slow. The value of a given item of durable equipment rests upon its expected series of future instalments (or its expected stream) of earnings or profits of operation. The present value or demand price of any *given* such stream depends upon the percentage per annum at which it is discounted. Given the relation of such profit-streams, in the aggregate, to the general output stream of which they are part, a change of the interest-rate will alter the ratio of the value of the economy's capital stock to the value of the goods annually produced with its aid, and it will do so in three distinguishable modes: first, by a general change in the present value of all *given* streams of expected profits; secondly, by a differential effect on these present values, those of streams extending far into future years being more affected than short prospects; and, thirdly, by inducing, through this differential effect on values, a gradual change in the technological composition of the economy's capital stock. Are such considerations serious, or even fatal, for a macro-economic argument such as Harrod's? They are certainly nothing of the sort. Slow changes are beside the point: no one supposes that Harrodian regular growth can continue for long at a given percentage per annum without upset from within or without. Even the arithmetical changes are likely to be small. The interest-rates which matter for the valuation of capital goods are the long or medium-term ones. For these, an alteration from 3 to 4, or from 6 to 8, within a year will be rather exceptionally large; yet even such a change as this will not markedly affect the present value of capital goods with a life of less than half the reciprocal of the interest-rate; say, of less than ten years.

After writing his fundamental condition for regular growth as above, Harrod immediately states the meaning he assigns to his equation and his reason for believing it important:

It should be noticed that the warranted rate of growth of the system appears here as an unknown term, the value of which is determined by certain 'fundamental conditions'—namely, the propensity to save and the state of technology, etc. Those who define dynamic as having a cross-reference to two points of time may not regard this equation as dynamic; that particular definition of dynamic has its own interest and field of reference. I prefer to define dynamic as referring to propositions in which a rate of growth appears as an unknown variable. This equation is clearly more fundamental than those expressing lags of adjustment.*

'Propositions in which a rate of growth appears as an unknown variable.' This is indeed an illuminating definition. When Sir Roy implies, however, that his model dispenses with lags of adjustment, we had rather say that such lags *disappear* when the condition, which is the hinge of his theory, is fulfilled. Fulfilment of the condition consists in a precise *échelonning* of orders and completions of equipment, such that the later, larger orders absorb the newly completed extra capacity which has sprung from earlier orders. This, of course, is not how Harrod thinks

* *Economic Journal*, vol. XLIX, p. 17.

of the matter. He formally abolishes lags by a resort to the telescoping process which is characteristic of the differential calculus. Essentially, nonetheless, lags remain implicit in his model.

Harrod proceeds, in his 1939 article, to 'prove' the validity of his equation, but does so by a curious detour via its *ex post* interpretation, which adds nothing to our understanding of its logic, except in so far as it reveals a kind of 'period analysis' underlying Harrod's thought. This period analysis could have been equally well performed in *ex ante* terms, and the fact that Harrod at first avoids them shows how hard it is for a new idea, however powerful and salutary, to make its way in unaccustomed minds. It is fair to say that Harrod presumably learnt of the *ex ante* construction from Ohlin, who is by no means the most convincing user and expositor of it. Harrod completes the laying of his foundations by a curious remark which reappears in some of his later expositions and is, we think, bound to puzzle his reader. Writing C_p for the *ex post* or recorded ratio of extra equipment to extra output, and G for the recorded growth-rate, Harrod says that 'if $C = C_p$, then $G = G_w$, and $G_w = s/C$'. This is evidently to solve two unknowns from one equation. G_w, the warranted rate of growth, can only be defined as that growth-rate which fulfils an equation in which C and s are *given*. To regard *both G and C* as fluid at the same time is to render their conjunction meaningless (unless we have some further constraint or equation, which we have not). One or other of G and C can be said to have a 'required' or determinate value *given* that of the other. Harrod proceeds to consider the relevance of *ex ante* conceptions for his purpose, but with a curious hesitancy and ambiguity of language:

To use terminology recently employed by distinguished authorities, [Professor Ohlin's articles on the Stockholm School had appeared two years earlier] C_p is an *ex post* quantity. I am not clear if C should be regarded as its corresponding *ex ante*. C is rather that addition to capital goods in any period, which producers regard as ideally suited to the output which they are undertaking in that period.

' . . . which they *are undertaking*'. This phrase in this connection suggests that the essence and meaning of the *ex ante-ex post* distinction has been missed and misconceived. That distinction points to a *qualitative difference of nature* between the time in

front of us filled only with our individual imaginations, intentions, hopes and fears, in forms of unlimited diversity and in-
compatibility; and the time behind us, a matter of records which
can in principle be partly public, consistent and agreed. The
point is not a quibble. It may seem that 'are undertaking' can
easily enough be read as 'intend to produce' or 'have decided
on'. But we cannot afford to blur the issue. 'Are undertaking'
hankers after the mechanical conception and the abolition of
the difference between past and future. It is a question of the
highest relevance and importance for the purpose of this book
to consider why a mind of such originality and power should in
1939, and, it would seem, in all the subsequent years, have
found the Myrdalian conception difficult and alien. Not only
Harrod but Keynes and many others have found it so, for
Keynes also in the *Treatise* uses similar expressions which
deliberately blot out the question of the temporal viewpoint.
The reason, I believe, goes very deep. It is the wish to preserve
the economic subject-matter as something rational and rationally understandable. To admit that actions spring from an
immense variety of un-coordinated and un-coordinable thoughts
based upon insufficient evidence and interpreting that evidence
with all the freedom which that insufficiency allows, producing
from it mutually incongruous expectations and plans which by
that very incongruity are largely condemned to disappointment; is not this to admit that economics and all the studies of
the genetics of history are a discussion of essential *disorder*, an
attempt to impose meaning upon the accidental or chaotic?
Without an underlying discernible repetitiveness, science is
impossible. By sticking to the observable and measurable
external aspect of things which *have happened*, by accepting as
real only the *ex post*, we turn our eyes away from that disorder
and keep them fixed on what has become, at any rate, a single
narrative instead of a multiplicity of conjectures.

Harrod points out that the definitions and constructions of
the *Treatise on Money*, where saving and investment could be
unequal, 'may still be a useful aid to thinking if we substitute for
"Investment" *ex ante* investment'. Why, with this insight, did
Harrod himself not subsequently take that road?*

* The present writer's *Expectations, Investment and Income* (Oxford University
Press, May 1938) was an *ex ante* interpretation of the *General Theory*.

Harrod's dynamic theory is propounded in three steps: the statement of a condition; the proof that this condition can at best be only occasionally and precariously fulfilled; and the tracing of a variety of circumstances and consequences of its non-fulfilment. As to the prescription for regular growth, it ought really to comprise two conditions. Harrod's equation tells us what relation regular growth requires between the speed of percentage growth of general output (the time which output takes to grow by one per cent of itself) and the percentage of general output which the society is willing to leave unconsumed, this relation depending on the number of 'units of general equipment' (comprising all sorts of goods involved in the productive process) required, or desirable, per unit of output. But the incentive to order extra equipment (the incentive to invest) which Harrod ascribes to the desire of business men to increase their output, will not work unless the *existing* equipment is no more than what is desirable, or required, for the *existing* general output. For if the existing stock of equipment is greater than this, an increase of general output can be obtained by working this existing stock at a load nearer to, rather than further from, the optimum. Thus a second condition ought to state that regular growth can only start from a position where existing equipment is employed at the desired or optimum load, so that its relation to the existing general output is that of the desired capital–output ratio. Even when this initial condition is fulfilled, however, the precise matching of intended net investment and intended saving, even in their respective aggregates, seems as if it must depend largely on chance. But even the slightest failure to achieve this matching must, Harrod shows, immediately destroy the relevance of the former equilibrium growth-rate and lead to a cumulative upward or downward explosion. The paradoxical nature of this instability, and its sharp contrast with the stability normally ascribed to 'demand and supply' relations in a static model (except when lags of adjustment lead to the 'cobweb' phenomenon) is a discovery which Harrod regards as one of the chief fruits of his work:

The dynamic theory so far stated may be summed up in two propositions. (i) A unique warranted line of growth is determined jointly by the propensity to save and the quantity of capital required by technological and other considerations per unit increment of total output. Only if producers keep to this line will they find that on balance their production in each period has been neither excessive nor deficient. (ii) On either side of this line is a 'field' in which centrifugal forces operate. Departure from the warranted line sets up an inducement to depart farther from it. The moving equilibrium of advance is thus a highly unstable one. The essential point here may be further explained by reference to the expressions over-production and under-production. We may define general over-production as a condition in which producers representing the major part of production find they have produced or ordered too much, in the sense that they find themselves in possession of an unwanted volume of stocks or equipment. By reference to the fundamental equation it appears that this state of things can only occur when the actual growth has been *below* the warranted growth—i.e. a condition of general over-production is the consequence of producers in sum producing too little. Over production is the consequence of production below the warranted level. Conversely, if producers find that they are continually running short of stocks and equipment, this means that they are producing above the warranted level.*

The extreme paradox which Harrod here achieves has contributed justly and greatly to the fame of his theory. It contains a highly important element of truth. Yet like all paradox it must have its rational explanation. And that explanation lies, yet again, in Harrod's reading too much into his own exploitation of the differential calculus in a quasi-mechanical application. It is when business men are *planning, intending,* to produce an output which exceeds recent output too far for available prospective additions to equipment to support it, that they will feel restricted by an insufficient willingness of society to save. When the *orders* they give for extra equipment drive up too far the prices of this equipment (or lengthen too much its delivery dates), because it cannot be produced in the desired quantities within the desired time except by costly pressure on *existing* productive capacity, the business men, the would-be investors in this equipment, will find themselves 'over-producing', that is, *intending* to produce more than is economically feasible. The lags between the phases of the phenomenon turn out, after all, to be essential. It is not when business men *have* produced a great deal more in the just-elapsed period than they did in the preceding one, that they will feel that they have under-

* *Economic Journal,* vol. XLIX, pp. 23, 24.

produced. It is not *ex post* production which can perversely disappoint by being too big and therefore seeming too small. To think this is to force the paradox into absurdity. It is *ex ante* production which can be too great for *ex ante* saving out of an income which, at first, in the *immediate* future, will be no bigger than in the immediate past.

It is when he seeks to analyse the nature and consequences of a departure from warranted growth that Harrod finds the absence of an explicit apparatus of time-lags most inconvenient. He is driven to admit the need for such a scheme, though in a very confusing way:

The foregoing demonstration of the inherent instability of the moving equilibrium, or warranted line of advance, depends on the assumption that the values of s and C are independent of the value of G. This is formally correct. The analysis relates to a single point of time. s is regarded as likely to vary with a change in the size of income, but a change in the rate of growth at a given point of time has no effect on its size. C may also be expected to vary with the size of income, e.g. owing to the occurrence of surplus capital capacity from time to time, but the same argument for regarding it as independent of the rate of growth at a particular point of time applies. It may be objected, however, that this method of analysis is too strict to be realistic, since the discovery that output is excessive or deficient, and the consequent emergence of a depressing or stimulating force, takes some time, and in the interval required for a reaction to be produced an appreciable change in s or C may have occurred.*

The main question raised in this passage (namely, whether s can be regarded as an increasing function of G, and whether, if so, a higher rate of growth might be able to induce the necessary extra flow of saving) need not concern us. The supposition, as Harrod proceeds to show, is not worth considering. We ourselves are concerned, first, with the ambiguity which here reappears about the meaning of C. If C means the technologically based required or desired ratio of capital-in-use to output, why should it vary appreciably with moderate short-period changes of output? If it means the *ex post* ratio of capital which actually was available in comparison with the output which actually was produced, then its variations are a consequence, and not a cause, of dis-equilibrium, that is of the

* *Ibid.* vol. XLIX, pp. 24, 25.

failure of growth to proceed at a percentage per time-unit which just absorbs in investment the output left unused by consumption. Secondly, we may note that in the latter part of our quoted passage Harrod defines two time-lags, the first of which, at any rate, would be highly useful in dissecting the *process of departure* from warranted growth. And he does in fact proceed to make use of this 're-action time' in an argument about the degree to which s might increase with G. He speaks (pp. 25, 26) of 'the time required for an undue accretion or depletion of capital goods to exert its influence upon the flow of orders'.

The third step of Harrod's argument is to trace the types of behaviour which an economic system, broadly conforming in character to his fundamental equation, would show in various combinations of circumstances. The statement of these circumstances themselves requires a third version of his equation, in which the rate of growth is the one permitted, as a long-term trend, by the combined effects of the growth of population and the improvement of technology:

Next it is desirable to relate these two equations (viz. the fundamental equation in its meaning of a *condition* for self-justifying growth and in its meaning of an *ex-post* record of events] to that steady rate of advance determined by fundamental conditions. [We may write] G_n (n for natural) for the rate of advance which the increase of population and technological improvements allow. G_n has no direct relation to G_w. G_n represents the line of output at each point on which producers of all kinds [viz. all suppliers of productive means, not merely entrepreneurs] will be satisfied that they are making a correct balance between work and leisure; it excludes the possibility of involuntary unemployment. G_w is the entrepreneurial equilibrium; it is the line of advance, which, if achieved, will satisfy profit-takers that they have done the right thing.*

Thus *maintainable full employment* in Harrod's system requires $G_n = s/C$ or $G_n = G_w$. We have taken the foregoing passage from Harrod's book of 1948, rather than from the last pages of his 1939 article. In that article, Harrod introduces the notion of long-range investment (investment not related to or induced by the intended growth of output) before coming to the discussion of disequilibrium in the simplest possible growth model. It

---

* *Towards a Dynamic Economics* (Macmillan, 1948), p. 87.

is by studying the possible relations between the actual (re-corded, realized) growth-rate G, the warranted rate G_w, and the natural rate G_n, that Harrod provides the materials or com-ponent parts which Sir John Hicks later assembled into a pre-cisely articulated trade-cycle machine. In a few lines, in terms of these relationships, Harrod sets out a complete scheme of explanation of the origins and governing circumstances of prosperity and depression. Perpetual alternations of boom and collapse, on one hand, or under-employment equilibrium, on the other, are seen as natural conditions of an economy which relies for its inducement to invest mainly on the accelerator mechanism:

The relation of G_n to G_w is clearly of crucial importance in deter-mining whether the economy over a term of years is likely to be preponderatingly lively or depressed. Whenever G exceeds G_w there will be a tendency for a boom to develop; and conversely. Now if G_n exceeds G_w there is no reason why G should not exceed G_w for most of the time. Consequently there is no reason why the economy should not enjoy a recurrent tendency to develop boom conditions. But if G_w exceeds G_n then G must lie below G_w for most of the time, since the average value of G over a period cannot exceed that of G_n. Therefore in such circumstances we must expect the economy to be prevailingly depressed. In a revival, in which unemployed resources are brought back to work, G stands above G_n. When full employ-ment is reached it must be reduced to G_n. If G_n stands below G_w then a slump is inevitable at that point, since G has to fall below G_w and will, for the time being, be driven progressively downwards.*

This simple frame of ideas is exploited in Harrod's various 'dynamic' publications with extraordinary virtuosity and imaginative subtlety. He supposes and accounts for variations in s and C_r during the course of output fluctuations and con-siders the consequences of this; takes account of the distinction between goods in process and durable instruments; considers the influence of interest-rate changes and brings in the notion of 'deepening' as distinct from 'widening' of equipment; and finally relaxes his tacit concentration on 'real' events and allows price-level changes to play a part. It is of course out of the question to quote enough to follow out these intricate speculations. The claim that Harrod has, in this work, had

* *Ibid.* pp. 87–9.

most notable and powerful insights, and that as a whole it constitutes a great discovery, is, we think, irrefutable. Before we
turn to ask what antecedents are to be found in the literature,
we may notice his own cautious words:

> While the equations clearly show the instability of an advancing
> economy, they do not in themselves provide very good tools for
> analysing the course of the slump.*

In 1962 the *Journal of Political Economy* marked its seventieth
anniversary by collecting into a book twenty-four articles
judged, by a panel of the *Journal's* former or current editors, to
be the most original and seminal that the seventy volumes had
included. Amongst these articles were two which are of special
concern to us. John Maurice Clark in 1917, in 'Business Acceleration and the Law of Demand: a Technical Factor in
Business Cycles', not only was one of the (at least) three writers
who independently of each other introduced the acceleration
principle into economic literature, but he also, to a remarkable
extent, anticipated the modern accelerator–multiplier theory
of the business cycle as a whole. The development of this latter
theory during the 1930s by Frisch, Hansen and above all by
Harrod was traced and systematized in 1939 in two famous
articles by Paul Samuelson, one of which is included in the
Journal of Political Economy volume and is the second of those
which specially interest us. John Maurice Clark thus explains
the accelerator:

> There is one circumstance which can convert a slackening of the rate
> of growth in one industry into an absolute decline in another. Every
> producer of things to be sold to producers has two demands to meet.
> He must maintain the industrial equipment already in use and the
> stocks of materials and goods on their way to the final consumer, and
> he must also furnish any new equipment that is wanted for new con-
> struction, enlargements or betterments, and any increase in the stocks
> of materials and unsold goods. A change from one year to the next
> in the rate of consumption has a temporary effect on the demand
> for the intermediate product which is greater than its permanent
> effect, in just about the proportion by which the total amount of
> investment in the intermediate product exceeds the amount annually
> spent for maintenance.

* *Towards a Dynamic Economics*, p. 90.

This latter statement is formally demonstrated thus:

Let t = years elapsed between two dates, t_1 and t_2.

Let C = rate of consumption at time t.

Let $C + \Delta C$ = rate of consumption at time t_2, the increase being distributed evenly through time t.

Let I = investment [*stock* of producers' goods] necessary to produce output at rate C.

Let L = average life of instruments included in I, in years.

Then maintenance is required at the rate I/L. The demand for new construction during time t is $I\,(\Delta C/C)$, an annual amount equal to $I\,(\Delta C/Ct)$.

Demand for new construction is to previous demand for maintenance as

$$I\,(\Delta C/Ct) : I/L \text{ [that is, a ratio]} \quad \frac{\Delta C}{C}\frac{L}{t}.$$

This final expression admirably condenses the essence of the accelerator principle. If, between one year and the next, consumable output increases from one steady level to another, the demand for investment goods increases, between those two years, by a percentage which results from multiplying together two factors: first, the ratio of the increment of consumable output to the former level of that output, and, secondly, the durability in years of investment goods on the average. It is, indeed, the durability of much equipment which, by reducing the annual replacement to a small fraction of the first cost, gives net investment so powerful a weight in the total demand for investment goods. The disturbing consequence is, of course, that unless consumable output rises between the second and third year, and so on perpetually, investment goods demand will fall back to virtually its level in the first year.

The acceleration principle shows how a change in the *pace of growth* of the monthly quantity of goods consumed can, and must, induce a change in the same direction in the monthly *quantity produced* of equipment and producers' stores. But this is not enough by itself to explain the business cycle, for we have still to ask why the monthly or the annual increments of the flow of consumption should vary in size or sign. Clark himself had his hand upon the answer, yet strangely abandons it:

The demand for consumers' goods fluctuates quite decidedly [in the statistics assembled by Wesley Mitchell] but the greater part of its fluctuations appears to be the result of changes in the amount of unemployment which result from the business cycle itself.

The mathematically directed economists of the 1930s, Ragnar Frisch, Tinbergen and Kalecki, would introduce in those years the conception of an inherently oscillating system, and Samuelson would interpret this general conception on lines already, before he wrote in 1939, proposed by Harrod and visible in the work of Alvin Hansen, namely, the combined and interlocking operation of the Accelerator and the Multiplier. Clark makes no reference in his article of 1917 to any other proponents of the acceleration principle, and he is no doubt its most careful early expositor. He was, however, anticipated by two other writers. In 1913 Albert Aftalion published his *Les crises périodiques de surproduction* which contained the suggestion, and in 1914 F. Bickerdike published in the *Economic Journal* an article called 'A Non-monetary Cause of Fluctuations in Employment'.

For the theory of business cycles the year 1936 was the Apocalypse: the revelation and the end. It was the end because in the intervening thirty years we have had no business cycle of the kind which is discernible throughout the nineteenth century and the first third of the twentieth, reaching a fearful climax in 1930–3. Recovery and boom swung up to a peak in 1937; by 1938, employment, output and prices were again on their way down; but the new cycle was killed by the plain imminence of war, and never matured. Nor has anything remotely comparable with 1929–37 happened since. The year 1936 was also the beginning of the end for business cycle theorizing, for it provided so powerfully convincing a basic general model, that the task of filling in the details, brilliantly accomplished in various versions by Harrod, Kalecki, Samuelson, Kaldor and Hicks during the decade following our period, began to pall, and has not since been resumed. That model, the immediate consequence of combining the Multiplier and the Accelerator, each defined in a time-lagged form, was first stated in print by Harrod within six months of the publication of the *General Theory*. It was the first of what I have ventured elsewhere to call the Keynesesque*

---

* The same name for Keynes-inspired but variant models occurred to Sir John Hicks but he shrank from it. See his *Capital and Growth*, p. 104, and my *A Scheme of Economic Theory*, p. 99. We had no knowledge of each other's books, both published in the summer of 1965.

models of macro-economics, models where Keynes's decision to treat investment as autonomous, that is, not explicable by reference to the other variables of the system, was reversed, and investment was made to depend in very simple style on the level or the movements of general output. Harrod had enjoyed the advantage of reading the *General Theory* before publication. But so had several others. Among them all it was he who seized with impetuous urgency the chance to make a great suggestion and broadly indicate its massive implications. *The Trade Cycle* appeared in August 1936, during the Oxford meeting of the Econometric Society where, on a remarkable occasion, three classic and still-famous critiques of the *General Theory* were read by those respectively who are now Sir John Hicks, Professor James Meade, and Sir Roy Harrod himself. After his paper, Sir Roy was asked whether, when he used the expression 'output is increasing', he meant 'output has been increasing', or 'output is expected to increase'. But he was thinking in terms of physical mechanics, 'dynamics' in the sense of the forces bearing on a particle, and would at that time have nothing to do with *ex ante* and *ex post*. Physical analogies could still channel the thought of a brilliantly originative mind. Nor dare we suggest that in this he followed a false trail. Theorizing is simplification, abstraction. Who is to say that abstraction from the effects of ostensible human uncertainty and non-empty* decision is not essential for some insights? It is a view from which we may dissent, but not one which we can contemn.

The new business cycle theories had in common a power, simplicity and internal unity which make the pre-Keynesian ones seem tiresome tinkering by comparison. Nor can we doubt that the exuberance of new business cycle thought sprang straight from the seed-bed of the *General Theory*. Yet there was an ironic twist. The *Treatise* was concerned with phenomena central to the business cycle and regarded as interesting largely on that account. We may say that the *Treatise* was a piece of economic dynamics in something like the modern sense. But the

---

* By this expression I sought in my *Decision Order and Time* to suggest the distinction between a decision which is empty in the sense of merely registering the implication of adequate information, and decision which contributes something to fill the gap of uncertainty.

General Theory turned away, concerned itself ostensibly with states or situations rather than events, adopted a formally equilibrium method, and relegated the business cycle to a single chapter, as a mere illustration of the new theory's powers. And when next Harrod himself wrote on the Multiplier-Accelerator nexus it was as a theory of growth and not of the business cycle. The business cycle continued to be the object of complex and ingenious thought: but in 1966, pending the collapse of prosperity which some have been long awaiting, these works now appear in the light of *oraisons funèbres*.

To read *The Trade Cycle* again after thirty years is to be astonished at the list of ideas, adopted since by others as part of the presuppositions of their work, which seem to have first been made explicit in its pages. Harrod's first chapter at its outset explains the case for regarding economic life, in its purest essentials, as an orderly, self-regulating process, where any unbalance brings its own plain penalties and people will be led, by their natural response to circumstances, to manage their lives efficiently and 'economically'. This picture of order and equilibrium applies, however, to an economy which manages without money. Money conceals and disguises the effects of the ultimate pressures and conditions, viz. the need for sustenance and shelter, the distastefulness of effort, and the facts of technology. Money is a 'destabilizer', perhaps causing, but at least allowing, by changes in its abundance relative to prevailing prices and output, or in its velocity of circulation, the size of general output to fluctuate widely in spite of the virtually un-varying strength and the steady operation of the three (or four) basic stabilizers. As to whether money, and the banking system which administers it, play an active or merely passive role in the mechanism of fluctuation of output, Harrod pronounces no verdict. He does not reject those explanations which ascribe the business cycle to purely monetary causes. He appeals to the nature of money merely as an explanation of how another cause, the one he wishes to suggest, can operate in the face of the three basic stabilizers. This other cause is the combined operation of the Relation, as Harrod calls the Accelerator, and the Kahn–Keynes Multiplier.

To establish the reality of the Relation, Harrod confronts with one another, on one hand, the statistical facts of the business cycle so richly analysed in the 'thirties by Wesley Mitchell and his assistants at the National Bureau of Economic Research, as described by John Maurice Clark, and on the other the evident theoretical relation of growth of output to growth of equipment. The latter, he suggests, explains the former:

In order to maintain output at a given level, replacements [of durable equipment] of a constant amount are necessary. In order to increase the output of consumable goods, additional capital goods (net investment) are necessary. The amount of these latter depends on the rate at which consumption is increasing. Thus if consumption were advancing at the rate of 2 per cent per annum, only half as much net investment would be necessary as would be required to sustain an advance of 4 per cent. And, since net investment is responsible for a large proportion of the activity of capital goods industries, a cessation of the advance of consumption, without any decrease in its absolute amount, would entail a vast falling off in the activity of capital goods industries.*

And then the Multiplier:

[Mr Keynes] propounds the view that the general level of economic activity is determined by the amount of investment taking place, in such wise that, given the community's propensity to save, the activity must be just so great as to give people an income from which they will choose to save the amount that is required for that investment. The ratio of the increment of income (= the increment of output) required to make people save an amount equal to the increment of investment [to that increment of investment] is called the Multiplier. It is the contention of this essay that by a study of the interconnexions between the Multiplier and the Relation the secret of the trade cycle may be revealed. The theory of the multiplier implies that the level of activity is not otherwise predetermined and is in accord with doctrines regarding the monetary de-stabilizer already put forward.†

Harrod's account of the actual process and mechanism of the cycle (p. 71, last three lines, to p. 75) is remarkable for two things. Implicit throughout this tracing of a *sequence* of phases and events, there is the idea of *lagged* influence of one variable on another. Only the word *lag* itself is absent. Secondly, there is

* R. F. Harrod, *The Trade Cycle* (Oxford: The Clarendon Press, 1936), p. 55.
† *Ibid.* p. 70.

here implicit the idea of the distinction and vital difference between expected and realized quantities. Only the expressions *ex ante* and *ex post* are absent. Thus there is a strange phenomenon observable in the work of these two writers, Keynes and Harrod. Both of them, in the fresh and uninhibited first response to a challenge and an inspiration, describe what happens in a world of humans, whose prime requirement before they act is some data and recorded facts about what others *have been* doing, and who must form on the basis of these data some expectations and intentions about what they themselves *will* do. Both of them, in this first fine frenzy, write Myrdalian dynamics. The *Treatise* and the *Trade Cycle* are full of the natural give and take of a world where people must find out, compare, decide, before they act; then register results and make fresh plans and decisions. But when we come to the *General Theory* and *Towards a Dynamic Economics*, all this has been banished in deference to the formal respectability of 'equilibrium'. There is a most curious psychic twist of unconscious argument in all this. Theories give knowledge, and so (it is unconsciously felt) knowledge must be ascribed to the people who play a part in our theories. It is almost as though the writers said to themselves: We cannot theorize rationally about conduct which is not completely rational. The dominance of the equilibrium idea, in one or other of its many forms, goes very deep in economics. Is it beneath the dignity of humans to recognize the human predicament of uncertain expectation? The *General Theory*, of course, is wholly concerned with uncertain expectation but still allows itself (except in chapter 22, on the Trade Cycle) no liberty to connect sequential states of mind with each other.

Let us turn lastly to Samuelson's appraisal and sublimation of the Multiplier–Accelerator theory of the business cycle.

In two brief articles Samuelson brought rigour and system into the field of Multiplier–Accelerator interaction. In 'Interactions between the Acceleration Principle and the Multiplier' (*Review of Economics and Statistics*, May 1939) he showed by an arithmetical example that if today's consumption spending is proportional to yesterday's income, and today's net investment is proportional to the difference between the consumption spending of yesterday and the day before, never-ending cyclical oscillation can be self-generated in the system. The same will be true if, for example, net investment is made to depend on the difference of today's and yesterday's consumption, or on the difference of income, that is, the sum of consumption spending and net investment, for the two successive days. Perpetual oscillations, however, are only one possible type of behaviour of such a system. In 'A Synthesis of the Principle of Acceleration and the Multiplier' (*Journal of Political Economy*, vol. XLVII, 1939) Samuelson puts the Relation, β, on the horizontal axis, and the marginal propensity to consume, α, on the vertical axis, of a Cartesian diagram, which is then divided by curves into four regions:

For the special linear case the results can be briefly summarized. With any given value for the propensity to consume, small values of the Relation yield no cyclical behaviour, merely asymptotic approaches to stationary equilibrium. For the same α, slightly larger values for β lead to cyclical oscillations which become smaller and smaller. Still larger values of the Relation result in cyclical oscillations becoming greater and greater but oscillating around the position of stationary equilibrium. Very large values of β lead to explosive cumulative movements growing at a rate of compound interest.

Such systematic exploration is done by expressing the mutual lagged dependences of income, or consumption, and investment as a difference equation, and a rich field of theoretical subtleties is thus opened up. Whether statistical data can ever enable us to pin any segment of real history on to the precise but essentially rather simple frame of such an equation is a quite different question.

Samuelson expresses in conclusion an evident deep admiration for Harrod's work together with the cautions that he feels bound to attach to it:

A comparison of the foregoing results with Harrod's brilliant chapter ii [of the *Trade Cycle*] will reveal many discrepancies. Upon rigorous analysis his exposition will be found to abound with non-sequiturs and over-simplifications. On the whole, Harrod's intuition surpasses his reasoned conclusions—of what investigator worth his salt is this not true?

CHAPTER 17

LEONTIEF'S 'TABLEAU ÉCONOMIQUE'

Industries supply their products to other industries, as well as to consumers. The number of physical units annually demanded of a product is thus made up of two parts: the quantity taken by those who will put it directly to some purpose of human sustenance and enjoyment, and the quantity taken by those who will use it in making some further product. For each product, the total quantity annually demanded may thus be altered by a change in consumers' direct demand for some other product. When all products are considered together, the effects of a change in the relative quantities annually demanded by consumers, upon the total quantities which will have to be annually produced, thus depend upon an intricate web of interlinked productive 'recipes' or production functions, each stating for some one industry the quantities of other industries' products that it requires for making one unit of its own product. The central purpose of Wassily Leontief's input–output analysis is to make possible the calculation of the respective *total* quantities annually required of all products, from a *given* list or 'bill' of the quantities to be supplied direct to consumers.

Far-reaching simplification is required. Industries and products are assumed to be in one–one correspondence: each industry makes only one product, each product is made by only one industry. Any industry and its product viewed as supply can be denoted i; any industry and its product viewed as purchaser and absorber of another industry's product can be denoted j. Thus an industry or product may be called in one context i, in another j, and each of these symbols, or labels, is taken to range over the whole list of industries and their products. Use of a product to make another product we call an *intermediate* use; use of a product by a consumer for his sustenance and enjoyment we call a *final* use.

The central notion of input–output analysis is the *input coefficient*. It states the quantity of product i required for making one unit of product j. Accounting simplicity and coherence is served by measuring all quantities as value at fixed prices, since quantities thus expressed can be added up. Statistics tell us how much in some recent year was produced of product j, and the total purchase in that year by industry j of output i. This relationship is assumed to represent a quasi-permanent technological necessity. Dividing the annual production, X_j, of product j into the quantity thus absorbed, X_{ij}, of product i we get the input coefficient

$$\frac{X_{ij}}{X_j} = a_{ij}.$$

We now write down for some industry i a series of terms, of which a typical term $a_{ij}X_j$ shows how much of product i is absorbed by industry j. Having written one such term for each industry j, that is, for each intermediate use of product i (including a term showing how much of i was used in producing i itself), we write also a term Y_i showing how much of product i we are supposing to be annually taken for final use by consumers. The entire series of terms then adds up to the total quantity annually produced of product i. It *accounts* for this output, X_i, by showing how it is disposed of and absorbed, and it thus expresses X_i as *dependent on* the final demand Y_i for product i and on each of the *total* annual quantities produced of all the products including i. Now what we desire is an expression of this total annual requirement of product i in terms, not of the *total* quantities annually required of all the products, for their intermediate as well as their final uses, but in terms of their *final* use quantities only. We wish, in fact, to transform the system of equations, each of the form

$$X_i - \Sigma\, a_{ij}X_j = Y_i,$$

(where, instead of writing out the terms individually with plus signs between them, we have used the Greek capital sigma, Σ, to mean 'add together all terms of which $a_{ij}X_j$ is a general representative') into another set each having the form

$$X_i = \Sigma\, r_{ij}Y_j.$$

The central operation of input–output analysis is the *solution* of the former set of equations so as to derive, from the information they contain, the numerical values of the new coefficients r_{ij}.

The Leontief system, and the operations involved in solving it, compellingly invite expression in the notation of matrix algebra. A matrix is a table of entries (numbers or more general symbols) in which each entry stands at the intersection of a row and a column of such entries, so that with m rows and n columns there are m times n entries in all. This scheme provides, in the first place, a highly compact and also a self-checking means of book-keeping. The double-entry principle, whereby an amount which has to be transferred from one account to another is recorded in both accounts, one showing it as having been subtracted and the other as having been added, is here served by a single entry, the amount of which is deemed to pass from the account represented by the particular column in which the entry stands to the account represented by the row in which it stands. Thus when one industry buys from another a quantity of the latter's product, the value paid is written in the column labelled with the name of the purchasing industry and the row labelled with the name of the selling industry. One and the same sequence of industry names being used in assigning a row to each industry, and a column to each industry, and the industries being labelled with numbers in this sequence, the entries representing purchases by an industry from itself occupy the 'main diagonal' from top left to bottom right of the matrix. When each entry in some one column of the table is divided by the total quantity annually produced, in value at a fixed price, by the industry to which this column belongs, each resulting quotient is an input coefficient. In this way the initial 'transactions matrix' is transformed into a matrix of input coefficients, each of which can be linked to the selling industry and the purchasing industry involved by writing as subscripts the numbers which label these industries, so that the value of product i annually sold for intermediate use to industry j per value-unit of product j is noted, say, a_{ij}.

Two matrices can be multiplied together provided that, when they are written side by side, the one standing on the right has as many rows as there are columns in the one standing on the left. Then the first column of the right-hand matrix is deemed to be lifted bodily and superposed on the top row of the left-hand matrix so as to form pairs of entries. Within each such pair, the two members are multiplied together. The results of these multiplications are then added. A similar operation is performed between the second row of the left-hand matrix and still the same, first, column of the right-hand one, then with the third row, and so on. Next the second column of the right-hand matrix is multiplied with each row of the left-hand matrix in the same way, and its third column, and so on. In the end there results a new matrix with as many rows as the initial left-hand matrix and as many columns as the initial right-hand matrix. Thus when the right-hand matrix has only a single column, whose m entries stand for the total quantities annually produced by the m different industries, and the left-hand matrix has m columns and m rows of input coefficients, the result of multiplying them together will be a column of entries, each of the form

$$\Sigma a_{ij} X_j$$

showing how much of product i is annually purchased for intermediate use by all industries taken together. The pattern for three industries is as follows:

$$\begin{bmatrix} a_{11} & a_{12} & a_{13} \\ a_{21} & a_{22} & a_{23} \\ a_{31} & a_{32} & a_{33} \end{bmatrix} \begin{bmatrix} X_1 \\ X_2 \\ X_3 \end{bmatrix} = \begin{bmatrix} \Sigma a_{1j} X_j \\ \Sigma a_{2j} X_j \\ \Sigma a_{3j} X_j \end{bmatrix}$$

where $\Sigma a_{1j} X_j$ is the total annual requirement of product 1 for *intermediate use in all industries* (including industry 1) taken together; $\Sigma a_{2j} X_j$ is the total intermediate use of product 2; and so on.

Two matrices can be added or subtracted provided they have the same numbers of rows as each other, and provided they have the same numbers of columns as each other. Then addition or subtraction simply consists in adding or subtracting corresponding entries: the entry in row 2 and column 3 of one matrix is (e.g.) subtracted from the entry in row 2 and column 3 of the other matrix. Thus when X_i stands for the *total* annual production of industry i, and Y_i stands for the annual quantity of product i demanded by consumers for *final* use, we can write

$$\begin{bmatrix} X_1 \\ X_2 \\ X_3 \end{bmatrix} - \begin{bmatrix} a_{11} & a_{12} & a_{13} \\ a_{21} & a_{22} & a_{23} \\ a_{31} & a_{32} & a_{33} \end{bmatrix} \begin{bmatrix} X_1 \\ X_2 \\ X_3 \end{bmatrix} = \begin{bmatrix} Y_1 \\ Y_2 \\ Y_3 \end{bmatrix}$$

or using a single capital letter in bold face to stand for an entire matrix, we can write this equation with its four matrices

$$X - AX = Y.$$

The identity matrix, whose role in matrix algebra is that played by *unity* in ordinary algebra, leaves unchanged any matrix with which it is multiplied. It can have any number of rows, and must have the same number of columns. For three rows and columns it is

$$I = \begin{bmatrix} 1 & 0 & 0 \\ 0 & 1 & 0 \\ 0 & 0 & 1 \end{bmatrix}$$

Thus instead of $X - AX = Y$

we can write $IX - AX = Y,$

or $(I-A)X = Y.$

This expression simply states in matrix language that the total annual production of each product i, less the quantity of it annually required for intermediate use by other industries, is equal to the quantity annually available for consumers. So far we have done nothing but express the relations imposed upon the quantities by the necessity of accounting coherence. The vital step is to change this equation into one where X, instead of Y, appears all by itself on one side of the 'equals' sign, and Y, instead of X, appears, multiplied by a coefficient, on the other side. This exchange of roles by X and Y, the former becoming the 'dependent' instead of the 'independent' variable, and vice versa, is the solving of the matrix equation, that is to say, the solving of the *system* of equations each of the form

$$X_i - \Sigma a_{ij} X_j = Y_i.$$

This solving operation, expressed in matrix language, requires us to find for the matrix $(I-A)$ an *inverse*, written $(I-A)^{-1}$, such that $(I-A)\ (I-A)^{-1} = I$. If we can find such an inverse, say $(I-A)^{-1} = R$, we can multiply by it both sides of the equation

$$(I-A)X = Y$$

and get $(I-A)\ RX = RY,$

or $IX = RY,$

or $X = RY$

and this will be the solution we require. The matrix R will be a column of those coefficients r_{ij} which we declared ourselves, on page 273, to be seeking. $X = RY$ can be written out in full

$$X_1 = r_{11}Y_1 + r_{12}Y_2 + r_{13}Y_3$$
$$X_2 = r_{21}Y_1 + r_{22}Y_2 + r_{23}Y_3$$
$$X_3 = r_{31}Y_1 + r_{32}Y_2 + r_{33}Y_3$$

and when, having inserted, at will, numerical values for the Y's, we perform the multiplications indicated on the right-hand side of the equals sign, we get on the left-hand side numerical values for the X's which are the respective *total* outputs of the three products sufficient, and only sufficient, to make available the prescribed Y quantities for consumers.

Leontief sought a means of filling in, with measurements taken from some real nation, the Walrasian conception of an economy as a skein or system of inter-necessary, mutually sustaining and quantitatively coherent activities. Production and consumption in the detail of their composition, the distribution and the disposal of money incomes, and the purchase by one industry of the products of another (and even, going beyond Walras, investment in equipment and the saving which, in the record, necessarily matches it), were to be included in an empirical illustration of general equilibrium. One view of such a system is given by a comprehensive set of accounts. These, whether expressed in general (i.e. algebraic) symbols or in numerical values, exhibit and require coherence: fully listed parts must be equal to their wholes; quantities transferred from one account to another must leave the total of the two accounts unchanged, and so forth. When such accounts give a picture of an actual economy, they of course consist of numerical entries, each such entry being the result of actual statistical measurement. But, in general, we can perform a given type of measurement, on material belonging to one activity of one and the same group of people, many times in various circumstances. Thus we shall get many different numerical values which can all be regarded as belonging to one and the same *class* of measurements. Such a class of measurements, when extended to include potential as well as actual ones referring to the same material, is the practical embodiment of the mathematician's notion of a variable quantity.

The state of some real economy at some historical epoch re-flects, on one hand, what we may call the design-features of that society; the tastes, skills and institutions of its people; and on the other hand, some more casual and contingent circumstances, such as the state of demand for its products by the rest of the world, the political situation, and even the quantities of natural or man-made resources which it happens to possess. If we accept such a dichotomy, we are free to ask what the state of that same society, identified by its permanent characteristics, would be if one or more of its 'casual' circumstances were differ-ent. In that case we shall have to look on many of the entries in a set of accounts describing the economy, not as uniquely valid features of the economy, inseparable from its identity, but as particular values of variable quantities, that is, as particular measurements each belonging to some class of measurements of which there are other members. Let us call a set of numerical values, one from each of a specific list of variables, a *vector*. Then a rule which permits the association together of some sets of values of this list of variables, but excludes others; a rule which, that is to say, defines a class of vectors in the space composed of these specific variables, is a *function*. The design-features, the permanent mould and identifying character of an economy, can be described by mathematical functions which express by their *form* the permanence of such features while allowing, by the mutability of the values of their variables, the expression of the variability of circumstance.

A rule defining a class of vectors is, of course, ordinarily expressed as an equation. The equation $2x - y = 0$ confines our attention to those vectors (x, y) such that $y = 2x$. What is common to all vectors of the class is specified by coefficients, as 2 in our example, and this common element, viz. the stipulation, in our example, that only those pairs of values (x, y) are to be considered where y has twice the value of x, is what we mean by the *form* of the equation, and this is the permanent or invariant feature of the equation, contrasting with the free choice open to us concerning the numerical value assigned to x, or alternatively to y.

Now the question arises, what scope is open to the policy-maker? When he sees the economy in some particular state, in what respects can he alter it? The answer will depend basically on the political institutions of the economy. In a society where everything is left to market forces, it may be appropriate to regard the entire list of variable quantities, such things as the output and price of every good, the quantity annually supplied, and the price, of every factor of production, and hence the incomes of the suppliers, and so forth, as all mutually determining each other in a system which, so long as tastes and resources remain what they are, has no freedom at all to change. Resources will, of course, be changing if knowledge is advancing or if investment in extra equipment is proceeding, but in a sufficiently 'short' period these processes may have no perceptible effect. Then we can say that there prevails a general static equilibrium such as Walras conceived. This complete determinacy of the state of affairs and of all its composing elements may find its formal reflection in our being able to write as many equations (no one of them derivable from others) as there are variables. These equations may then interlock in such a way as to assign one and only one numerical value to each variable. We can in fact write every equation so that it formally as well as impliedly involves every variable of the system, and it is the system of equations as a whole, and not one individual equation, which is to be conceived as determining each variable. The values which the system of equations determines for the variables will be governed by its structural parameters, the 'constant' coefficients by which the variables are shown as having to be multiplied. These parameters are the expression and embodiment, in the equational description of the economy, of the economy's 'permanent' design features. Our inverted commas for the words 'constant' and 'permanent' are meant to indicate that though these features have a greater stability than that of the 'variables', it is none the less necessary to assign some meaning to the notion of altering them. For in a purely free-market economy, if the policy-maker wishes to change the state of affairs he can only do so by changing either these parameters or such environmental conditions as the supply of natural forces or the available quantity of equipment. A real economy, however, is not a Walrasian system of free markets working in an environment wholly given by Nature. There are circumstances under the policy-maker's arbitrary, or free-choice, control; in especial, the rates of taxation and the fiscal system in general, and the quantity of money and the monetary system as a whole. Under some institutional arrangements, he may have direct control over the quantities of the various goods annually taken by consumers for final use. It is this latter supposition which gives to Leontief's analytical tool its most widespread application. Under this supposition, the policy-maker is free to ignore some equations of the complete system. He may, for example, be in a position to disregard those equations which, in a free market, would make the offers of productive services by 'households' depend in their quantities on the supplies of consumers' goods offered to households. To discard in this way some subset of equations is to turn the closed system into an open one where the policy-maker is free to name at will some subset of variables and to assign at will a value to each of these variables. This freedom is often made use of to specify a 'bill of goods' for final use, that is to say, a list of annual quantities, one for each of the distinct products which our descriptive scheme recognizes, which we propose to make available to consumers and other non-industrial users. By solving the truncated system of equations which remains after we have replaced some equations by an equal number of arbitrary final use quantities, we calculate the required total annual output, for intermediate and final use taken together, of each product. For the general economic plans, such as 'five-year plans', of developing or other countries, the Leontief scheme, with its various extensions and developments, is practical and valuable in the highest degree, and must surely be thought one of the best things an economist has ever invented.

Leontief's basic attitude throughout has been a conviction of the theoretical truth and practical relevance of Walras's conception. That conception is mathematically embodied in a closed system of equations, showing, in its ultimate refinement, that one and only one set of values of the variables by which we elect to describe the economy is compatible with the assumed tastes, skills and circumstances of its people. Leontief's original purpose was to quantify in this way the United States economy of 1919 and 1929, and he describes his method and results in the first edition, published in 1941, of his book *The Structure of the American Economy*. Besides the task of description, however, econometrics has that of educing the alternative goals open to policy, and the means and implications of their attainment. The basic knowledge required for this pragmatic purpose is already contained in the closed system of equations. All that is needed is to 'open' that system by disregarding some of its equations and treating some appropriate set of variables thus released as having values freely choosable by the policy-maker, subject to the known or assumed ultimate constraints consisting in the scarcity of labour and natural resources. It is as an 'open' system that the Leontief scheme has in more recent years chiefly become famous and has been applied in several dozen countries of the world. Leontief's own, concise and lucid statements must be quoted, if only to show the contrast between their author's modest outlook and his massive achievement. We shall refer to the second edition of his book, published in 1951, since although its date is outside our period, the retrospect which it contains is in every way relevant:

We are dealing here essentially with attempted application of the economic theory of general equilibrium to empirical quantitative analysis of the concrete national economy. The economy is visualized as a combination of a large number of interdependent activities; that is, of various branches of production, distribution, transportation, consumption, etc. Each one of these activities involves absorption of commodities and services originating in other branches of the economy, on the one hand, and production of commodities and services which in their turn are transferred to and absorbed in its other sectors, on the other. The commodity and service flows (transfers) taking place between the separate branches of the economy within some specified period of time, say a year, can be conveniently described by a rectangular input–output table. The main body of the table contains as many rows and [as many] columns as there are separate sections of the economy, and every row and the corresponding column are labelled accordingly. The allocation of the total output of any one industry among all the others is shown by the series of figures entered along its particular output row. The distribution of all the inputs absorbed by any one industry by origin is at the same time represented by the sequence of figures entered in the appropriate input column. Since everybody's output constitutes somebody's input, the figure entered, say, in the intersection of the 'Lumber and Timber' row and the 'Cotton Yarn and Cloth' column, shows the amount of lumber and timber products absorbed by the Cotton Yarn and Cloth industry ('Double entry' book-keeping!). By dividing all the entries in each input column* by the total output of the industry [whose] cost structure that particular column represents, we find how much of every particular kind of inputs had been absorbed per unit of the finished output.†

He proceeds to explain how the structural description of the economy, which these input-ratios give us, can be used to discover the implications of various government policies and measures. The 'closed' and complete system of equations must be relaxed into an open one by setting some equations aside; the place of these equations having been taken by free or arbitrary assignments of numerical values to variables, the remaining equations must be solved as a system. The solution will show each sector's total output as a function of all sectors' respective annual quantities required for final use. Our quoted passages are taken from the final division of part IV, a part which was added in the edition of 1951 to the three parts which constituted the original edition. At the beginning of part IV (pp. 140–52) the complete series of steps involved in discovering the technological structure of some actual economy, and in using this knowledge to find the implications of a specific 'final use' bill of goods, is spelled out by Leontief with the utmost lucidity and patient care. *The Structure of the American Economy 1919–1939* thus adds the virtues of a superlative textbook to its claims as the record of a massive pioneering exploit in practical econometrics.

The statistical study presented in the following pages may be best defined as an attempt to construct, on the basis of available statistical materials, a *Tableau Economique* of the United States for 1919 and 1929. When [in 1758] Quesnay first published his famous schema, his contemporaries and disciples acclaimed it as the greatest discovery since Newton's laws. The idea of general interdependence among the various parts of the economic system has become by now the very foundation of economic analysis.

Thus in the first words of his book Leontief defined its spirit and looked back to the most famous of his precursors in the sche-

---

* Leontief here writes 'row', but, according to his own convention, evidently means 'column'.

† Wassily W. Leontief, *The Structure of the American Economy 1919–1939*, 2nd edn (1951).

matic picturing of interdependence. Quensay's conception is precisely that of the mutual, and quantitatively coherent, support of each sector and activity by the others in a self-sufficient, closed and stationary economy. Erich Roll has admirably explained how the elements of Quesnay's *Tableau* fit together:

We start with an annual gross product of five thousand million livres. [For simplicity, let us call this 5 units.] Of this, 2 units are at once deducted in kind as the necessary expenses of reproduction (the farmer's food, the seed, etc.) The *produit net* is 3 units, of which we assume 2 units to consist of food and 1 unit of the raw materials of manufacture. In addition to this *produit net* in kind the farmers also hold the total amount of the nation's money, say [the money-value of] 2 units. The proprietors [landowners] hold nothing, but have a claim upon the farmers for rent to the amount of 2 units; while the sterile class [Quesnay thus refers to those who manufacture goods in contrast with those who aid nature to grow them] possesses 2 units' worth of manufactured goods produced in the preceding period. The farmers now pay the proprietors their 2 units [in money] as rent. The proprietors buy 1 unit's worth of food from the farmers, who thus receive back half the amount of money they had paid out. The proprietors then spend the second half of their rental revenue on the purchase of manufactured goods from the sterile class, who spend the money thus received on buying food from the farmers. The farmers now spend 1 unit in buying manufactured goods from the sterile class, who send the money back in return for raw materials. The process is now completed. The farmers are left with 2 units in money, which will serve to set the whole process going again in the next period.*

The *Tableau* shows us two circulations, that of goods and services useful in themselves, and that of money which, by flowing in the opposite direction, acknowledges and registers the transfers of real goods and services. The real flows include that of the services of land which are deemed to pass from the proprietors to the farmers. In each of these circulations separately considered, the total ingoings and the total outgoings of any one sector are equal. This can be seen by tracing the affairs of each sector in turn in Roll's account. Thus the farmers part with 2 units of food plus 1 unit of raw materials, and receive in exchange 2 units of services of land and 1 unit of manufactures.

* Erich Roll, *A History of Economic Thought*, p. 133.

The proprietors part with 2 units of services of land and receive 1 unit of food and 1 unit of manufactures. The sterile class parts with 2 units of manufactures and receives 1 unit of food and 1 unit of raw materials. But what a pedestrian labour is involved in this item by item enumeration. The whole matter can be expressed in three rows and three columns of an input–output table, in a form which is assimilable at a glance. In his *Economic Theory in Retrospect* (1964), pp. 26–9, Professor M. Blaug has set out such a table, and has even re-expressed it as a Leontief matrix or system of three equations, with an explanation of the meaning of the symbols. Quesnay's *Tableau* itself, with its arrows showing the direction of transfers and its numbers showing the matching of their totals, was a bold innovation in means of statement. Leontief's own adoption of matrix algebra was, no doubt, one more instance of the mathematician's natural and almost instinctive reflex to a need for manageable notation and compact schematism. But notational inventions or new applications can yield immense gains in insight and conceptual grasp, and in scope for empirical discovery. Let us bring our direct contemplation of the Years of High Theory to a close with this modern Leontian statement of a conception now more than two centuries old:

Producing industry		Purchasing industry			Total output
		I	II	III	
I	Farmers	2	1	2	5
II	Proprietors	2	0	0	2
III	Artisans	1	1	0	2
		5	2	2	9

Finally, is it not tempting to look back far beyond Arthur Cayley and Sir William Rowan Hamilton, and the other nineteenth-century inventors of matrix algebra, to a scheme in use by the clerks of a medieval king, where a 'square array' was employed to make money transactions verifiable by sheriffs who could not read or write?

The Exchequer took its name from the system of auditing, on a table resembling a chess-board or 'chequer' (scaccarium). The table was divided into columns representing sums of money, and the accounts of each sherriff, and so the whole royal revenue, were worked out by moving counters about in these columns. The new system of addition, brought in from the Arabs at about this time, not only speeded the arithmetic, but made it possible even for illiterate officials to follow what was being done by observing the movements of the counters.*

Tradition and invention, ever climbing on each other's shoulders!

* Christopher Brooke, *From Alfred to Henry III* (Nelson, 1961), p. 111.

CHAPTER 18

THE LANDSLIDE OF INVENTION

Insight into the *thing in being* of which we form a part, whether we attend chiefly to its non-human or its human aspect, cannot consist in a knowledge of its nature or meaning in any ultimate, absolute sense. All we can seek is consistency, coherence, order. The question for the scientist is what thought-scheme will best provide him with a sense of that order and coherence, a sense of some permanence, repetitiveness and universality in the structure or texture of the scheme of things, a sense even of that one-ness and simplicity which, if he can assure himself of its presence, will carry consistency and order to their highest expression. Religion, science and art have all of them this aim in common. The difference between them lies in the different emphases in their modes of search, the stress upon the promptings of inborn longing and intuitive or inspired conviction, upon reason and experience, or upon the imagination of beauty. Our own purpose is concerned with the conceptions of the scientist and philosopher, but even these, and even in their most general, abstract and basic formulations, are extremely diverse.

A sense of order and consistency is needed, not only to satisfy a detached curiosity, but also to make practical life possible. Whether our decisions contain any element of *ex nihilo* origination, or whether they are the pure reflection of desire and external circumstance, they are powerless to further our interest unless they can count upon some non-arbitrariness, some conformity to discernible rules, in the sequences of situations or events that we observe. Perhaps the most unassuming expression we can give to this idea is to say that we discern recurrent configurations of particular circumstances, configurations involving both simultaneous association and temporal sequence, and that we ascribe to this recurrence a permanence, a power of survival, a claim to belong to the nature of things, a guarantee of future as well as past validity. Let us call such configurations, *stereotypes*. The fixity of pattern in which we have habitually found certain appearances associated, enables the observation of part of such a pattern to suggest that the rest of it will in due course be observed. A stereotype can thus be the instrument of (scientific, that is, conditional) prediction. The observation of a part of such a pattern may also suggest the presence of its antecedent parts, and we have a basis and meaning for explanation. And if the earlier sets of circumstances which compose such a stereotype can be deliberately brought about, it may be reasonable to expect the rest to follow. The stereotype in such a case has provided guidance for practical action. A type of thought-scheme which offers the possibility of prediction, explanation and technology is a theory, and we may in large measure identify our notion of stereotype with that of theory. It is the *content* of an invention or discovery that is in some sense novel, not the mode of making that invention or discovery. There does not seem to be any essential reason why stereotypes should not be sought and discovered in the mode of making inventions and discoveries, including the invention of theories. Such stereotypes have been in this book our object of search. We have now to put in order the suggestions which our material has offered.

Alongside the simple discernment of recurrent patterns of circumstance, theorizing requires also reason. Its role will lie in discerning essential likeness amongst ostensibly diverse patterns, so as to embrace many formerly distinct stereotypes into one more general form. Its means will be the invention of axioms concerning entities or elements which in the first place will remain undefined except by the interrelations imposed upon them by the axioms. Upon these axioms it will construct systems of further propositions obtained from the axioms by logical inference. Finally a likeness will be sought between the structure of some such system and some observed stereotype, whose composing elements may then be identified with the elements or concepts of the logical system, and the inferential properties of the latter ascribed to the background of real events within which the stereotype was discerned. The scientist's ultimate aim is to see everything as an illustration of a very few basic principles incapable of further unification, hoping perhaps that at the last this unification will end in his apprehending the single Secret of Nature. But such reduction of the

vast richness of phenomena to some statement of the final
ground of things belongs rather to the material sciences than
the moral sciences. In the former, we can believe ourselves to be
penetrating deeper and deeper towards the heart of things,
even if this sense of approach is illusory, as many have believed.*
But in the sciences (so-called) of men and their affairs, the investigator may be said to impose rather than discover the orderliness which constitutes knowledge.

Theoretical advance can spring only from theoretical crisis:
either internal crisis, as when, for example, the analytically
indispensable assumption of perfect competition is recognized
to conflict with the notion of economies of large scale, or when
the notion of a unit of utility is found to be incapable of
operational definition; or external crisis, as when the established
theory of value seems to declare general heavy unemployment
impossible, in self-destructive contradiction of the facts, or as
when political alarms at the doctrines of Marx called for a
replacement of the labour theory of value. The chief service
rendered by a theory is the setting of minds at rest. So long
as we have a satisfying conceptual structure, a model or a
taxonomy which provides for the filing of all facts in a scheme
of order, we are absolved from the tiresome labour of thought,
and the uneasy consciousness of mystery and a threatening unknown. It is when the scheme is suddenly perceived to be
internally inconsistent or to fail to accommodate observations
or to support the interests of our own portion of humanity, that
it is attacked, destroyed, re-built on fresh lines or replaced with
a radically new conception. Theories in natural science are, of
course, useful summaries of technological stereotypes, they provide a readily-consulted filing-system for recipes and sets of
working instructions. But they are not ultimately indispensable
to the technologist, who in the last resort needs only rules of
thumb and not far-ranging generalized interpretations or
abstract structures of thought. Theory serves deep needs of the
human spirit: it subordinates nature to man, imposes a beautiful
simplicity on the unbearable multiplicity of fact, gives comfort
in face of the unknown and unexperienced, stops the teasing of
mystery and doubt which, though salutary and life-preserving,

* 'The universe is not merely stranger than you imagine, it is stranger than you
can imagine' (J. B. S. Haldane).

is uncomfortable, so that we seek by theory to sort out the justified from the unjustified fear. Theories by their nature and purpose, their role of administering to a 'good state of mind', are things to be held and cherished. Theories are altered or discarded only when they fail us. What shortcomings did the nineteen twenties and thirties reveal in the Great Theory, the general equilibrium conception built between 1870 and 1910, the legacy of the Age of Tranquillity to the Age of Turmoil, handed on across the great divide of the 1914–18 war?

The change of circumstance alone would have sufficed to render obsolete any theory concerned with social and political affairs. For the British people in 1914, a hundred years of peace and of naval supremacy had established the unquestioned assumption that tranquillity and safety were part of the natural order. Wars were rare, brief, remote and on a minor scale, they were disappearing, they scarcely touched or concerned the ordinary British man or woman. The free market system, though in fact subject to restraints, was dominant and legally entrenched. There was room enough and time for equilibrium to find itself. 'There was', as John Maynard Keynes says, 'nothing to be afraid of.' Long thoughts, long vistas, long preparations for still longer decades of family and business prosperity were fostered by this guarantee that the harvest sown with labour and thrift would be garnered in due course. Perfect competition was not a fact, but it was not yet a gross and obvious absurdity. Resources were allocated by a market where the value of the currency was stable. For such a world, 'general equilibrium' was an image miraculously successful in combining simplicity with an all-inclusive explanatory power and a recognizable resemblance to the facts.

One and a half generations of ostensible political and social peace in Western Europe from 1870 seems in retrospect to have been marvellously apt as a setting and illustration of the subjective, marginalist theory of value. The most essential and powerful difference between this world and the world of the 1930s was the loss of tranquillity itself. Problems of 'the price of a cup of tea' as Professor Joan Robinson put it, no longer counted much against the problem of unemployment arising, so Keynes explained, from the failure of the incentive to invest, which failure itself was due to the sudden oppression of business minds by the world's incalculable uncertainties. There was no longer equilibrium in fact, and there could no longer be equilibrium in theory.

The Economics of Tranquillity, that is, of Confident Foresight, the economics of a world where changes of circumstance are believed to proceed no faster than the physical decay of equipment, so that we have the equivalent of a hand-to-mouth connection between act and result, the economics which we call the theory of value and income distribution, was essentially, logically, by its basic presuppositions, incapable of explaining general heavy unemployment. The use of scarce versatile resources according to reason applied to a complete, precise and certain knowledge of what states of mind would be brought into being by this or that allocative pattern, within a free market system, cannot leave idle any part of the available resources. The fatal assumption is that of perfect confidence in the possession of perfect knowledge. However, in a barter system, or one where money serves only as a *numéraire*, knowledge is *effectively* bound to be perfect. For nothing can be sold except by the concomitant purchase of some other resource-embodying thing. Without money, we cannot put off deciding what to buy with the thing we are in the act of selling. If we do not know precisely what use a thing will be to us, we are compelled nevertheless, by an absence of *money*, to override and ignore this ignorance. It is *money* which enables decision to be deferred. And it is not by accident that the Economics of Employment, that is, the Economics of Uncertainty, were approached by way of the theory of money. But the theory of money which could serve this purpose was not the mechanical Fisherian Quantity Theory, not even the more human Cambridge desired cash balance theory, but Wicksell's theory of the natural and the money rate of interest. The basic failure of General Equilibrium Economics, as an instrument for understanding the 1930s, was its assumption of a stable, knowable and foreseeable world. Its more concrete failure was to offer as a theory of money, a sort of Hydraulics of Currency which could hardly have stood in more complete contrast to the Psychics which was needed.

The Great Theory constructed by Walras, Pareto, Jevons, Menger, Marshall, Wicksteed, Wicksell and John Bates Clark was in some sense a calculus of scarcity for the use of perfectly informed economic man, whose society, because of his perfect knowledge, had no need for storable general purchasing power, only for an accounting unit. The theory of employment and general output, which emerged from the work of Wicksell, Keynes, Kahn, Joan Robinson, Harrod, Hicks, Meade, Kalecki and Lerner; and from that of Myrdal, Lindahl and Lundberg; with aid and refinement from Ragnar Frisch, Alvin Hansen, Paul Samuelson, Nicholas Kaldor and others; was an account of the consequences of the natural and ultimately unavoidable *lack* of information suffered by human decision-makers. The Victorians derived from first principles an account of the ideal, the neo-Georgians derived from experience an account of the real. The Victorians are not to be condemned: their Age was perhaps a mere accidental pause in humanity's career of violence; but it was for them present reality, the only thing available for direct inspection. When, in 1914–18, the settled assumptions of life for ordinary people dissolved, the economics of tranquillity became inadequate and partly inappropriate. Its obsolescence, becoming abruptly evident as soon as there was time again to think, after years of war and of absurd, gigantic inflations, is the greatest single explanation of the theoretical ferment of the 1930s.

Doubtless also the war was a psychic release. The young economists of the 1920s were not spell-bound, like those of earlier decades, by the glow from a great focus of convergent thought where all the world's economists seemed to pour in their blending illuminations. The fires on that hearth were out. A fresh start could be made. Perfect competition could be questioned as to consistency as well as realism; money, after its debacle in Germany, central Europe and even France, could be studied as a source and not mere servant of events, an active and inherently restless factor; the phenomenon of growth on which Gustav Cassel had insisted could come into its own; strands from Marshall and from Pareto, those very different kinds of mathematical economist, could be spun by Hicks and Allen into a new version of part of the old theme. So much for the *reason* for a great theoretical renewal. What of its methods?

The rebuilders of economic theory fell, as we saw, into two classes in respect of their approach: the mathematicians who wrote down in formal algebra the conditions to be fulfilled, and found the solution by formal manipulations of kinds which their training, experience and the nature of mathematical thought suggested to them; and the conceptualists who saw before them on the intellectual work-bench a number of component parts, some still serviceable, some perhaps requiring to be reshaped, some obsolete; and who then tried to conceive a workable composition made from such parts, a machine as much like the old one as possible, improved in just the indispensable respects but not radically transformed. The mathematicians were incisive and efficient. The formal authority and finality of their results, the swift economy with which their answers were attained, seem sometimes to deride the labours of the conceptualists. Yet there is something superficial about all this. The mathematicians incline to regard economics as the study of mechanism, and with mechanism we are able, sometimes in practice, always in abstract argument, to abolish the distinction between past and future, to design a system where 'ignorance' can no more affect outcomes than it can affect the operation of gravity, to treat all as determinate, fateful and calculable. And this view of human life is at odds with all experience. The mathematicians had great triumphs. Leontief's perception of the vital practical importance of the input-output problem, his formulation of the problem and its means of solution as a series of essentially simple steps applied to a square table or matrix, were a great landmark in logical–quantitative economics, 'econometrics'. Cournot's sharp tool reappeared in the hands of Yntema, cutting a rapid swath where the conceptualists would struggle to unlace the tangled stems. Frisch, Tinbergen and Samuelson taught the economic world by means of difference equations that *lagged* relations between two or more variables can generate a perpetual leap-frog game in which each variable in turn stimulates and lifts, or hinders and depresses, the other, continuously and without any feed-in of impulses from outside the system. This last example is plainly beyond the power of verbal analysis. Arithmetic can illustrate it but not provide a general conception and insight, nor a classification of its cases. Yet even this unarguable case of mathematical ascendancy needs interpretation in terms of human thought, knowledge, choice, audacity and error.

The mathematician 'sees things whole', but his sense of the indivisible unity of an argument, of the equal indispensability of every step and every element in it, is not always an unalloyed advantage. For it inhibits him from singling out such elements and giving each of them an identity and separate existence of its own by naming it. Thus the derivative of {output times price} with respect to output is, for the mathematician as such, just a derivative, one by-product of his analysis. But for the economist, 'marginal revenue' and the marginal revenue curve are almost personalized objects of thought, real tools whose feel is comfortable and confidence-inspiring, the focus of many problems and the means of answering them. Which attitude is best? We have the strange case of Marshall's writing down (as an accustomed user of the calculus could not help doing) marginal revenue in algebra, and leaving it nameless and unnoticed, while Mrs Robinson seized upon it as the one central and vital clue to the theory of imperfect competition. There is some danger, as well as suggestive power and inspiration, in too definitely objectifying the elements of a structure of reasoning. In the older economics 'increasing returns' and 'decreasing returns' sometimes seem to be in themselves actual forces or principles of nature, beings with a capacity for making trouble, which must be carefully kept under control. 'Inflation' suggests a cause instead of merely the numerical answer to a sum. It is conceivable that a supremely able mathematician could describe the whole human metabolism by means of a differential equation, but it is not conceivable that a doctor's patients could consult him by its means. The names of organs are necessary, their functions, however interdependent, must be separated in thought. In just this way, the mythological type of linguistic economics is indispensable. We need a 'bestiary' and not merely a taxonomy, a taxonomy and not merely a machine. The list of such terms is impressive: 'the demand curve', 'the supply curve'; 'the contract curve'; 'the short, or long period'; 'the indifference map'; 'the laws of returns'; 'the accelerator', 'the multiplier', 'the ceiling'; and very many more. We are, indeed, mechanics and engineers rather than abstract logicians. In the theories we have studied in the foregoing chapters, this value and importance of names is very visible.

In economic theorizing, three worlds, three levels of thought, are involved. There is the world of what we take to be 'real' objects, persons, institutions and events; on the axis of abstract-concrete this world is at the concrete pole. There is the logical or mathematical construct or machine, a piece of pure reasoning, almost of 'pure mathematics', able to exist in its own right of internal coherence, as a system of mere *relations* amongst undefined thought-entities; this world lies at the abstract pole. And between these two worlds there lies the world of names, linking the real-world elements with the undefined entities of the abstract machine, the real-world events with time-spanning comparisons in the pure structure of reasoning. The name-world is vital, not merely in its role as setting up the correspondence between percepts and the terms of logic, but in its heuristic capacity as *suggesting and revealing* these vital links which are in themselves the very essence of theory. Language is often said to be the chief and indispensable instrument of thought. Names are the vehicles and receptacles of ideas, and to attempt to do all our theorizing in the medium of algebraic symbols alone would be nonsense. The rich and fruitful theory is a structure, not of nameless quantities existing only in relation to each other, but of named concepts, images, enjoying an almost personal life in our minds. That is why neither the mathematicians nor the conceptualists can be allowed to bear the palm alone.

In the 1930s the Great Theory was destroyed and not replaced. To the zealous theoreticians who performed it, this work of destruction was unexpected, disturbing, often undesired and regrettable. Sir John Hicks openly declared against imperfect competition, Keynes ignored it. Those who had seen the need to modernize the neo-classical edifice were often bemused by the visible difficulties and dangerous consequences of what they were doing, but they had to wait till the very end of the decade to hear the plain report by Hicks and Triffin: they had levelled the old building to the ground. The Great Theory, the General Equilibrium, rests on two indispensable assumptions: of perfect competition and perfect rationality. Rationality is only perfect when relevant knowledge is perfect, and relevant knowledge includes knowledge of the consequences of actions. But the consequences of actions do not yet exist at the moment when choice amongst those actions is being made, and it follows that direct knowledge of the objective, publicly assessable consequences of still-choosable actions is logically impossible. Perfect rationality belongs only to the timeless equilibrium in which all actions conform to a general simultaneous solution of the pooled statements of the tastes and resources of all participants. When economic theory elects to bring in imperfect competition and to recognize uncertainty, there is an end of the meaning of general equilibrium. Economics thereafter is the description, piece by piece, of a collection of fragments. These fragments may fit together into a brilliant, arrestingly suggestive mosaic, but they do not compose a pattern of unique, inevitable order. One vital aspect of the process of theoretical innovation is its destructive aspect.

In the aims and operations of several of our theorists, there is a visible conflict of piety and discontent. Sraffa and Harrod honoured the language of Marshall and of much earlier writers, but they plainly felt that there was something wrong. Myrdal set out to clarify Wicksell, and ended by introducing a vital and fundamental reform of economic thinking: or at least, by making explicit, and coining into a phrase, what had only been vaguely felt and still more vaguely expressed. Keynes in the *Treatise* felt himself to be treading old ground in a somewhat different way; in the *General Theory* he felt himself to be breaking quite new ground. The *Treatise* is written with serenity, the *General Theory* is up in arms. The innovating theoretician needs a ruthless self-belief. He must overturn the intellectual dwelling-places of hundreds of people, whose first instinct will be resistance and revenge. Yet reconstruction must inevitably use much of the old material. Piety is not only honourable, it is indispensable. Invention is helpless without tradition.

It is as teachers that we confront the most remorseless need for a theory which is simple, self-consistent and relevant to the times. If need be, existing theories must be hammered and wrought to satisfy this test. 'Immanent criticism', criticism and evaluation from within, is an activity of a teacher, one who is striving to express a theory in his own forms of thought and his own words, and in doing so is compelled to make it yield sense that satisfies him and that he is prepared to sponsor and be held unanswerable for. Only a theory that one has come to terms with can be taught with zest and conviction; but this deep assessment of a theory implies a consciousness of its weaknesses and possible alternatives, as well as of efficiency and beauty. To have courage to question, alter and rebuild an established theory, a teacher needs aid from contemporary fact. When a long-accepted view visibly fails to meet the modern situation, then we pluck up courage and start to dismantle it. If there must be destruction and clearance of the site for new architecture, let history herself do some of the demolition. The middle 1920s brought to those then beginning to teach economics a great release from inhibitions. So much of past theory was plainly unsuitable to the times. And there was in those years perhaps another kind of liberation. The great figures of Victorian economics were disappearing from the scene. The twelve years from 1840 to 1851 produced Menger (1840–1921), Marshall (1842–1924), Edgeworth (1845–1926), Pareto (1848–1923), Wicksell (1851–1926), Wieser (1851–1926) and Bohm-Bawerk (1851–1914), seven of the greatest figures of our discipline all born in virtually one decade, all but one dying in the six years 1921–6. By that last year, which we have taken as the first of our Years of High Theory, the great Victorian cohort had at last withdrawn into antiquity. A fresh start could be made without these giants peering over men's shoulders. Thus need and freedom beckoned.

INDEX

Geldzins und Güterpreise by Knut Wicksell, contained a theory of output as a whole, 228

'The General Theory of Employment', article in the *Quarterly Journal of Economics*, 112, 130
    and convention as the sole basis of stability, 247
    and Keynes's ultimate nihilism, 247
    and society's resort to convention as a substitute for reason, 228
    expresses Keynes's ultimate insight, 132, 152
    Keynes's sole attention in it to the effects of our ignorance of the future, 135
    the view it expressed had been distilled in the preface to the book, 162
    was a 'third edition' of the *Treatise-General Theory*, 136
    was concerned exclusively with 'one big thing', the nature of the investment-decision in face of ignorance of the future, 136

General Theory of Employment, Interest and Money, 6, 89, 98, 111 n., 112, 124, 135, 137 and n.
    a foreshadowed *ex ante* version of, 227
    and correspondence with Myrdal's *Monetary Equilibrium*, 126
    and employment as a measure of output, 166
    and human institutions, 149
    and liquidity preference, 217
    and mechanical defects of the old system of economics, 135
    and society's economic anatomy and physiology, 130
    and the classical theory of employment, 137
    and the confrontation of two bodies of thought, 149
    and the Dalton incident, 222
    and the 'many things' which Keynes found wrong in detail in the older conception of economics, 136
    and the Multiplier, 201
    and the speculative motive for holding money, 216
    and the stability or mutability of liquidity functions, 217
    anticipated in the *Treatise*, 182, 183
    as a formal system, was based on the speculative motive for holding money, 209
    as illustration of a book with a focal chapter, 124
    attempted a rational theory of semi-rational conduct, 129
    central core of, is in chapter 12, 132
    chapter 12 of, may appear an intruder into the main current, 133
    compared with the views of the Stockholm School by Ohlin, 227
    comparison of, with the *Treatise*, 161, 162, 209–15
    divides inducement to invest into two parts, 174
    does not link together the two theses of chapter 2, 139, 140
    falls into two natural divisions, 145, 146
    gave rise to new business cycle theories, 267
    has two natures or modes of being, 129
    its method depended on *accidental* equilibria, 240
    its nature misunderstood, 129
    Keynes's essential thesis present, but not clear, in chapter 12, 132
    liquidity-preference theory of interest was intimately necessary to, 145
    message of, is that investment is non-rational, 130
    pays deference to formal methods, 270
    shows us a tableau of posed figures, 182
    signs of strain in, 162
    source of its mystique, 162
    the anatomy of, summarized in its chapter 18, 158